KILLED OUT

KILLED OUT

Hunting the Corporate Herds

LION J TEMPLIN

Copyright © 2021 Lion J Templin
41 20210215
United States

lion.fm

All Rights Reserved. The moral rights of the author have been asserted. No part of this book may be reproduced, in any form or by any means, without permission in writing from above mentioned copyright owner.

Company or product names mentioned herein are trademarks or registered trademarks of their respective owners. Names and surrounding information of individuals and organizations in this book have been changed.

The Lion Logo is Copyright © 1998 Lion J Templin
Cover design by Pinguino Kolb at pinguinokolb.com
Published by Keil Capital Publishing

ISBN 978-1-7364971-0-4 (eBook)
ISBN 978-1-7364971-1-1 (paperback)
ISBN 978-1-7364971-2-8 (audiobook)

First Edition: March 2021

*There's no nobility in the things we do,
they're just the things that must be done.*

TABLE OF CONTENTS

PREFACE 1

CHAPTER ONE
King of the Wild 15

CHAPTER TWO
Fight Club 25

CHAPTER THREE
Shop! 37

CHAPTER FOUR
Sheeple Aren't Baaad 49

CHAPTER FIVE
The Hunters 59

CHAPTER SIX
World Traveler 69

CHAPTER SEVEN
The Document Riot 81

CHAPTER EIGHT
Do You Want Blood? 91

CHAPTER NINE
Are You Not Entertained? 107

CHAPTER TEN
Breaking Stuff 125

CHAPTER ELEVEN
Breaking People 139

CHAPTER TWELVE
One Last Gig 153

CHAPTER THIRTEEN
Being Run Out 173

CHAPTER FOURTEEN
Synergy 207

CHAPTER FIFTEEN
A Kill Isn't a Death 223

CHAPTER SIXTEEN
The Red Queen's Race 239

POSTSCRIPT 245

ACKNOWLEDGMENTS 247

PREFACE

"The preface is that part of a book which is written last, placed first, and read least."

—Alfred J. Lotka

To me, the concept of an office is a loose one. As a turn-around consultant, I have travelled the world, stepping into the center of businesses in trouble. That comes with a certain amount of flexibility on what an "office" really is. Folding tables in a dusty warehouse basement? Sure. Lavish conference room overlooking prime real estate? Absolutely. But none of my offices was as beautiful as the one I shared with a handful of coworkers spread across a million acres of Canadian wilderness.

This is one of their stories.

CANOE TRIP JOURNAL TO THE ONTARIO WILDERNESS

BY BOBBY WAHL

DAY 1. EARLY JUNE, 1995

I wanted to floor it, to hammer the engine and race the last few miles to the end of the road, but no dice. The gravel under the van was a mixture of loose stone and the beginnings of washboard ruts not yet worn in by constant summer traffic. So I took the curves of the barely two-lane road at a gentle pace. Wrecking the van this far out from civilization isn't on my list of things to do.

Jim is sitting next to me—well, next is relative when the passenger seat is several feet away. I can only assume he's watching the road like I am. I'm not about to take my eyes off it when at any moment the path could swerve suddenly around another tall granite outcropping masked in ancient pine trees. Jim's been the other driver on this trip, sharing the last 1,300 miles. Until the last four hours of gravel winding through the desolate forests of northern Ontario.

It is a beautiful place. The trip so far has featured nonstop incredible scenery ever since we made it past Toronto. Ted, asleep in the back of the van—or at least I assume so, given that's mostly what he's done for the last 26 hours—made a point of how beautiful the trip across the Trans-Canada Highway would be. He wasn't wrong at all; the northern shores of Lake Huron and Lake Superior were stunning. We saw an actual bald eagle, its white head and tail unmistakable in the bright sun of the afternoon. Jim was driving, while I and the rest of the guys stared out of the windows at it. Amazing. I've only seen maybe a dozen in my entire life.

The air inside the van has a mixture of bad odors. The worst offender comes from a bag of gas station burritos we picked up at an Esso on the northern edge of Thunder Bay. Other smells contribute: the back of the van is packed with camping gear, and that stuff has its own aroma that the van only intensifies. Us, without showers, add mightily to the stink. Dave smokes—not in the van, of course—but I can still smell it. I'd say we shouldn't have stopped for the burritos, but they were more of an afterthought. Our enormous Ford Econoline 15-passenger van, on loan from our church, drinks gas like a college student at an open bar. Only the cheapest gas would do. This Esso was the last stop we could make before starting the long, dusty road to Armstrong. Craig did warn us that cheap burritos and twisty gravel roads would spell disaster, but besides the smell, I'm feeling more excited than anything.

We pass another red and white radio tower on the right side of the road. We are so far away from the rest of the world that anyone living up here has to use this long chain of towers, each with antennas pointing south to Thunder Bay and north deeper into the wilderness, to make a simple phone call. And that is it: a desolate gravel road through a rough landscape of craggy, barren granite and hearty pine trees with an occasional radio tower to remind you that people do, in fact, live this far out. When we reach the end of the towers, we are there.

I stop the van next to a cluster of other trucks and vans in a dirt parking lot, and we pile out. It's quiet, no engines, no noise, just the breeze. The far edge of the lot has a huge painted wooden sigil looking over it:

canoes on a lake, trees, all surrounded by curves of white, red, black, and yellow. This is the gateway to living in the real wilderness: Mackenzie Lake Canoe Outfitters. This is the beginning of a vacation of a lifetime. The five of us are about to embark into the unknown, surviving with only backpacks and canoes.

We arranged for a guide. There's nothing like this back in Pennsylvania, so we are going to need help. A small group of them are leaning against a fence a few dozen feet from the gate. I approach, introduce myself, and an unassuming 20-something steps forward.

"I'm Bill, I'm your guide."

I am shown into a log cabin turned into a reception area for an hour of paperwork. So maybe we're not that far from civilization.

After that, Bill starts us on the move. As in "move your stuff." We hike the gravel road carrying everything we have to the far side of the canoe base. Turns out we have a lot of stuff and it's not the easiest to carry. So we stumble, dropping things occasionally, to a squat, octagonal wooden hut with a half-height door. This is apparently where we will stay tonight, this eight-sided wooden structure with low benches on the outside walls. Tomorrow, we venture into the wild. We dump our stuff and head off with Bill to prepare.

We sit on wood benches in a huge log cabin–style hall, huddled close to the front, where a map of the wilderness hangs on the wall. Bill lays out for us our pick of three different routes for our four days "on the water," which means paddling and portaging our canoes and gear between every lake. We're good with what Bill calls the "medium difficulty" trip: we'll start out on Caribou Lake, where the base is, then do a big loop around Smoothrock Lake. I'm excited to live out in the wild for the next few days.

We are directed to yet another log building for food. Wow, for only four days that's a heavy pack! It's a big plastic box-shaped thing with black nylon pack straps. It's solid, but it must weigh 60 pounds. Bill's taken care of the food; all we have to do is check it to make sure it's all there. Bill's going to make dinners out of a lot of staples; rice and pasta make up most of the supplies, with some vacuum-packed meat to add to the flavor. No bland freeze-dried camping food for us!

We proceed on to a long row of giant canoe racks. These are our transportation for the trip, and we have to pick out the two we want. They all look the same, 17-foot gleaming aluminum canoes. We lift a few up at random, and it turns out they're all heavy. We pick a pair that look like they're in good shape. I can lift one with effort, so I'm carrying that one. Bill says he will take the other canoe, since he's the guide. That makes sense. The rest of the crew have to carry the packs. Three of us will occupy each canoe, and we split up who goes in which canoe. Ted, Craig, and I in one, and Bill will take Dave and Jim.

By the time we get back to our cabin, it's dark and we're shot. Before we try to sleep on the benches, Bill has us perform the shakedown. We go through our gear to make sure we have the right stuff. Bill checks all of our personal equipment to weed out what we shouldn't take, which is plenty. Apparently, we only need one can of bug spray. Dave doesn't have a dry place to keep his cigarettes, so he goes back to the van and grabs a Ziploc bag for them. When we're through, Bill leaves us until morning.

Right before bed, we step outside into the dark and look up. It is like staring at every star in the universe. No city lights get in the way, and the sky is brighter than I've ever seen it. I feel small. We drove for hours from Thunder Bay on a desolate road into the most middle-of-nowhere I've ever been. It's clear that out here you're on your own. There's nothing nearby, no hospitals, no civilization. Armstrong is hardly even a town, more like a small collection of buildings around a gas station and a rundown diner. Tomorrow, we will go out into the wilderness on our own. It's all on us. What we don't bring doesn't exist. And, if we get into trouble, there's no one to save us.

I guess the wood benches are good enough, because I collapse on one and nod off.

DAY 2

We get under way at 10:00 a.m. It's a beautiful day, with only a few white clouds in the sky. This is amazing! We're in what Bill calls the "Canadian Shield." A massive lava rock flow that happened millions of years ago covers all of northern Minnesota and up through Ontario. There's not much soil, so the landscape is stark. The trees grow only in small plots of dirt and in the cracks between huge slabs of stone. Pine trees, birch, and aspen are all mixed together. We paddle our canoes across Caribou Lake easily, enjoying the sunshine. All that time paddling up and down the Susquehanna River back home has done us good. Our canoes glide across the lake straight as an arrow.

Our first portage is interesting. This is where we pick up our gear and canoes and carry it all to the next lake. Bill explained how we're supposed to do this, but I don't think any of us are making it work. He has a system for carrying the stuff, but somehow we're not getting it. After 10 minutes of Bill talking through the process, my only take-away is that the guys carrying the packs aren't supposed to help the guy with the canoe. Jim and I look at each other, shrug, and then Jim helps me lift the canoe up onto my shoulders. I don't know how I'm supposed to do that on my own, because the canoe is heavy and unwieldy. The trail to the next lake is rocky and narrow, so we each take it at our own pace. Bill is trying to keep us all together, but it's difficult. Dave takes off on his own, leaving us all behind. Thanks, Dave.

I guess we're not supposed to walk around the mud, we're supposed to walk through it. The trail is lined with big stretches of little pools. Bill yells at Ted after he skirts around a pocket of mud, brushing up against the tree limbs. I don't understand why we're not supposed to walk around the stuff, but Bill is mad about it, so I don't ask.

We conduct a total of five portages today, every one narrow, rocky, and muddy. I don't feel they're that bad, and I'm having a great time. This is real wilderness! How we're doing them still isn't going right, though. Bill keeps getting upset with us after each portage. Dave keeps hauling down the trails without us, and Jim helps me with the canoe again. Both of these make Bill mad. At least we're not trying to avoid the mud anymore. At one point, Bill tells Jim to get moving and then tries to teach me the right way to mount the canoe up on my shoulders by myself, but it still doesn't make sense. I finally grab the thing and muscle it up there. That is more work than I expected. When we reach the end of the trail, we discover Craig left a pack behind. Bill is angry about going back to get it. Oh, well.

We arrive at our campsite on Smoothrock Lake in the late afternoon. We're on the very east end of the lake, on a series of long, thin bays. Looking at the map, I see this lake is huge. It's absolutely beautiful out here. We haven't seen another person outside our group since we set out this morning. Our campsite is pitched on a rocky point within 20 feet of the water. Wow.

Bill makes dinner, using first the frozen stuff in the pack instead of our rice-and-meat supplies. It was supposed to be beef stew made with thawed hamburger, but it's really just a weak soup. Oh, well! I'm still hungry! Bill builds a fire and cooks on it, which is impressive. Even if the meal doesn't turn out right, I've never cooked on fire before.

I am glad we brought the bug spray. The black flies are awful here. The mosquitoes are bad, sure, but these are far worse and tiny. When they bite, you can see the chunk of skin they take out of you as it starts bleeding. The bites then turn into awful sores! The back of Craig and Dave's necks are bitten badly; bloody and very swollen. Bill advises us to use the bug spray more often, so we'll pass the can around tomorrow as we portage.

DAY 3

Bill gets us up early. We break down the camp while Bill cooks oatmeal on a small camp stove. In no time, we are back in the canoes, paddling happily. It is another blue sky day, the morning is absolutely gorgeous. This is still amazing!

We stop for lunch on an island. I pull out my maps to study them, but with all the bays around the lake, I have no idea where we are. I'm glad Bill knows.

After lunch, we return to the canoes and continue to follow Bill's lead. Eventually, we end up in a swamp, a really big one filled with rushes, lily pads, and this floating bog stuff Bill calls "moose muck." Moose muck is a floating layer of mud and plants that look solid, but if you step on it, you sink right through it. Lots of small saplings and tall weeds grow in the muck. We can't see over it or get on top of it; we can't see anything but what's right in front of us. The part we can paddle through is a narrow slot of water that twists and turns. I quickly lose track of where we're at.

Bill seems pretty certain of himself, so we keep heading deeper into the swamp. The rest of us aren't so confident all of a sudden. Bill never mentioned a giant swamp in our planning, and Craig tries to decipher our map to pinpoint where we are, unsuccessfully. After a few hours of fighting our way through the muck, Craig finally tells Bill to stop. We float in our canoes in this little open spot filled with reeds and a foot of dirty water on top of the mud, while Craig politely argues with Bill over the maps. Craig is certain we're not going the right way. Bill tells him the narrows that he pointed out before were in the swamp and that we're almost to the other side. Eventually, Craig agreed—well, gives up—and we go back to following Bill.

After that, the passage gets worse. By 4:00 p.m. we still haven't made it out of the swamp and Bill is looking nervous. We make slow progress trying to paddle through the thin channels in the muck. At one point, Bill tells us we have to get out of our canoes so we can push them through a short section where the water isn't deep enough. Dave gets out first and sinks right in. He can't stand or swim. We fish him out with paddles. He comes up soaked from head to toe, including his cigarettes. That's not going to go well for him.

We are still stuck in the swamp by 7:00 p.m. Bill said the sun is going down in two hours, so we need to find a place to camp. Oh shit, this is serious: he really doesn't know where we are. We push on, trying to find places we can guide the canoes closer to the tree line, closer to what might be dry land. An hour later, we find a flattish, rocky area with a few trees that we can stand on. Bill makes dinner with the camp stove since there isn't any dry wood on our tiny, muddy island.

While Bill is cooking, we sit down with Craig to look at the maps. He was right all along. We aren't anywhere near where we are supposed to be. Craig pieced together about lunchtime that we needed to turn north, but what had happened is that Bill turned us south. He led us into a giant swamp in the southern part of the lake miles in the other direction from our route. Damn.

Bill serves dinner; he has burned the pasta to the bottom of the pot, but food is food, I guess.

It's late. We're all exhausted and in bed well after sunset. Jim and Ted are downright pissed, and the rest of us are pretty unhappy. Dave is covered in mud and now he's really missing his cigarettes. He's been trying to dry them out on a rock, but he hasn't made much progress. Everyone is hounded by the mosquitoes and black flies.

I thought this guy knew what he was doing.

DAY 4

In the morning, we pack up and leave the rock to forge our way out of the swamp. We had to paddle back through all the little channels of water in the moose muck, fighting it as we did yesterday. This time, though, Craig keeps an eye on the maps. None of us want to be stuck in here any longer than we have to.

By 1:00 p.m. we finally emerge back in the lake. Thank God, this is so much better. Open water, a light breeze to keep the flies away, and no more rotten moose muck. We stop on a rocky point just outside the swamp for lunch. Jim and I sneak away and talk about Bill while everyone is eating. Jim thinks he's merely inexperienced, while I think that the guy is dangerous. It's a million miles to civilization and Bill has no idea what he's doing. The canoe base said all their guides are well trained, but how do you explain getting lost in a swamp for 24 hours?

We stop for the night at a campsite on the main part of the lake, and this time we know where we are. We set up camp while Bill starts on dinner. He retrieves the camp stove he used for breakfast and refuels it from a steel fuel bottle. The stove is one of these things that you have to pump up with a little thumb pump on the fuel canister. You fill it with white gas, close it up, and the pumping builds pressure to run the burner. It's like a small version of my two-burner Coleman camp stove at home, except the gas tank is right below the burner. Bill pumps it up, lights it, and it bursts into flames. Bill freaks out. He looks terrified as he picks it up, throws his arm back, and then chucks the stove at the lake. Which I guess isn't the best plan ever, because now a pressurized fuel tank, on fire, is flying through the air over a lot of sharp, broken granite rocks. We watch in horror. It never gets even near the lake. It falls well short and hits a rock that punctures the fuel tank, causing it to explode, which then rockets the stove out into the lake. Seriously. We all stared in shock as the fireball hurtles through the air. Jim loses it, yelling at Bill that he could have killed us. Craig carries on about shrapnel and how everyone's damn lucky. Ted glares at Bill with a cool rage I know him for.

After the yelling stops, we go back to setting up our tents. Dave makes a fire and cooks our dinner while Bill sulks. Our adventure isn't going as I expected.

DAY 5

This morning, we took things upon ourselves. It was hard to get away from Bill to talk about him, but we had to. We gathered back in the woods, quietly without our guide. Everyone agreed Bill was trouble and we couldn't trust him. Craig wanted to leave him in the wildness and let the canoe company deal with him; Jim agreed, but he wouldn't actually do it. Ditching him wasn't really an option. Everyone agreed to just tell him to be quiet while we traveled back to the canoe base. Which Bill did, for the rest of the day, across the portages, and back to the base on Caribou Lake.

When we got back that afternoon, we took hot showers and had a real meal that night. No one talked about Bill while on base. It felt like a taboo subject with so much anger toward him, or maybe we were just thankful to be alive.

DAY 6

So Craig and I were elected to go talk to the base's management before we drove home to Pennsylvania. We met with the head guy, Sandy, in his office. We told him about everything Bill had done, including getting lost in the swamp and blowing up the stove. Sandy listened intently and then simply announced, "Bill's not going to guide again." Wow. Good. That's a relief.

Overall, we're glad to be alive. This is a trip neither I, nor my buddies, will ever forget. The stove explosion was serious, because if anyone had been hurt, we couldn't have called for help. Ted and Craig are pretty good at first aid, but not "exploded stove shrapnel" good. Being lost in the swamp overnight was not a good time for any of us either. What if we weren't able to find our way out before the food ran out? We were all pretty relieved to load into the van and head home. I could actually say I'd be good with the next 20-some hours in an uncomfortable white van with bad smells.

END OF JOURNAL

I grew up a hunter. My wilderness was a beautiful place, filled with the constant drama of living things doing what was needed to survive. I existed on the side of the predators. It was my job to hunt and kill. That made it necessary for some ... not to survive. I saw that nature was a complex balance of life, death, and change. Without that intricate balance, nothing would survive.

Life didn't change much when I started my career in corporate. The same patterns of nature played out in front of me. The mass of people in their surroundings of steel and glass looked as natural as the deer herds of the wild. My role had not changed. Ever the hunter, I did what was natural.

Seeing the patterns of nature at a young age left an impression that helped define the world. Those patterns are important to me: they represent that intricate balance, the way nature keeps surviving into the future. The forest floor became a carpeted floor in a high-rise office tower. My camouflage became a starched shirt and a plastic ID badge. I could only bring to bear what any other predator could: their natural abilities. My wits would have to be the tools of my trade.

I learned those tools by sharpening my mind in college, play-fighting like any young predator should. I realized that a person so motivated could bring terrific force upon unsuspecting prey. Physical prowess gave way to mental agility. The world was no less savage.

Meanwhile, like any good predator, I honed my observation skills, seeing people in their natural environments and teasing apart their habits. The job world for a young man wasn't complicated, but it revealed far more about how people worked together and what they had in common.

I would find that commonality drives all of society. It is ingrained in us, and often celebrated in ceremony. But, among the celebration, there were problems: some people didn't measure up. They caused trouble. In the everyday fight for survival, they made everyone's workday harder.

Poor performance in the wilderness doesn't get very far, and the end is likely to be at the jaws of a predator. That is the part of the intricate balance I know well. In the world of humanity, predators are just as necessary.

Some people go too far, get away with too much; their bad ideas become their identity. They are empowered to harm those around them. They can be bad at their job, have a bad attitude, or worse. If left unchecked, their view of the workplace spreads. Life in the office becomes hard for everyone.

They have their own games to play. They can exact undue force with process; they can command just by hoarding knowledge; they can justify their actions through force of will. I have witnessed multi-year projects laid waste by just a few individuals who refuse to change with the times.

But I am still a hunter. I know weak prey when I see it.

My boots, black Vietnam–era combat boots with drain holes above the sole that resemble the bottom of a shower stall, ground each step into the dusty, crushed gravel with an intent pace.

Bill and I both worked for the same guiding company in the wilderness of Ontario. We both wore the same plastic name badge while on base, his with BILL cut into it, mine with LION. Bill and I trained together, and we took our capstone training trip into the bush together under the watchful eye of an experienced guide.

But Bill wasn't my friend. He was only along during that training week out on our own. There was nothing too memorable about him. The story of his first trip out was the first I'd heard of him since we both shipped out with our own crews: a hurried conversation outside the shower house that started with "Holy shit, Lion, have you heard about Bill?" My eyes got wide, then narrow, as the journal above was retold like some guide-culture oral history lesson about the dangers of being outrageously stupid in the deep woods.

The story had circulated the base for two days prior to my return, which meant it was spreading like wildfire across the expanse of wilderness I generously called "my office." I must have missed it on my wandering route back to the base for the last couple of days. So this whole Bill fracas was a surprise.

I set out for the administration building. Bill's story appalled me. I was pissed. He could have killed someone.

On paper, this wilderness belonged to the Canadian government, an almost endless expanse as long as you didn't cross the loosely-marked border with the United States to the south or wander into the barren permafrost called the Arctic Circle to the north. If you went far enough you would see the Hudson Bay, Lake Winnipeg, and the mighty Gitchigumi: Lake Superior.

This place, filled with swamps, hardened granite pilings, tall jack pines, and so many lakes that you can walk between them and get almost anywhere, is what I call my backyard. My father took me here when I was young, insistent that I learn the ways of the wilderness. When I grew up, I joined the ranks of guides, taking the often unprepared for the real wilderness tour. I was proud to show off my backyard.

I was not proud of Bill. I took the steps, built of old railroad ties, two at a time, purposefully heading up the stairs to the administration building. This guy could not be allowed to go back out with a crew again. Ever. I banged the door open with an elbow.

"Oh, hi, Lion." Our secretary, Judy, sat behind a desk beside the entrance. She wasn't new to drama; Judy clearly had seen everything the wild could do to the guiding company a dozen times over. Sheer willpower kept her driving the long road out to the base decade after decade. I doubt she'd ever retire.

"I want to talk to Sandy." I paused, considering my next words. "About Bill."

Judy's face brightened and she almost laughed. "Bill who's leaving to go back to Michigan tomorrow?"

"Oh?"

"Yeah, he won't be coming back."

So close, I almost got him.

We tend to think of predator and prey as a simple relationship of who kills who, but nature is far more subtle than that. Many talk about the idea of balance, as if nature is some delicate machine set evenly on the head of a pin. In reality, nature is messy, chaotic, brutally dangerous, and has no value, good or bad, for anything in its path. It is ruthless, uncaring, and unmerciful. Nature is an incredibly complex system that's slowly built itself up over millions of years, through good times and bad, to today, to you, right here, reading this book.

Nature has been wildly successful.

That success is because it maintains balance. Parts of nature must work against each other in order to survive. Eliminate predators and terrible things, like disease, consume the prey instead. Bring back predators and entire ecosystems change and flourish. That is an incredible realization: nature's own organic conflict drives improvement.

This book applies that dynamic. I will show you the details of these two parallel worlds, the wilderness and the office, and how they both embody the same need for predator and prey. The stories progress through adventures I've had in life, from deep in the northern forests to deep inside corporate jungles. There's rarely been a dull moment.

I'm also not alone. My peers — other predators — have been just as successful. Their stories span small businesses, large corporations, and governments. This is an inside look at predators in action at the heart of their kills, allegorical blood and gore shown in detail to demonstrate this side of nature. None of what prey does in these stories is particularly unusual. You will recognize all of them. What is unusual is the predator and the outcomes. Every story in this book is real.

In nature, when ecosystems are in balance, life abounds. In our workplaces, when the aberrant, the poor fits, and the bad actors are held in check, happiness and productivity make work worth doing. Balance will be maintained.

In both nature and the office, everyone has their place.

My paddle, a thickly lacquered wooden plank, bright and new, arced vaguely parallel to the water, losing droplets as it swung forward. It rolled, suddenly, as I plunged the blade edge-on into the lake with a splash. I pulled back, twisting the wooden shaft, turning the drowned blade, pushing the stern to my left, causing the canoe to gently swing around the corner to the right. I pulled the paddle from the water again, swung it harshly, and repeated the cycle anew.

I looked up as the canoe slowly bent around a rocky point cutting into the water, watching the bow, seeing the passengers, their gear, and most important, the canoe's heading. I stared at the far end of a bay, only a few football fields in size, trying to spot the portage trail. You never know where it is when it's your first time.

I think I see it, just to the left of my bowman's head, next to a clump of bushes. I make to swing the paddle again and stop in mid-throw.

The terrain surrounding the bay seizes me; it is a bowl, an amphitheater, a stadium. The broken granite climbs from the water in an even grade, all the way around, as if built rather than just the product of natural glaciation. Upon the rock, all the way up the grade, all the way around the bay, are ranks of red pines: tall, straight, serene, commanding. The wind blows through their thick needles with the familiar sound of the northern wilderness. The afternoon sun burns down through them, striking bright flashes on the wind ripples in the bay.

The canoe glides on, straight for the portage trail, unaware of the occasion.

I stare at the trees around me. Even in the wind, they refuse to move. They are waiting in judgment. On my first trip as a guide, only days in with my first crew, with my gear and technique poorly suited for my work, the wilderness is looking into me, judging me. Who would this man be? What would he become? My youth was spent in this wilderness under the attentive eye of my father. No more. Now I sit in the back of the canoe with the lives of others under my watch.

The trees still haven't moved. I know, I haven't blinked.

I shall find my place.

CHAPTER ONE
KING OF THE WILD

THE PHILOSOPHICAL TENET that states, "No man is an island," dates back to a work of poetry in 1624 by John Donne. In modern English, it reads, "No man is an island entire of itself." The point is one of connectedness, that humankind is worth more than the sum of its parts. If one of us passes beyond life into death, we are all lesser for it. "Ask not for whom the bell tolls," it tolls for all of humanity. Donne is making a bold statement for the value of human life, both on an individual and societal level.

However, this accepted universal teaching is only a perspective. It holds true as long as you adhere to that specific perspective. Stray from that viewpoint and "no man is an island" becomes deeply false in a very different context. Allow me to show you.

Every man and every woman lives on a solitary island with an infinite gulf between them and everyone else. We see the world through our eyes only. How we interpret the world around us, what we decide is true, how we live our lives, is set in motion by this singular view: our own personal perspective. While we may not know our own mind down to the most minute of details, we will never truly know the mind of another. We live out our days trapped on the island of our consciousness with no hope of rescue. It's lonely here on our islands. So, we try as best as we can to see the perspective of others, in hope that we might understand a glimpse of what is going on in their own island of thought.

Seeing another person's perspective is not easy. Their view of the world could be just as ineffable as the two views of "no man is an island." Both are true at the same time: no man is an island and yet, at the same time, we are all isolated from birth to death. It depends on how you look at it.

What this book is about, in essence, is my perspective as presented through the imperfect smoke signals of language. A view of the world, a way of understanding it, and the set of motivations that drive my decisions. Perspective is not easily shared. It is difficult to see the world through another's eyes, more so when the view is not one you're accustomed to. So, to see my perspective, I will show you me, in the hope that you see a little of the world the way I do.

I grew up in the wilderness. I was born into a small 900-square-foot home built by my father at the end of a rough forest road. Our property abutted a 23,000–acre state wilderness to the west, a dense unadulterated collection of wetlands and thick timber woodland. By the time I could walk, I had developed the habit of wandering into its depths. My mother wasn't too happy about my adventures, but my father encouraged them. At an early age, he pressed a crude wooden mockup of a rifle into my hands with the expectation that it would always accompany me. That wooden rifle, combined with a wide-brimmed felt hat, turned me into a very small version of my old man, the hunter.

The wooden rifle wasn't a toy, it was training. A few years later, I was awoken from a sound sleep by my father on a dark fall morning about 4:00 a.m. I was excited: first grade was on hold for the day because I had much better things to do. Dressed in warm clothes and clutching a BB gun, I sat in the bow of an old fiberglass boat as the little motor pushed us across a dark lake ringed with numerous bays filled with cattails. This is where his real instruction began.

"Look at the way the cattails form protected coves." I could only make out the faintest outlines in the dark morning, but enough to see what he was talking about. "Ducks look for those coves to rest and feed. The shallows have food, plants, and weeds for them to eat, and the high cattails protect them from predators." His left arm waved over the lake. "Out there in the open water, there is no protection. So they stick close in, hiding in the bays where it's safer. So that's where we'll hunt them."

The sun was still vaguely considering rising as we set up 50 plastic and rubber duck decoys. We had a pile of dark green canvas bags filled with them; I would dig decoys out one at a time and hand them to my father. He would unwind a long cord with a lead weight on the end, then drop each one in the water of our chosen reed-encircled bay. "The decoys look like real ducks to the ones flying above. From altitude, they'll see their own kind down here, peacefully at rest. They'll see their peers are safe, so they'll think they're safe to land here too."

"Can't they tell our decoys are fake?" I asked, still digging in the canvas bags.

"They won't. The skies are gray, and the light isn't great. All they need to see is the shapes on the water to feel the desire to come down to safety."

With the boat's motor off, my father used an oar to push us into a pocket of reeds at the back of the bay. This would be our spot for the day, carefully camouflaged in the thick cattails. We had an excellent view of the decoys and the skies above. We both hunkered down in the boat, using the green canvas bags to cover our bodies. My father's 12-gauge shotgun lay hidden, and my little BB gun remained stuffed under the canvas as well.

"Now we wait, son. I can't hit any of the ducks that are passing overhead, they're too high up. We need to coax them down to our decoys, where we can take them as they land." He took to scanning the sky with a pair of black binoculars. "Ducks fly in groups, and this time of year they're migrating south, leaving to avoid the cold of winter. If we convince one duck in the group to come down here to rest, the flock will follow."

Hunting involves a lot of waiting, more so than anything else. My father would tirelessly watch the skies. Sometimes, the horizon was clear edge-to-edge, and I was allowed to crawl out of my canvas covers and shoot cattails with my BB gun. It was fun for me. I'd miss the fat brown cattail heads a lot, but when I hit one, I'd have a little celebration.

"All right, son, slowly get down."

He saw something! I grinned as I carefully buried myself in the old canvas. I had to move slowly. I needed to keep my face down and hands hidden, because the color of my skin could be seen from high above and would spook the flock. My father started to blow through a handheld tubular device that mimicked the sound of a duck. He had a half dozen of them attached to cords hanging from his neck. Each call was for a different species of duck. It had to sound natural, so he had to judge the altitude of the flock, the species, and direction before he could choose which one to use.

The sound of the call was loud, almost piercing in the little bay. He was trying to get the flock high above us to notice the peaceful cove filled with friendly ducks and absolutely no predators. They heard him. The flock changed course and started to descend.

"Stay down, son. Don't move. Here they come." My father's whisper was loud in my adrenaline-pumped ears. Ducks have great eyesight, and if they saw even the slightest thing wrong, they'd fly off. We'd miss our prey. I stayed motionless under the canvas.

I heard the slightest tap of my father's wedding ring against the steel of his shotgun. I held my breath. Then a loud explosion as the gun went off, immediately followed by the metal-on-metal racking of a new round into the chamber. Another shot fired, another sharp clack-clack of the pump, and one more massive boom. The echoes of a round going off bounced back to us from across the lake, sounding like distant thunder.

A moment passed, almost infinitely long, before he said: "Okay, you can come out. We got two." We would have duck for dinner tonight.

Six years later, we had moved to a different wilderness. While not quite the 23,000 acres of my first home, this was on the west edge of a surveyed section: 640 acres. There was much more if I wanted to wander farther, but 640 seemed enormous in my young mind. Our home, once again, was at the end of a long, gravel road that snaked through the woods. But, instead of an expanse of state forest, everything was privately owned. That hardly stopped me. At 12 years old, I felt property rights were determined more by who did the walking than who waved a piece of paper.

The school bus would travel on the old roads: the surveyed lines that divided the woodlands into those 640-acre sections. When I got dropped off at the end of our driveway, I'd have a long walk down a gravel road to get home. In winter, it was cold and snowy. In spring, it was raining and wet. In late spring, the deer flies would cloud around my head and try to dig through my hair to bite my scalp. But in fall, just as school was beginning, I'd have two months of the most beautiful strolls down that dusty road.

Growing up hunting came with a lot of lessons. For one, everything in nature paid attention. Both sides of the equation, predator and prey, had keen eyes for the world around them. The ducks were hard to fool. The partridge easily spooked just out of range. The pheasants ran into deep brush rather than flying into the sights of shotguns. Deep woods whitetail deer were the most difficult. They had keen eyesight in black and white with a little ultraviolet: they saw every detail around them. Wash your clothes with the wrong detergent and you'd stand out like a spotlight. Move even the slightest and you'd be made. They had a tremendous sense of smell as well, and things upwind of them didn't stay upwind.

Deer seemed to have this sixth sense to danger, deeply embedded in their survival instinct.

Predators paid close attention too. They are constantly watching, always observant of the world around them. Subtle differences could be important. On one walk home, I noticed something back in the forest away from the road, visible only from one specific angle. It was a thinness of the trees, following a straight line through the dense underbrush. I wouldn't have noticed it if the leaves hadn't recently started falling. Straight lines don't usually exist in nature, they stand out. Something about what I was seeing was off. Curiosity drove me to climb through the ditch into the woods to find out what it was.

I was no stranger to the hundreds of acres surrounding our home. It was sliced up among a number of different owners, none of whom spent any time on their property. They held old logging roads, a couple of small fields planted with corn, but mostly uninterrupted hardwood forests. This was my backyard, and something new in my backyard deserved investigation.

I pushed my way through the brush to the spot I could see from the driveway. I stopped to assess. It looked like an old, straight track cut through the trees, roughly 15 feet wide. That made it a logging road from probably 30-50 years ago. It hadn't been used for vehicles since then, however. Ah, there, the old road had become repurposed. It was now a deer trail. It was the easiest way through the woods for them, so of course they'd follow it. Time for me to follow it, too.

I walked quietly through the woods, as I always did. Growing up hunting ingrained good habits. Somewhere along the way, I passed onto someone else's property, I think. This was not a concern to me. I watched for deer sign: hoof prints, scat, old buck scrapes, anything to tell me how well this trail was used. It was well defined, but bore no recent activity. Maybe it was a seasonal trail. Maybe the deer's patterns had changed recently.

I eventually came to a clearing. I could see it through the trees as I approached, because the sunlight reflects differently on the distant trees even if you can't see the clearing itself. I was in uncharted territory. Is this a small crop field? Someone's back yard of a home I didn't know about? I wondered. No, as I stood hidden at the edge of the clearing I could see it was only a grass-filled opening in the middle of the woods. The size of half a football field, oval in shape, the space was drenched in warm sunlight across waist-high grasses and flowers.

I stood my ground at the edge. Edges were important: they were spaces of change, and when things changed, the rules changed. I needed to understand the space and its rules before I entered it. The deer trail I was following passed into the grass in front of me at the southern edge of the clearing. If I stepped out I'd become visible from a distance, and everything out here knew humans were predators. So I stood slightly behind the trunk of a tree, watching and considering. What created this clearing? Was it human or nature? Is the clearing slowly closing up as trees creep in around its edges? Or was it getting bigger, forming the start to a shallow swamp? Was the grass disturbed by some— Wait, what's that?

On the far side of the clearing stood a wooden structure made of two-by-fours. It was a small shack covered in plywood no more than a few square feet inside, elevated on four sloping legs to stand ten feet in the air. In front, facing the clearing, was a ladder leading to a door. Crude shutters hid obvious windows. This was a deer stand. By the look of the golden-yellow wood, it was brand-new.

This was a predator's hide, a structure designed to conceal the hunter's visual and olfactory tells from the deer. Now I understood. The trail I'd been walking is used by the deer in late fall as they went from their deep woods bedding areas to sources of food. Their trail crosses the clearing at the south end. The stand is at the north end and high in the air, giving the hunter a clear view of anything entering the clearing. The shutters were closed, the stand was empty. Deer season was still a couple months away.

I picked my way through the trees at the edge of the clearing, heading north to the stand. It was new. I climbed up into it, and there were no signs of use beyond assembling it here sometime this summer. Sure enough, I could watch over the entire clearing. I sat there in the open door, relaxing. A light breeze ruffled the tall grasses, the smell of fall woodland was strong in my nose, and the sunlight coursed over me, making me warm. I could hear nothing but the wild around me. It was beautiful.

The wilderness has patterns to it; everything has a reason. When I followed the deer trail farther, I found I was right. The deer slept in the safety of a swamp and traveled to a farmer's field for food. In the middle of this daily routine was this clearing, an open spot the deer crossed because it was the easiest way to get from point A to point B. They followed the old logging road. East of the clearing, the logging road was more distinct, more used. This was where the builder of the deer stand had come from. It was erected at the other end of the field because that was the easiest place to catch the deer in the open.

The clearing became part of my own routine: I visited it often, in all seasons, watching the patterns of nature in this little place. The trees would slowly overtake the open space as their seeds drifted into the sunlit void. The grasses started small in spring, grew tall in summer. Some of them were sharp to the touch, then turned golden in fall, only to be knocked down by freezing rain and covered in snow by winter. When the weather was wet or cold, I'd stay only for a few minutes. When it was warm and bright, I'd lie in the grass, soaking up the sun with a smile. I never hunted here, and to this day I don't know why someone built that deer stand. It was never used. I watched it carefully. Over the years, it would turn gray with weather and disuse.

The clearing and the deer stand did serve as a poignant message, one about the relationship between the whitetail deer and humankind, of people and nature, of patterns and rules. This place was a symbol for all I grew up with, of what I was to become. I am a hunter, a predator. I am not separate from nature, for I am as much nature as my prey.

A few years later, I stepped off a bus to see a white pickup truck parked on the edge of our gravel road, halfway down it. I didn't recognize the vehicle. I knew almost everyone who lived out here, so this had to be a stranger. The pickup was parked near the deer trail.

Bow hunting season was on, and perhaps someone had gone to my clearing. This wouldn't do. I inhabit this forest, I thought, this is mine. I knew what I would do. I dropped my backpack to drag on the ground and began stomping down the thin trail. Sure enough, I could see signs of the hunter's passing. Busted twigs and boot prints were easy to spot. I broke my rules: I snapped twigs too, I dragged my backpack loudly, I even started singing an inane song. Loud enough to be heard, but not loud enough to be obvious. I kept my eyes open. He could be somewhere, likely in a tree above me. And there he was.

"What are you doing?!" he yelled from the impromptu tree stand he'd erected just outside the clearing.

I looked up, smiling. "Oh, hi! What are you doin'?"

The guy looked angry, scowling at me. "I'm trying to hunt. Now get out of here!"

I feigned surprise. "Oh, I'm sorry! I'll get going right away!" I turned, resumed singing my vapid song, swinging my backpack, and noisily wandering back along the trail. When I eventually reached the driveway, I laughed lightly. Deer have a great sense of smell, and I had spread a high school backpack's worth of scent all over the trail. I sang my stupid song so he'd identify me as a kid well before he saw me and not shoot me. I stomped on the way just to be that much more obvious. To him, I was some idiot high schooler who had innocently stumbled upon his hunt. He might be pissed, but he'd never realize that I had intentionally tainted the whole area for deer. His hunt was over. He never came back. Ever.

It was a frigid day up on the ridge as the wind picked up and cut its way over the top of the forest. I never hunted in my 640-acre backyard. My father and I wanted even more isolation: we hunted in the depths of a million-acre wilderness to the north. This was untouched federal land, and the nearest town was an hour away via narrow gravel roads. If you got there, you'd find the town only had one church and two bars. We built a ground blind for me up on a ridge overlooking a gap in the long, curving glacial esker that separated two huge cedar swamps. It was natural for deer to move between the safety of the two swamps here, since any of them that climbed up the ridge could be seen for a long distance. Which is why I was here trying to stay warm in the middle of a snow-covered wilderness. The blind consisted of trees piled waist-high in a U shape, and I was seated on a crude box in the middle. I could move my legs, but any movement of my arms and chest would be seen by any animal looking up toward the top of the esker. That meant the top half of me would freeze.

You will find these swamps mixed among the high ground in the northern wilderness. Cedars prefer just the right kind of wet ground. There's nothing like it: it's not a common marsh, filled with reeds or open water covered in floating bog. They're dark, foreboding places where the cedars grow so close together that sunlight doesn't reach the swamp floor and you can't see more than a few yards in any direction. You can walk through them if you're careful, but the only solid footing is the roots of the cedars before they dive into the dank pools of water below. In winter, the pools only half-freeze because the swamps trap heat. These belong to another world, which is why the middle of a cedar swamp in winter is one of my favorite places. You do not want to kill a deer in here, though. Dragging the carcass out is an interminable nightmare.

Crunch. I freeze. I hear the sound of something stepping in the snow, just slightly louder than the wintry breeze. I try playing back the sound in my mind while my ears continue listening. Too soft for a person. Is it a squirrel?

Crunch. It's slightly louder this time. Off to the left. I stare into the thick wall of the swamp while my gloved hands tighten my grip on the rifle.

Crunch, snap. There, at the edge, a deer is about to step out into the gap. My gap. I slowly start raising my gun.

My heart is racing. This is my first season of deer hunting on my own, I'm just old enough to have my own license. My rifle is brand-new. This is it.

With another step, the deer emerges halfway out from the cover of the swamp. Two points on his antlers form a fork, thin and light. The buck can't be much more than a year old, if even. I slowly shoulder my rifle.

I watch over the top of my scope as the buck picks its way among the rocks and downed trees, heading for my gap. It'll be in range in moments.

I can barely contain my nerves. This is it. I'm going to pull the trigger.

As the buck takes another slow step forward, my mind snaps back to a history lesson of my firearms instructor years ago, condensed into a momentary thought:

"We killed the wolves. Nature demands balance, and the role of the predator must be maintained. We humans do that now. We hunt deer because we are now responsible for keeping that balance. We are their only predator."

I work to steel my nerves while I peer through the scope, trying to line the crosshairs up on the chest of the young buck. The scope won't stay still. For a clean kill I need to hit him slightly back and down from the shoulder, in the heart. Why won't the crosshairs sit still?

The buck is now right in the middle of the gap. It's time. I apply pressure to the trigger, slowly, fighting the erratic circling motion of the crosshairs. And then, in one moment, the trigger sets home and the gun goes off. I jerk back slightly from the recoil, and I look at the deer over my scope. He's just standing there.

And then he tries to run. He stumbles. His right front leg is swinging wildly. He stumbles again and then stumble-runs straight into the depths of the swamp.

I stare, unmoving. I can see it clearly in my mind's eye: I hit him in the shoulder. I missed the heart, even the lungs. I destroyed his shoulder. Fatal, but miles and maybe days deep into the swamp fatal. I failed.

I sit silently for some time, playing back the tape in my mind.

Crunch. That's a boot, a person on the ridge behind me. My father is coming to find out what happened.

I don't know what to say to him when he arrives. I explain as best I can what happened, trying to stick to the facts. He leaves me on the ridge as he inspects the gap, carefully picking over the spatter of blood and bone among the rocks and snow, trying to reconstruct the scene in his mind. When he climbs back up the ridge, he announces that the buck was severely injured, but it would run a long way on three legs before eventually bleeding out and dying. It was not a clean kill.

The next morning, the guys down the road in the next hunting camp picked up my buck's blood trail. They said they followed it, painstakingly, for three miles before giving up. They said there's no way the buck would live past another below-freezing night. The blood loss would guarantee it. Life and death are a daily occurrence out here in nature, and now I was part of it.

CHAPTER TWO
FIGHT CLUB

"You're wrong, Lion." I sat on the edge of a dirty couch, staring at Wade, sitting across from me in an equally dingy chair.

Wade continued. "That's a slippery-slope argument. That's like saying that, because the administration is cutting back on the hours the dining hall is open, students are going to starve. That's a logical fallacy. Your whole argument is invalid. You. Are. Wrong." Damn.

The apartments on my college campus were thick Cold War–era cinderblock constructions, carefully designed to withstand something worse than nuclear exchange: college students. The four friends of mine who lived in this apartment were certainly putting the design to the test. Cleaning was a chore done once, right before move-out at the end of the year. The beige walls held no artwork—no metal band posters, no half-burnt-out Christmas tree lights taped up for mood lighting. Bare. The rectangular bricks were fairly uniform, save for an occasional hand-sized stain smeared horizontally in places. The tradition of move-out dumpster diving had paid off for these guys: grubby chairs and couches passed down through generations of students via the leave-a-couch, take-a-couch philosophy made for places to sit, or at least raised horizontal surfaces for junk to collect. And wow, did it collect. One of the guys had a freeze pop addiction. Nearly empty sugary plastic tubes of dayglow radiator fluid were everywhere, as if the entire apartment was situated on the forest floor underneath a dense canopy of Mister Freeze trees that constantly shed dead freeze-pop wrappers.

I shifted uncomfortably on the couch. Wade was grinning at me, happy in another victory against one of his "friends." I vaguely shrugged and stood up. "All right, fine, I, uh, need to go. See ya, Wade."

Wade was an interesting guy, from the "may you live in interesting times" category of interesting. It was all perfectly normal back then, because our group of friends threw a lot of different, often conflicting or confusing, personalities into a mix that tried to be cohesive. Such is the nature of college friendships: they were born of physical proximity, not of common interest. They were sustained by the inertia of familiarity, not shared values. Wade was a philosophy major. At the time, I didn't know what to make of that. I was in the College of Science and Engineering. Math was a concrete subject: either you were right or you were wrong. Liberal arts seemed like a whole different world.

Wade made a point of bringing up Nietzsche on a regular basis, flaunting it like he was some kind of dark villain. The best any of the rest of us managed was a vague sense that Nietzsche's views were bad somehow. Today, in retrospect, it seemed like Wade was trying to be the philosophy equivalent of a goth: dark and brooding nihilism with a healthy dose of black clothing. I didn't figure out what nihilism was until two decades later. Seems kind of pointless now.

What Wade did do well was beat people up intellectually. He was smart, well-read, and had a knack for arguing. The ubiquitous late-night philosophy debates so common to college were Wade's home turf: he would drag people into his world of rational point-to-conclusion argumentation and then beat them down with his command of concepts like logical fallacies. It was a humiliating process. He had this smug confidence that he would roll into every statement he made, every argument, every point, every counterpoint. He wasn't wrong either.

I was smart enough to avoid getting into it with Wade most of the time, preferring to stay out of his debates with my friends. I'd sit back and root for pretty much anyone but Wade, and then witness my friends getting demolished. Whenever I voiced my own immature musings on life, I was sure to say them far away from the guy.

That day, however, I had accidentally wandered into an argument, and after all of his non-verbal gloating, I finally learned something. I recognized what Wade did as a pattern. He had a skill he'd worked on and developed. He'd wait for one of our friends to get into some light sophomoric debate, then jump in and dominate the discussion. No one won against him.

It was a long walk across campus back to my dorm. Still stung by my defeat, I made a conscious decision that I too needed to develop this skill. My choice wasn't only based upon what Wade had done to me. I didn't actually respect him, despite his intelligence. But Wade's ability to conduct arguments was a tool that, when mastered, would serve me well. So, how do I approach this, how do I generalize it to the everyday, how do I learn it?

The little I knew about Wade centered around his degree program: philosophy. I had no knowledge of his upbringing. The only place he could wield this tool was on his home turf. He didn't challenge anything that was outside his expertise. I had this vague sense that philosophy was an intellectual pursuit very different from math. Somehow that pursuit gave Wade his skillset.

So, I marched over to the College of Liberal Arts the next Monday to declare my minor: philosophy.

My first philosophy course was a classic 1001: critical thinking. I had great expectations of fights. This was critical thinking: the very title draws you to challenge everything! As the first few weeks rolled on, it began to dawn on me that this was a required course in many liberal arts degree programs. The signs were obvious on the faces of the students: disinterest, boredom, low energy, a "let's get this over with" fatigue. The lethargic course barely registered for most of the students. Potential argumentative topics were trotted out by the professor in a "look but don't touch" manner. The students would quietly take notes and never speak up. Well then, it was time to change the music.

"There are unassailable facts," the professor droned on, "such as two plus two equals four." Or are there?

I raised my hand and spoke without pause, taking the initiative. "Sure, except when two plus two equals five for extremely large values of two."

The professor stared at me, a little confused, a little annoyed. She put her hand down from the chalkboard. "What?"

"Yeah, two plus two equals five for extremely large values of two. It's just math."

She paused, then nodded. "All right, well, moving on."

Two plus two equals five has a lot of cultural connotations. Its most common meaning was used by George Orwell in his book *1984* to demonstrate conformity in contradiction of obvious facts. In this sense, I was calling out the conformity of the class. The attempt was ham-fisted at best. Orwell's use was patently false, and I could be easily shut down if I had left it there. To wage a real argument, I needed to add to the challenge a mathematician's joke: for extremely large values of two.

For the next few weeks, I repeatedly brought it up as I clumsily tried to undermine the "what is truth" lessons of the professor. I was cruising for a fight, not just with her but with anyone in the room. I assumed my half-awake peers were wondering what the hell I kept going on about. But no, as I watched the body language of the class, nothing was registering. Flat line. Don't care.

Eventually, I had to be stopped. The professor put her chalk on the rail and stepped away from the board, frustrated. "All right Lion, are you capable of defending your position on this?"

Yes! It was time! Inside, I was excited and nervous. I was facing off against the professor. Bring it on! "Of course I can."

"Then come up here and explain yourself."

As a junior, I was late to the philosophy game. The class consisted mostly of freshmen. But my mathematics game was top notch. The math stinger to the joke has to do with how decimal numbers are stored inside a computer. They're not stored as "3.14159," but as at least three different numbers that interact. By doing so, it introduces a very small amount of inaccuracy. If you draw out that built-in inaccuracy really far, you come to the ridiculous claim that two plus two equals five for extremely large values of two. This is what I showed them, on the board, down to the bit level with all the right terms. By the end of my laborious explanation, I had covered the chalkboard in many patterns of zeroes and ones and consumed at least 20 minutes of time.

I turned back to the class, trying to look triumphant. "So, that's how the error is introduced and how that can overflow to five. It's both right and wrong." I stood with hands at my sides, scanning the room for a response. They were all looking at me, but their eyes told the entire story: still don't care. The professor had the same look.

She nodded. "All right, Lion, we believe you."

I sat down, feeling a bittersweet victory. What I had just committed was a little fraud covered by a lot of domain-specific technical knowledge. Did they buy it? Probably begrudgingly. Not because they thought I was on the level—my nervous body language betrayed me—but because none of them knew enough about math to duke it out with me. None of the students rose up, the professor just went with it, and it was over.

I got bored with the class after that. I joked my way through it, probably to the irritation of everyone. Some jerk was disrupting their sedate "have-to-be-there" class. At the end I begged off the final exam. I convinced the professor to let me write a paper explaining why the class failed to teach critical thinking. At least I was trying. I didn't think I'd get into a fight with the professor by then. I just wanted her to know that I knew her 1000-level philosophy class never went past rote execution. Decades later, when I'd take up teaching college myself, I'd come to really dislike students like me. She did give me a B+ on the paper, though.

Not everyone's a winner.

Next, I had to take two ethics classes: one required for my degree titled "Ethics for Scientists" and another for my minor called "Philosophy of Ethics."

Ethics for Scientists was interesting, and this time there was at least some energy in the room. We spent a lot of our time discussing the ethical consequences of our labors. What were we researching? What effects would it have on humanity? What are the ethical implications of the pursuit of certain kinds of knowledge? While the room had a baseline agenda of "Do good, not evil," interpretations of that theme varied.

Then, one day, the debate turned ugly. The subject was the continuation of a decades-long debate on humanity's impact upon the environment. It started slow, as the professor laid down the concerns of technology versus nature pretty lightly. My fellow students took the cudgels from there.

"Man cannot be allowed to destroy the earth!" Passion was starting to build among the class.

"We have a responsibility to ensure that people do not damage our ecosystem with our work!"

"Ethically, we cannot win over nature!" The discussion was getting a little bit off the rails now, so this was the moment.

I stood up, dead center in the room, surrounded by everyone. They stopped talking in mid-sentence and stared.

I held no illusion that there exists some kind of dichotomy of man versus nature. We adapted to our world. For instance, 40 degree below zero winter days were not to be taken lightly. We stocked extra wood in the cellar to heat the house. We kept thick jackets and outer gear to survive outdoors. Our habits were driven by our environment. The weather had more to say than we did. The deer would change their habits to their environment as well; trails would move according to the seasons, what fields were planted by farmers, and what traps were laid by hunters. Neither deer nor man would dare stand up to nature. The forest is littered with the crumbling foundations of old barns and farmhouses, the decades-enduring skeletal remains of one kind of death. You would only see them if you stumbled across that rare straight line through the trees and recognize the vague outlines in the moss.

I set my jaw. "Humanity is driven by evolutionary pressure. We change and adapt to our surroundings, like every organism. Survival of the species is our top goal. As we change the world around us, the world changes too, maybe unexpectedly. Our tool use is our evolution, and maybe our pathway is survival through those tools. Maybe evolution will require that we all wear gas masks." It wasn't my most eloquent moment, but the statement landed like the knight's gauntlet it was supposed to be. The room erupted as I sat down, and incensed gibberish filled the void. There wasn't a cogent response in the fray. Good. I was finally seen as a threat. I had spooked the herd. I was learning.

Philosophy of Ethics was an elective course, which meant more investment, more interaction, and more arguments. Here I figured out what philosophy really is: an attempt to classify and explain the unexplainable. It is the pursuit of understanding humanity, applying rules to it, failing, and then for some, trying to force humanity to follow those ill-fated rules. I find it incredibly important to have a philosophy, an understanding of one's self that is guided by a deep conviction or principle. It's also just as important to know when to bag it and go on with life anyway.

This began what I had been looking for all along. My attempts to start arguments, the point-to-conclusion kind, weren't met with apathy or profanity. Instead, the professors encouraged it, nurtured it, gave it guard rails early on, only to remove them later when we would not go off the road. We fought, testing ourselves, our wits, our command of history and literature. We failed, we succeeded, we learned. Some days were tranquil dispensations of our instructor's lesson plans; others thrust us into an intellectual pugilists' ring where friends respectfully attacked, feigned, and defended.

Philosophy of Language showed us the deep meaning of words and how they structured the mind. Epistemology started at "justified true belief" and ended up with intellectual brawls about rocks in fields that looked like sheep. As the cohort progressed from class to class, we got to know each other, our styles of thought, how each of us saw the world. We never raised our minds in anger, far from it. This was fun.

My cohort and the professors came to know me as a fighter by the time we reached the 4000 level: Ethics of Life. One professor decided to take what we had built and made it the main feature. We would argue about abortion, euthanasia, and who lived and who died. What was a life worth? When you had to decide, what would guide you and who would you choose?

In the event of everyone agreeing, I would take the opposing view to keep the class going. I didn't let on that I was doing this. I was learning how to take on everyone for a tenet I didn't even believe in.

One day, I spent the last 45 minutes of the class arguing that trees had "interests." Their biological function manifested as more than a biochemical impetus to proliferate. The class had argued against me with fervor. Even I didn't buy my own arguments. I couldn't win against the class, but I held the line. That was enough.

"Okay, we have to stop here. We're out of time." The professor waved his hands in a friendly gesture of "enough."

I smiled and put my hand up, palm out. "Hey, sorry, guys, I only wanted an argument. I don't really believe that trees are like that." The room burst out in a combination of laughs and sighs of relief.

One student addressed me as we all stood up. "I'm glad you said something, Lion. I thought you'd gone crazy!"

My last philosophy course wasn't actually in the philosophy department at all. Philosophy of the Native Americans was part of the Tribal Management degree program, serving the significant native populations of the north. I took inventory of the class makeup when I sat down for the first day. The students were half native Ojibwa and half whites who would go on to work government jobs surrounding the Anishinaabe population. They didn't intermingle much in seating. While I sat absolutely in the center in the classroom, the Ojibwa were on my left, the whites on my right. The Ojibwa were the normal ones in my eyes, looking like everyday students. The whites all had this new-age look to them with their hemp clothes and crystals tied around their necks. Odd.

The instructor was an Ojibwa professor in his 50s, portly but respectable. With every class he would take us into Ojibwa oral traditions, dissecting the meanings and underlying themes of the stories. Every story had an objective lesson, such as don't treat your neighbors poorly, or respect your parents. To me those lessons seemed obvious. To my left, the natives would get a little into it being their own ancient tales. To my right, the whites treated the stories with reverent mysticism. I would quietly wait for everyone to weigh in, then simply say something like, "This story warns against excess in eating."

I wasn't looking for a fight at first. Through all those arguments leading up to this, I had honed my mind by deliberate practice. My words could hurt people. I had to be responsible. They weren't to be wielded unless it was really necessary. I didn't become Wade, careless and severe with his intellect. When my turn came in class, I'd say my piece, everyone would listen to me, and then continue on.

Except when it came to the final paper. It wasn't an unusual ask: write a paper and give a presentation on your research and opinion on a topic in Native American philosophy. The professor wanted check-ins, status reports, data to show him each of us was making progress. I ignored him. I knew I was going to create conflict, and I wouldn't have it blunted. Buried in the library stacks, I pulled history books recounting the events of the last days of the Plains Indians.

The class, including the professor, watched in horror as I dismembered the Ghost Dance movement of the late 1800s, reaching the ruthless conclusion that the Lakota people were responsible for their own cultural destruction. The beliefs, the symbology, all spoke volumes of willful ignorance of their own fate.

When I finished, I passed out copies of my paper. "These are to demonstrate that I am accountable for every word I've said today." I panned the room, looking everyone individually in the eye. "Are there any questions?"

Only one student spoke up. "You're hardcore, aren't you?"

"Yes. Yes, I am."

I met the professor in his office right before the semester ended. I wished him the best of luck with his class and program, and he wished me luck with my life and where I was going. Not much more was said, because not much more needed to be said. It was a farewell of mutual respect.

Low clouds scudded across the sky, threatening to snow on my spot halfway up the gully wall. Thirty feet above me, out of the valley, the wind was blowing enough to keep me down in this pocket. Despite my thick blaze orange jacket, I would have been chased off the peak quickly. It was a steep, 40-feet drop down to the frozen creek. I could walk down if I wanted to, picking my way through the trees for support. During the summer, the creek was at most a few dozen inches deep in places, but in winter it was frozen solid and snowed in along with both sides of the gully.

My blind, hastily constructed of tree branches and snow before dawn, once again hid me from the waist down. I kept my orange hat pulled down low, keeping the cold at bay while my rifle sat on my lap and my gloved hands stayed in my pockets. The wind was such that I wouldn't hear anything moving on the slope across from me. That worked both for me and against me. If I couldn't hear deer moving, they'd have trouble hearing me. With their eyesight, though, a deer could still see me move.

I considered it an exercise in thinking like my prey: considering the weather, the terrain, the path between shelter and food, then setting up where the deer would be even slightly disadvantaged. They are clever, and catching them at a disadvantage isn't easy. I tried to understand the deer while surveilling the valley, to view this area through their eyes. This is the practice of hunting. I need to know the literal landscape of the valley and its surroundings as well as the figurative landscape of my prey's motivations and capabilities. It is detailed work.

I waited.

The clouds began to lighten as noon rolled around. The wind was still whistling lightly in the forest above. I considered the venison jerky in my pocket for lunch as a way to pass the time.

Not yet.

The trees were mostly bare, having dropped their leaves a month ago. A single spruce was still green a short distance up the valley. It was maybe 20-feet tall. I smiled at it like a friend—we're both still alive out here, but conserving energy.

I catch a flash of movement on the other slope. My eyes dart toward it, my body staying still. I stare, unblinking.

Again, movement, small, brief. My eyes hone in.

Brown. White-tailed deer colored brown. A brown leg emerges from between the trees.

My line of sight isn't clear up the valley to where the deer is. I need it to get closer, to come down the valley almost directly across from me. I can't move until the last moment, until it's time to fire.

Time has come to a stop as the deer picks its way silently across the slope, heading my way. I barely breathe, trying to obscure the clouds of vapor from my lungs. It keeps moving, slowly, carefully, watching.

Buck. It is nearing the tiny clearing where I can make the shot. I finally make out the antlers among the leafless tree limbs. It steps again. I raise my rifle slowly, carefully, eyes never leaving my prey. The stock slips against my shoulder naturally, and my left eye closes as my right dives into the scope.

The crosshairs move in a predictable figure eight. I line the center on the buck's midsection, down and back from the shoulder blade. He steps again. I adjust. I slowly let my breath out of my lungs, and right before I run out of air and the crosshairs slide over the point I want to hit, I apply the last bit of pressure to the trigger.

The rifle goes off with a deafening crack, echoes quickly dissipating in the wind. My right hand flashes against the bolt, a quick snapping in another round. I don't look up from the scope. Nothing else moves.

The buck falls.

It's a hit.

I stare through the scope at the buck. He's down but still alive. He looks peaceful, head up and alert, but he's not going anywhere. I must have nearly hit his heart and punctured the lungs. He probably doesn't have the ability to get up. Now it's a waiting game to let him bleed out.

I set my rifle down.

My father arrives sometime later, quietly working his way down the slope. He kneels next to me in my blind and we watch. Nothing happens: the buck's head is still erect, eyes still watching.

My father looks down at my gun. I watch his gaze dip, then come back up to me. Right.

Shouldering the gun again, I set the crosshairs so that it circles on the thin sliver of the buck's head I can see. Relaxing into the trigger, the gun goes off and the buck's head snaps back and onto the ground. A perfect shot.

My father pats me on the back with a gloved hand.

CHAPTER THREE
SHOP!

MY WORLD OF part-time work back in college was a small box, 8 x 10 feet, with a raised countertop and lower workspace, two extra-large IBM terminals in beige, and stacks of paper carbon forms. The gray laminate countertops were brand new, unmarked as if the plastic shipping protector had come off them only moments ago. Upon them were set a few clear acrylic sign holders, each bearing an exciting ad for my store: Shop! Above me, the Shop! logo hung on a large rectangular sign bearing in all capital letters the words "SERVICE DESK."

From the service desk, I could see the whole store. Rows and rows of clothing hangers were laid out for hundreds of feet. On my right, spanning from the far wall to well past the middle of the store, was various women's clothing. That right wall had the practical heart of all women's clothing: the changing rooms. On my far left, beyond the row of six checkouts and against the other wall, was men's clothing. Another box out in the sea of hangers was enclosed in glass cases. Above it, the same Shop! logo and the word "JEWELRY." In the far back of the store were long retail shelves bearing odd home furnishings, luggage, and an ever-changing landscape of whatever came in off the truck: Department 88. These were curiosities that defied description. Colorful, sometimes almost classy items that when purchased, went to a home, and sat upon a shelf to garner the unspoken questions, "Why would you have that?" or "Huh, I wonder what that is?"

Shop! is a national discount clothing store, and when word got out that they were coming to my sleepy college town, I was almost first in line to apply. I had great part-time retail career credentials: I'd already worked for two major chain stores, from shell to grand opening. A brand-new store was what I knew, from an open expanse of tile floor to the first customers walking in the door.

This was now my third time watching the process of getting a new store started. The stores did mass hiring: fill out these forms, your interview is right now, your first day is Monday. My first Monday evening shift came quickly. Two store managers, Shop! lifers, came from other stores to head up the new one. I looked around the mass of people standing in the middle of the empty expanse of floor. We were mostly young, college on up, with a few middle-aged people rounding out the curve. This was the part-time evenings-and-weekends crew. None of us knew each other.

"Welcome to Shop! number one hundred and twenty-six!" The senior of the two lifers stood before us, dressed in slacks, white shirt, and tie. He stood there comfortably in his mediocre frame topped with short, dark brown hair. A plastic Shop! name tag adorned his left chest.

"I'm Rich, and this is Cheryl." He waved at the other lifer, a middle-aged woman in gray slacks and a white blouse. She waved at everyone, looking a little nervous. While Rich didn't register as being interesting at first sight, Cheryl looked bright, intelligent even, and charming in a classic way. Rich looked like your average retail lifer.

He held up both his hands. "I want to warmly welcome all of you new Shop! associates to the store." Associates, that was the term for employees here. Got it, that's important to know. "We have eight weeks to get the store from what you see now to full swing. We believe that all of us should become a team here at Shop! and both Cheryl and I know we'll come together. Everyone's been assigned a department already, so why don't you head over to where your department sign is, group up, and hang out while Cheryl and I get everyone started? Yay, Shop!"

I chuckled inside at Rich's excitement. I wasn't that excited to be at Shop! I mean, I was excited to make some cash, but I was not on Rich's Shop! level. I wandered over to the service desk, closely tailed by two women my age.

"You guys service desk too?"

"Oh yeah, go Shop!" one of my coworkers said, a touch sarcastically. We all laughed, acknowledging Rich's over-the-top enthusiasm. We were off to an excellent start.

As we were handling the basics of names and what college each of us attended, Cheryl walked up. "Hey, service desk people!" We made room for her in our little circle at the edge of the Formica countertop. "Like Rich said, I'm Cheryl." Sure enough, now I could read Cheryl's Shop! name tag clearly: a black strip of adhesive plastic with the name "Cheryl" in white punched into an oval with the Shop! logo at the top. She looked at me expectantly.

"Oh hi, I'm Lion." I quickly looked at the woman to my right.

"Christine."

"Hey, I'm Jenny."

Cheryl nodded. "Service desk is a complex place with a lot going on. I need you to take home the procedure manuals for the registers and learn all the steps for doing every kind of transaction. You'll do cashiering, returns, layaway, store credits, everything." She wandered back into the box as she talked. "Not only that, you're going to have to work the floor at times to cover people's breaks. So you pretty much need to know the whole place." She stepped inside the box and waved at us to join her.

"This is where you'll spend most of your time." Cheryl handed each of us a thick manual covered with the Shop! logo in black and white. "These are yours. Learn the stuff in them, and in a few weeks we'll train on the registers." Each of us flipped through the books, getting an idea of what we were in for. Nothing looked complicated.

"So, for now, you'll be working out on the floor, stocking. We'll get you time in every department." Cheryl surveyed the store. "Why don't you start in men's? It looks like they need help."

This was my third time through the process of opening a store, and by now I started seeing the patterns. Standing in the men's department, elbow deep in boxes of slacks, I realized the why of what was happening. We, service desk and floor people together, had been given a task: stock the racks with clothes. This task kept us together that night, working alongside each other, unpacking and hanging the endless supply of retail goods. We were forging a bond, one built on the requirement to get something done together.

The idea of a bond is the central driver in keeping people together in a group. A bond is an emotional attachment between people that is expected to continue forward into the future. Bonds vary in strength. Compare, for instance, the bond of a family to that of a community, to a state, a nation, and so on. The bond between my wife and I will last the rest of our lives. The bond between my younger self and the others unpacking boxes that night at Shop! would last until the task was done.

Task bonding keeps people together only as long as the work requires. It is a simple and weak bond built on the desire to achieve a greater whole.

When the task is done, the bond evaporates and everyone goes their separate way. At 9:00 p.m., we all left for our homes hardly knowing each other's names.

The next evening was more of the same: group up, unpack boxes, and hang clothes on racks. But more was developing than just the task. People are really good at bonding; it's in our nature as social creatures. We do it unconsciously. As we worked, we naturally engaged in two different activities that would build the next stage of bonding. We talked about ourselves and we paid attention to the rest of the group. Completely naturally, we each opened up about who we were, our past, our goals, and all the little details that take random strangers and turn them into known acquaintances. A lot happens when someone shows a little vulnerability in talking about oneself and then connects by reacting in kind to everyone else's stories.

Christine came from a German family, and she even spoke the language. Jenny went to the same college as I do, but majored in education. She wanted to teach young children. Cool.

At the same time we were sharing about ourselves, we were paying attention to each other. Again, unconsciously, we were evaluating the people performing the task with us. Do they seem like good people? Are they kind? Tough? Honest? Liars? Lazy? As we went back and forth between talking about the task and ourselves, each of us built up an impression of the others. Again, this process is completely unconscious. If one of us had not connected at least a little, we'd have this nagging sensation that they were somewhat "off."

The transition from a weak task bond to a stronger emotional bond worked to bring everyone at Shop! together as the exchanges back-and-forth between the work and ourselves were repeated throughout the store. Cheryl made sure Christine, Jenny, and I worked with every department, every person, and every job. As we approached the opening of the store, we all had an idea of who everyone else was. We knew, even if at a gut level, people's strengths, weaknesses, and character. It was as if we were becoming a team.

Rich was right. We had become a team because we had bonded in opening the store. Working together had unleashed significant bonding forces: shared common experiences, knowledge, and trust.

Opening a store is a bit of a greenfield exercise. There's no preexisting culture or deeply-embedded history that one needs to fit into. Instead, it's a unique experience to be part of creating the store culture from scratch. We all participated in that experience, we all had memories of it, and we all shared a common experience. Because of that, we had stories ("Do you remember when?"), language ("Oh, you pulled a Vicky!"), and the feeling that we all had arrived at the opening day together.

Shared common experience can even be a bond shared across people who have never met. Pilots new to each other can strike up a conversation and end up hours later getting asked to leave the coffee shop because it's closing. Pilots all have a lot of the same experiences. The frustration, fear, and elation of your first landing. A close call with another aircraft. A sunset from 10,000 feet. Or consider those from the military with basic training, the first deployment, enjoyment with the chain of command, enlistment contracts, bases, travel, and more. And never forget "Every Marine a Rifleman."

We also knew each other, well enough to work together. Jenny knew I was detail-oriented at the register, and she could count on me to handle complex work accurately. I knew Christine was focused, almost to a fault, in doing her job. I knew that if I cracked a joke and she didn't find it funny, it was probably because she was engrossed in doing something serious. That was fine. I sometimes spoke really bad German around Christine just to push her buttons in good fun. And we all knew Cheryl was easygoing. Over time, she proved to be knowledgeable, kind, and understanding. This part of the bond made us comfortable; we were walking into the store on any given night and greeting everyone warmly. It was good to see them again, honestly.

Finally, the most important part of the bond is trust. Without trust, humanity would still be fighting over the dirt under the trees we just came out of. Trust is a set of expectations combined with history combined with hope. I trusted that Cheryl was going to get our service desk team out of trouble if it cropped up. Up to now she'd had our back, establishing a history of backing us up with unruly customers. I had an expectation that when trouble came again, Cheryl would do well by us. I trust my coworkers will do a good job too, that they'll be there when they're supposed to be, and that we'll handle whatever comes next in our retail service desk world.

The bonds we formed throughout the store worked great for the first year. Until ...

"Martha?" I stopped my endless data entry on the IBM terminal and looked at Christine.

She stood next to me at her own terminal in the other corner of the service desk box. "Yeah, I heard she's in trouble."

"I don't know her that well. I mean sort of?" Data entry could wait, this must be something that merited attention.

She pushed a stack of return forms aside, an absent-minded habit. "She's over in women's, works the fitting room a lot. You know, the one with the curly hair and big glasses?"

"Oh, yeah, okay. I haven't talked to her much." I hadn't. Martha had always struck me as weird, but "over there" weird. The kind of weird that isn't a problem as long as it stays over there.

"So she came in late again today."

"Huh, okay." I didn't really care. I wasn't into gossip. My world of the service desk didn't extend as far as floor associates that were occasionally late and vaguely weird.

"I guess Rich should have a talk with her."

"She must have been really late, then."

"Yeah, that's my guess."

I looked over at the fitting rooms. Yup, there was Martha, sorting racks.

That was it, the end of the story. I went back to my stack of forms and data entry, and the issue of Martha went away. For a week.

The next weekend I was back in the box, staring at an inventory report on the terminal, when two associates stopped to pick up returns from the bin. I didn't look up.

"Did you see Martha today? Wasn't she supposed to be in the fitting room?"

Okay, I wasn't paying attention at first, but when Martha's name came up, I listened.

"I heard she switched schedules last night right before closing."

"What for?"

"No idea. I think Julie's back there, and she seems pissed."

They began to push their carts, now loaded with clothing to be restocked, away from the box.

"I heard that's the second time this week."

This was curious to me. Martha had shown up once in conversation in a bad light, and now independent of our service desk team she had been mentioned again, also in a bad light and for a different reason. Huh.

The next week, a cashier mentioned that Martha had been late another time. Was it gossip or was it real?

A few days later, Martha came up yet again. "Lion, can you look up these boxes in shipping for me?" Cheryl slid a paper with a series of handwritten numbers across the service desk counter.

I took the note. "Sure, Cheryl. Gimme a sec." I began punching numbers on the terminal. After a minute of button pushing, I heard footsteps outside the box.

"Cheryl, do you have a minute?"

"Yeah, Nancy, what's up?"

That was an interesting side effect of the service desk. You could see everything, but you were pretty much invisible. Nancy didn't even consider me within earshot.

"So Martha came back from break a half hour late. I was late to take mine, and no one could cover me."

Cheryl's silence was her thinking, remembering. I continued to punch numbers. "Yeah, okay, I'll talk to her about it. See if Jason in the back can watch your department."

"Okay, thanks."

I had been in the break room with Martha a half hour ago. I didn't think she was there any longer than normal. Was Nancy making things up, or was this only a misunderstanding? This is the first I'd seen something official against Martha, something that wasn't just gossip.

Right, so Martha had broken the bonds of the group; she had debonded. What we had all worked hard to build had come apart. That shared common experience was now meaningless and held no value. The knowledge of each other had turned against her: she was now known to be bad somehow. Most important, she couldn't be trusted. No one had come out and said that directly, but it was obvious. I didn't know details of what went on in that part of the store, I didn't see the genesis of the debonding, but it didn't matter how it all began. It was now a runaway train. All of the interactions that I witnessed told the story that something had happened and Martha was done.

In my mind, I gave Martha two to three weeks before she was fired or quit. Debonding is brutal. She was no longer "one of us," and that's a visceral emotion that will drive people to action. The store associates would make sure of that. Not management, not Martha, but the bonded group will use Martha as a lightning rod and pile on every complaint possible until she was gone.

"Uh, Lion?"

I looked up with a snap of my head. "Oh, sorry, Cheryl, I was lost in thought."

She laughed. "Any luck with those boxes?"

"Yeah, I have them here on my screen."

Three weeks later, Martha was gone.

A few years later, I would encounter the pattern again.

This one took place in a manufacturing company. They had a nice-sized factory and a sales team of 50 guys, covering every state. What I needed to do was get the sales guys out of the Stone Age with their carbon-copy paperwork and automate everything into a computer system I had to design. We called it "sales force automation." It was kind of CRM (customer relationship management) and ERP (enterprise resource planning) before those things were technology household words. I came in for a meeting, talked to all of management, we hit it off, and there I was a week later on a Monday morning, sitting in a generic cubicle in an office building attached to the factory floor.

I had a complication I wasn't prepared for: a direct report. I was some guy's manager. Looking back at my contract today, it says right there: "Clarence Jensen will report to Lion Templin to build the sales force automation software." Somehow, I missed that. It didn't occur to me that they'd assign me someone. Clarence had been working on building the software for a year before I got there, and I was assigned to be his new boss to get the project completed.

The strange thing was that I had never met him. Not during the interview process, not during contract negotiations, and certainly not before management gave me a disc with his work-to-date on it. I printed out his code, which was how I did things back then, and spent time going through it. I didn't try to run the software he had created to make it work. I didn't even talk to him to have him explain it. I just sat there for a couple days looking at a ream of paper that was one man's year-worth of work.

It was complete garbage.

The program wouldn't run, even if I had tried. It didn't have a cohesive concept. It was almost random in its nature, made up of huge, clunky blocks of code that didn't go anywhere. I was baffled by it. It didn't do anything. While I never met Clarence, I did know he was older, in his 50s, a software guy by trade, and had worked for the company for many years on a product database system that had been phased out long before I got there. He had been re-tasked to this project, and his delivery was awful.

On Wednesday morning, I took the ream of printouts into the CFO's office, my boss, and brandished them.

"Jeff, I can't use this." I told him.

"What do you mean?"

"The code Clarence wrote is terrible. There's nothing here I can use. I'll have to start from scratch." I thumbed the stack of paper and shrugged.

"Ok, well what about Clarence?"

I looked Jeff right in the eye. "He's useless to me if this is what he produces. I'd have to teach him how to program from square one."

Jeff nodded slowly. "Okay, so you're telling me you don't need Clarence?"

"Yeah, I don't need him, and I don't want him."

"Okay, he's gone."

That was it. The next day I saw an older guy cleaning out his cube as I passed through the office between meetings. Clarence had been let go. I had never met him, and now I never would.

It didn't strike me for some time what had happened. I got this guy fired. And he was old enough that his prospects of finding a programming job were slim, especially given his poor abilities and lack of technical relevance. That man was in serious trouble because of me. But, at the same time, I couldn't shake the knowledge that this was an easy decision for the company, and a necessary one. Clarence knew an old database system that wasn't used anymore. Management had assigned him to build a new system as a last-ditch effort to save him. Maybe, at some point in the past, Clarence had been an integral part of the team, but by the time I got there he had been languishing in a low-grade project that management was just watching to see if he delivered. He didn't.

After a year with the company, I found out the truth about Clarence. He had been on thin ice, having not produced anything that worked for more than a year after his old project was shut down. Clarence couldn't carry the weight everyone in the company was expected to carry. He had slowly debonded from the company. Not in an aggressive manner like Martha, but in a slow, inexorable slide. I arrived just in time as an outsider, free of the existing bonds, to pull the one last support he had, weak as it was, out from under him and give him the final push into the proverbial grave.

The terrain wasn't much to look at: low-quality hardwoods climbed the long slope of the hill behind me, while the forest gave way to a thick, frozen cattail swamp 75 yards down in front of me. Beyond the swamp was a marshy river: wet, messy, impenetrable. A few brave leaves that had ignored fall clung to the branches around me, and yet the thicket of weedy, barren branches made it hard to see anything that wasn't inside the 30-feet-wide swath cut down to the swamp by chainsaw. This was my deer stand, a permanent structure 15 feet in the air. It was a luxury; it had a roof and waist-high walls that obscured most of me while I sat. Inside, I had hidden a thermos of hot coffee, thick canvas tarps, and a paperback book to while away the time. It was comfortable, even in the biting cold of deer season.

It had taken a few seasons to understand that the edge of the swamp was a key part of the deer's habitat. They wouldn't go out into the swamp itself; even frozen it was too wet. They wouldn't climb up the hill into the hardwoods either, because that left them exposed. So, in their daily travels from the tangled mess of the lowlands to the open fields that recently grew corn, they kept to the edge of the swamp. I had taken a chainsaw to some thick trees down here, knocking down a thin, but long, clearing that was unavoidable. I had studied their habits carefully, then made a small change in the environment to force them briefly into the open. This was what my stand watched over.

I had hiked out in the pitch black of night, hefting my legs along the snowy trail, encased in inches of insulated parka and thick thermal pants. My rifle and various accessories hung on leather slings over my shoulder, swinging with every padded step. I arrived before sunup and watched the sky make its slow transition from black to deep blue to the first hints of dawn. Curlicues of warm vapor swirled out of the neck gaiter pulled up over my face before breaking against the blaze orange bill of my Stormy Kromer cap.

It was looking like a good day.

By noon I had had a cup of coffee, read some of my book, and had settled into a comfortable routine of slowly scanning the brush and letting my mind wander. I couldn't wander too far, since squirrels made occasional noisy forays into the brush that were just enough to snap my thoughts back to the hunt.

Then, the brown of a deer stepped into the chainsawed shooting lane, just at the end of the cut where a couple of cedar trees divided the tree line from the open reeds.

My rifle wasn't far. I slowly set the body of it on the railing, steadying my view through the scope.

I held my breath, didn't dare to move.

The deer took another step. Whoa, it's big, I thought.

Another tentative slow step. Look at that rack! Big, thick tines branched out from the top of the buck's head. Wait for it.

Again, a slow step. With my rifle steadied against the wood stand, I gradually let out my breath while I squeezed the trigger. The gun went off with a crack. My hand whipped the bolt back and forth, sending the metallic brass casing spinning off into the brush below.

The deer took one short leap and disappeared. Nothing made a sound. No crashing through brush, no bounding through the woods, just silence.

After a time, my father arrived below my stand. He had come down the hill slowly, picking his way along the trail as quietly as he could. Then, after him, another of our hunting party, Jim. Then, finally, my friend Mike. They stood below me, a knot of blaze orange in silence at the base of the tree. I climbed down, rifle in hand.

When we arrived at the bottom of the cut, we found the buck only a few feet into the woods. Dead. My round went straight through his heart. He had dropped instantly. Up close he was huge, the largest deer I'd ever killed. His coat was shaggy, gray in places around the muzzle, in good shape but not the picture of youth. The antlers told the whole story: they were thick, gnarled, and dense. This was an old swamp buck, long in years, not many left, having likely survived well over a decade. Smart all the way until the end.

I set my rifle against a tree and shed my jacket. I palmed a thin sliver of steel off my belt as I knelt before the belly of the animal. Around me, my hunting party stood in a loose semicircle, bundled up against the cold, watching silently.

I drew my hand as to hold a scalpel, fingertip held out along the top of the blade. I whispered under my breath what my father had taught me: "My knife is a precision instrument. It is an extension of me. I am a precision instrument, and I will cut true."

Blood pooled in the snow underneath the long, straight cut down the buck's centerline.

CHAPTER FOUR
SHEEPLE AREN'T BAAAD

THE CROWD GASPED as the roar of six World War II fighter planes ripped low over the airfield, leaving trails of smoke behind. They banked in unison, disappearing into the sun. The crowd shifted again, falling into its normal Brownian motion of people idly enjoying a beautiful early summer afternoon at a local airshow. This was a family atmosphere, with long rows of interesting planes set out without barriers; the kids could go right up and touch the machines. It had the air of a community festival, complete with fair food like hotdogs, tacos, and various meat and sugar combinations and lots of booths with folding tables and pop-up canopies, hawking the stuff that wasn't good enough to make it on "As seen on TV!"

Now, these kinds of places are not my usual thing. I'm alone in a sea of people gorging themselves on cotton candy and aimlessly wandering a huge stretch of asphalt on a Saturday morning. But I wasn't there to take in the sights. I was on a mission.

The year 2006 was going great. I was a vice president at a small hedge fund, I had a spacious office downtown, and we were making fantastic money betting on the future of renewable energy. Nothing, save for a one-in-a-million market crash, could get me down. I wanted to give back.

I had heard a rumor of a paramilitary organization that specialized in back-country search and rescue. Years ago, working as a wilderness guide, I had returned to base to drop off my crew and pick up a new one, only to find that one of my fellow guides hadn't come back. His crew, however, did come back. They had spent a few days traveling to the base and eventually reported they had "lost the guide and gave up looking for him."

I was incensed. I wanted to cancel all the outbound trips so I and my fellow guides could go find him. We knew the territory better than anyone else. Management wasn't on my side. The Canadian military search and rescue team said they had it under control and, sure enough, guides had reported seeing planes overhead from time to time.

The military never found him. He eventually rescued himself. After falling down a steep embankment and suffering a concussion, he had wandered through the deep forest for days in a fog. When the concussion had worn off, he found himself thoroughly lost. Surviving by eating insects and drinking from dirty ponds, he had finally come across one of the many lakes in the region. Another crew was on the lake, and after a lot of yelling, the lost guide hailed them and they brought him home.

So maybe the American paramilitary search and rescue crew, which I will simply call "The Org," could make a difference when someone went on an unintended walkabout in the wild again. The rumor I had heard was that this organization had a presence at airshows like this, so here I was.

And so was, in uniform, the guy making the difference, standing bored under a pop-up canopy next to a folding table.

I introduced myself to the tall gentleman in combat fatigues. After that, I went right to business: "I hear you guys do wilderness rescue work. Could you use an experienced professional wilderness guide?"

"Oh yeah, absolutely!" Fatigues responded, having switched from bored to excited.

I pitched myself, talking about my work in the Canadian wilderness. The uniformed man didn't care. He just seemed excited that someone was interested in The Org. Apparently, I had to attend meetings, talk to the unit commander, and go through FBI background checks. Okay, sure, no problem.

So I showed up at their next meeting. The place was full of other uniform fatigues busily planning. A number of people were doing what looked like book-work, and amid the chaos I stood in a corner and watched. I was mostly ignored, even though I stood out like a sore thumb among all the uniforms. Another civilian like me appeared, and both of us eventually reached a closed office that housed, apparently, the commander. I didn't have to pitch myself hard, for he barely listened. But he did say that I had to show up again a number of times before I'd be considered. Okay, clearly he wanted to see some commitment.

After four weeks of going to the meetings, I still didn't know what was going on. Everyone in uniform seemed to have a plan, but what they were doing wasn't obvious. Mostly I watched. The ever-busy sea of fatigues didn't reach out to me, but I still stuck it out. Here's the thing: I've spent my lifetime studying organizations, but I am not an organization person. I don't really fit in. So I'm used to watching.

The day I joined The Org was pretty much a regular day for me. I suppose I should have considered it a momentous occasion, but I didn't see joining an organization in that light. I had done the required show-up-and-fill-out-paperwork routine. They also took Don, the other guy that had been doing the same thing I had. Yet, even as we signed paperwork and took an oath together, our paths couldn't have been more different.

Militaries have used bonding to build cohesion since the dawn of a fighting force. The Western beginnings of this understanding came from ancient Greece, where soldiers defended the beginnings of nations. It was thought that close bonds brought out bravery and sacrifice; not only for their country, but for their fellow soldiers. Monuments to these fighting men still stand in Greece and Rome, honoring those who saved their nations from invading hordes or tyranny.

Clearly, times change, and modern militaries are orders of magnitude larger. But armies still need that emotional bond among soldiers to provide the critical will to fight. So, instead of bonds between a small number of individuals, they made the military your family. These were your brothers, and you'll go to your grave to protect them. They say, "Once a Marine, always a Marine." In order to get such a deep bond, you need some serious work done in bringing the troops together. This is why militaries and, in my case, The Org, are great examples of ritualized task bonding translating into emotional bonding.

It starts with an oath, a task. The oath is meaningful on its face; you are pledging to dedicate yourself to the 'Cause.' I've taken both the U.S. Government Oath of Office and The Org Oath in my life. They're closely related.

> *I, [name], do solemnly swear (or affirm) that I will support and defend the Constitution of the United States against all enemies, foreign and domestic; that I will bear true faith and allegiance to the same; that I take this obligation freely, without any mental reservation or purpose of evasion; and that I will well and*

faithfully discharge the duties of the office on which I am about to enter. So help me God.

5 U.S.C. §3331

That begins the emotional bonding process: a shared common experience. We all had to commit to the same ideals and sacrifices. Though I was poorly equipped to be a member of The Org, I became one of them. One of 'Us.' Don's case was different. He'd had prior service. My oath of office was to work as a government employee, but he had said the oath of enlistment to be a soldier.

A few years later, and two commanders later, Don and I would compete to be the commander of the unit. I'll tell you right away that I lost, but I knew the outcome going in. You see, even though we had joined on the same day, Don outranked me substantially. He stood there proudly in his dress uniform, covered in a highway billboard–sized ribbon rack on his chest. He looked exactly like the command staff that was choosing between the two of us, and I knew he felt right at home among them.

I didn't quite look like any of them. I, in my somewhat ill-kempt uniform, had only a tiny ribbon rack. The rank insignias on my shoulders were one step above "I just said the oath." It's not that Don had out-performed me and I'd been lazy. We both had worked hard for The Org. The difference was that Don knew at a gut level how to bond with the organization. As he stood there that day, with his spotless uniform covered in ribbons, he demonstrated that he shared that bond, that he belonged. The decision-makers saw themselves in Don; it was almost as if they were the same species.

Guess who didn't get command. Which, frankly, I'm thankful for. I ended up in another part of the organization that was perfectly suited for me: audits and investigations. Welcome to the misfits club. Oh well, someone's got to be that jerk telling you that you're doing it wrong. After a number of years in The Org, I bonded with my fellow auditors. We're all a special breed of misfit.

When you put people together in organizations, you need that emotional bonding, that sense of belonging, to build a community that lasts. Even I needed that to have a future in The Org. Shared common experience is a huge part of it: we all undertook the same training (preferably in the rain and mud), the same tests (reams of blurred photocopies-of-photocopies being our training material), the same rituals (saluting, formation, the awards ceremony), and the same story played out time and time again that results in such a similar nature in people that to outsiders we're almost indistinguishable as individual members. I can assure you that, when we are sent on-mission in our uniforms, civilians see just the uniform and ignore our only individual identification: a small name tape on our chest.

This isn't unique to The Org, or militaries, or even governments. When I worked retail, I had to wear a uniform with a plastic name badge. Today, I wear a uniform still: leather shoes, slacks, a neatly-pressed shirt, and a blazer. It's all tied together with a security badge identifying me as "Contractor."

Uniforms identify organization members to each other and to outsiders, making the choice of clothing critical to the bond as a group. What you wear, your plumage, the color of your fur, the presence of horns or other physical features, speaks volumes as to who is a zebra and who is a cashier at Shop! Underlying that uniform are the serious emotional bonds you'd expect: shared common experience, trust, and expectations.

I need to address some terminology here. For as long as I remember, being called "part of the herd" has been an insult. The term has been used maliciously to say people are drones incapable of independent personal thoughts, dreams, and goals. That's not even close to the truth. These people, this herd, have come together because they share many of the same thoughts, dreams, and goals. I know that, despite my significant differences with Commander Don, he and I both want to help our fellow countrymen in service of The Org. That doesn't make us incapable of being individuals. Far from it! Both Don and I have made significant positive impacts on The Org because of our differences. The herd benefits from a variety of people who can help make the herd a better organization. As long as we share the same core beliefs and emotional bonds, we'll stick together. There's honor, joy, and belonging in being part of something greater than yourself.

Because of this concept that many individuals make a greater whole, the herds of the world can do incredible things. Look at companies like Microsoft, Apple, IBM, or Exxon. Look at the great herds of religion. They've changed the landscape of the world beyond what any individual could ever possibly accomplish. Not even Steve Jobs on his own could achieve what Apple did. And how do you identify members of his herd? Everyone's required to display their security badge. We in the business call it a "cattle tag."

This is a world owned and operated by the herd, the property of prey. From the moment you start your education, you're surrounded by your peers, you're taught the rituals and the expectations of being a good member of society. You're rewarded for fitting in enough that people can connect with you. That's good, because we don't want to be left alone. But together, the herd can build pyramids, put a man on the moon, create a global society that everyone can electronically participate in from the comfort of their living room. Our great society isn't possible without the contributions of the herds of the world.

Now, it doesn't matter what herd you're a part of, you're always on the lookout for more like you. That's a core philosophy of every herd. Like Tall Fatigues (turned out his name was Dave), who was excited to have someone new show interest in joining The Org. New hires, recruiting and retention, pledge drives—these are all ways of growing the herd. Growth has a huge number of benefits. Particularly, the larger your herd is, the more your herd is capable of doing. And, in the end, the more people you have on board, the more fulfilling bonds you make.

Which brings me to Terrance. Terry had been a member of The Org for a decade before I joined. I didn't have much contact with him because he moved around The Org and I only knew the guys in my unit, where Terry made only occasional appearances. But I did end up working alongside him once. I remember getting called out on an emergency search mission with Terry.

Turns out my experiences on the ground in the wilderness weren't exactly needed in The Org. I ended up on aircrew, which meant I flew around in specially-equipped aircraft doing search and rescues. It turned out to be a lot harder than I thought, and it helped me to understand why the Canadian military failed to find our lost guide. I ended up piloting an Org aircraft over that same wilderness years later. We never did find our guy either.

Aircrews for Org planes are three people: a pilot, the "right seater" that handles a lot of the equipment, and the guy who sits in the back, whom we simply call "Here, hold this."

Flying on a clear day can be work, but flying during a live mission can be harrowing. At a minimum, you'll probably put in a lot of work. My commander, Shannon, was piloting that day I worked with Terry, while I operated the radios, sensors, and other electronic equipment from the right seat. In the area we were flying, I had to talk to air traffic control, our other aircraft, our guys on the ground, and our mission command center—all in the airspace surrounding a very busy international airport. Terry sat in the back of the plane, helping Shannon and me, keeping the mission log and being quiet. At least, that's what he was supposed to be doing. Terry was everything but quiet. I'm concentrating on radios, listening to the constant feedback of the equipment while holding three different conversations with other operators. Terry, doing the opposite of helping, was running his mouth in the back, making a tremendous racket. Which I guess wasn't enough, because he then started bouncing around back there, jostling both Shannon and me and making it hard for her to keep the plane straight and level.

Suddenly, the radio pitched up in tone, screaming over the top of the noise of Terry and the sensors. A female voice squawked out of the headsets: "Four Two Delta! DO YOU SEE THE SOUTHWEST SEVEN-THIRTY-SEVEN FIVE MILES AT TEN O'CLOCK?!"

Oh shit, that's close. I looked up from the equipment with a snap of my head. Shannon heard it too, and I could see the back of her hat as we both stared at the big Boeing gliding alongside us.

"Approach, uh, this is Four Two Delta, we see it, thank you." I transmitted back.

"I've been calling you! Why haven't you answered?" came back an annoyed woman's voice.

I swallowed hard. I hadn't heard her over Terry's bedlam. I don't even remember what he was talking about this whole time, but obviously he didn't care if we were listening or not. "Sorry, Approach, our mission radios are really loud. I'll turn you up. Won't happen again."

As Shannon gently banked away from the jumbo jet, she and I turned back at Terry almost in unison to glare at him. He was in the process of sliding the seat back and forth and wasn't even paying attention to what just happened. Seriously? Wow, Terry. Soon after, the mission was scrubbed by command and we flew home. Shannon and I raged silently at the idiot in the backseat. That was the last time either of us got in an aircraft with him.

That was pretty typical for Terry. In the years following the incident, I've watched Terry screw up over and over. Sometimes it's little stuff, sometimes it's really bad stuff. Misappropriation of equipment, violations of the regs, just plain terrible judgment. He's been demoted at least twice, been nearly thrown out, and every time he's gotten a reprieve. Why?

This is not an easy question to answer. To me, the way to deal with the problem was obvious: Terry had to go. But The Org refused to get rid of him, even when handed repeated opportunities by Terry himself. People stood up for him, sometimes to their own regret. The guy should have been fired on his first outing, long before he botched the mission with Shannon and me.

Terry is still with The Org today. Those around him try to keep him safe from himself by confining him in operational areas where he can't do too much damage. And they do it because of the bonding. You see, Terry's not a bad guy. I don't think he has an evil bone in his body. He just lets his excitement get in the way and he does stupid stuff. He's not bad, he's just Terry.

This is a feature of the bonding process. Organizations need these bonds so that they can flex over time through most conditions. In good times, the bonds are enhanced with fond memories and fulfilled expectations. In bad times, the bonds stretch to keep the organization together by preventing an over-reaction; everyone knows Terry is genuinely well-meaning. He's just a perpetual screw-up. The bonds also give people a vision of a future, via the good memories of the past, that becomes the goal of getting past the trouble of today. History is on our side.

Until it isn't. You can't have it both ways; you can't have long-lasting durable bonds that can be easily severed. Every organization has people that aren't a good fit. Is Terry really a good fit for The Org? Does he need to go? Probably, he's a huge liability. Being a good person isn't enough; you have to do good work too. In any workplace are those people that just aren't working. They survive because of that herd identity. When it gets really bad, the longest-lasting bond is familiarity. Familiarity is so powerful that people in abusive relationships stay in them because it's the evil they know. It's just as true in the wild: the herd absolutely will not kill one of its own. They circle around the sick and injured. They protect them, even when doing so costs them dearly. That is how Clarence kept on writing bad software for years after his usefulness ended, how Terry can make mistake after mistake and never be sent packing, and, most importantly, how unusual and personally vicious Martha's debonding was. Somehow Terry never crossed that line that Martha did. But once you do, there is no going back.

Deer camp consisted of an unfinished one-room cabin buried in the deep northern forests. It lacked power or running water, and the sink emptied into a bucket. Yet, we didn't care that the interior walls were sheathed in simple plywood, or that the sloped interior roof showed the paper backing of fiberglass insulation. The wood stove was happily packed with split oak. Its flames burned brightly as the iron and glass box radiated almost too much heat. For the next two weeks, this place was home.

Hunting season in this part of the country was a holiday for the whitetail deer herd's only predators. Businesses closed, schools showed movies for the unfortunate non-hunters, and the two-lane backroads were choked with pickup trucks vying to get to their camps. When all four of us eventually arrived at the cabin after hours of snow-covered backroad driving, we celebrated. The gas lamps were lit, casting bright shadows through the windows onto the trees outside. Country music blared over a cheap AM radio. We broke open a bottle of our deer camp's traditional alcohol: slivovitz.

"*Na zdravi!*" we said in unison, faces grimacing in the after-effects of the Czech plum brandy. None of us were Czech, not by a long shot. Somehow, this corrosive drink whose mere warning labels could not convey its dangers, had become part of our shared experience. I suspect, like most bad ideas, it had something to do with a bet many hunting seasons past. We never drank enough to get used to it, but we did drink enough to tolerate it.

My father raised his hand for attention and stood up. "So this year, I want to recognize one of us, my son, for his excellent marksmanship." He held up a small plaque that appeared to have a damaged bullet affixed to it.

I cringed. I knew what this was.

He continued, "While practicing shooting here at the cabin this summer, he somehow fired at a target, missed it, ricocheted the round off a tree, and then put the round straight through the outhouse. My son, the slayer of deer, is now also a slayer of outhouses and anyone who might be inside!" He beckoned me to stand up with him.

I stood next to my father, plaque and hands grasped in a grip-and-grin, while Jim took photos. I was, let's say, a bit sheepish. The story wasn't wrong. To be a good predator you need to practice. That summer day wasn't any different from any other weekend at the cabin with guns, working on our marksmanship. It just happened that I missed. Badly. That was unusual. As luck would have it, the bullet traced a most improbable trajectory right into the, thankfully, unoccupied outhouse. We had closely examined the hole in the side with the quiet appreciation of everyone present being regular.

So I stood there, drunk on Czech plum brandy, while my fellow hunters took what could have been a tragedy and turned it into a joke. We laughed, we toasted more slivovitz, we had good fun at my expense. It was a great night with my friends. We had to be in our deer stands early, well before sunup, and when drunk 4:00 a.m. seems like many hours away.

CHAPTER FIVE
THE HUNTERS

Sunlight flooded the cabin through the large south-facing windows. It was the start of an average winter, cold enough for snow but not frigid enough to make going outside a chore. That bodes well for a deer hunting season. Our little group usually would arrive a few days before the start of the season, and this year was no exception. We had to change mantles on the gas lights, bring in the wood we cut and split to feed the stove, and do all the normal preseason work.

I sat down heavily in a chair at the dining room table. It was called the dining room only because it was between the battered green, secondhand countertop that denoted the kitchen and the back of the plaid couch that created the living room. The surface of the table was old wood, an inexpensive build from a few decades ago that was surprisingly well taken care of. I sat in a wooden dining room chair, not the same style as the table or half of the other chairs. That was the way of hunting camp: castoff furniture and few amenities. This was the wilderness, not the Intercontinental.

"So, I guess I have a lot of tags." I thumbed open a plastic wallet and tumbled out a fat wad of folded-up papers. They looked like grocery store receipts printed on bright green strips.

Jim, seated across from me, pulled out a similar orange plastic wallet. "I have eleven."

Mike dropped his bundle on the table without comment, letting the pile sit there as proof of his results.

What we called a tag is a license to kill one deer, with specific limitations. In general, if you want to hunt, you have to pay to play, and you tend to pay the government. The practice in the United States goes back to the 1800s and, while the reasons for hunting licenses have had a varied history, how a license works hasn't changed a bit. These white-tailed deer tags play a crucial role in conservation of the herd.

Everything in nature exists in balance. Those that don't understand nature think this balance is some exquisitely-managed and maintained symphony of forces. They couldn't be more wrong. Nature's balance is determined by conflict: competition for resources and the unending quest to grow the herd or the species. This fierce fight is played out in every part of nature across a huge number of timescales. You might not notice trees competing, since their conflict of seeds and sunlight takes decades to play out, sometimes longer than a human lifespan. Because of competition, no opportunity in nature is left open, nothing goes to waste. Almost every niche of the biosphere has its occupants, adapted to a specific balance. You can see this in the forest flora; pine trees require a lot of light energy on their small needles to grow, while more meager plants spread large leaves to capture the faint sun that filters down through the pines. A cold-blooded toad requires less calories than a warm-blooded field mouse, which requires far less calories than a white-tailed deer, which are then eaten by another high-energy organism: wolves.

Rather, they had been eaten by wolves.

The natural balance can tip in a number of ways: too hot in summer, too cold in winter, fire, drought, starvation, or the action of a species that has adapted to competition. Those are the predators; they are the visceral representation of nature's competitive balance. The white-tailed deer of the north had been preyed upon by timber wolves; wild canines adapted to raw protein as food. They had to kill the deer to survive and, in turn, maintain their balance.

Then man changed that balance by killing all the wolves.

I looked up from my pile of paper tags. "I guess the DNR wants a lot of kills this year."

"It's the chronic wasting disease, isn't it? I've seen it on the news." Mike pulled back his stack of bright green paper.

"The herds down south are rife with it. It's been getting worse."

"You know what it does, right?"

"Starvation?"

Jim worked in medicine, so he knew better. "Sort of. It gets into an animal's brain and trashes it, slowly eating away the tissue. After a while, they can't do anything but wander aimlessly. They won't eat or drink. After a while, they die. The disease is easily transmissible to the rest of the herd."

"Holy shit."

Silence hung over the table, leaving us with our thoughts and the sound of crackling wood in the stove.

After a while I looked up. "We did this, didn't we?"

With the wolves gone, humanity had to take responsibility for the deer herds. And, for about a hundred years, we did. The conservation part of the tag system was the result of that responsibility. People in the Department of Natural Resources (DNR) estimated the size of the herd, judged its health, and controlled the number of tags and where you could hunt to maintain the balance the wolves once had. But another measure of balance had changed. Expansions of urban areas created rings of land around cities that were wild enough for deer, but not safe enough to hunt. Homes closely intermixed with the herd. At the same time, people gave up rural living for cities and left open acreage and hunting behind. Social pressure also mounted against the time-honored tradition of hunting. For a second time, the white-tailed deer's predators were dying off.

Deer populations exploded.

This is how nature works. Every organism does the best job it can to survive while balance comes from external sources. Things like weather, fire, and predators. The deer herd doesn't manage itself, for its balance is a byproduct of the interests of wolves or man. This is the true beauty of nature; everything fits together and balance is always maintained.

So when the deer population got big enough, it encountered another type of balance: disease. Again, balance is always maintained. But, this time, the cost was higher. Instead of dying quickly to the fangs of a wolf or a hunter's bullet, deer would suffer for months before eventually succumbing to CWD. It is a horrific death.

Suffering is a human concept. We are the only creatures in nature that can appreciate it. Left to its own devices, nature will do what is necessary to maintain balance, no matter the cost.

Jim looked serious. "Yeah, we did this. Now we have to cull the herd."

Crunch.

Thick granules of snow made up a hard crust of white above the softer layer underneath that went all the way to the ground. It had warmed at some point recently, then got cold again, recrystallizing the top of the snowpack into a solid band a few inches thick. Sunlight fell though the barren tree branches and glinted off the faceted grains. I should have brought sunglasses. Cloudless winter days are the brightest imaginable.

The snow crust wouldn't hold me. With every step, I'd press down with my foot and loudly break the surface. I wasn't being quiet, but at this point who was? Every hunter had their 11 tags on opening day, and they were making the most of their chances. This wasn't going to be a subtle season. The echoing thunder of rifles in the distance had been a constant presence ever since the clock ticked over to morning. I could only assume this is what a battle sounds like.

I had left my stand late morning to slowly stalk through the forest. The old patterns of the deer herd went up in smoke with the heavy presence of gunfire. Today, there was no point in waiting. So I wandered, intent on a chance encounter.

Crunch.

I felt bad, not because of the number of deer dying today, but because we had done wrong by them. Grievously wrong. Disease is the worst way to die; it's long, painful, and drawn out. We hadn't held up our side of the bargain and they were suffering. Not that they'd recognize that. Guilt, too, is a human concept. What we were doing today was mercy.

Crunch.

I thought of the butchers that would be busy in the coming weeks. We had our pole up with two dead bucks and a doe hanging on it already, frozen. We're predators, and nothing would go to waste. We'll have enough to feed four families when the week is up. Even the hides are donated to charity. The neighboring section of land was owned by a huge farm family, and they were ruthless in deer season. They had a lot of people to feed.

Crunch.

I scanned the trees, the snow, the rolling hills and ridges, swamp and valley, and the meandering creek in front of me and thought about … Stop! Movement. I froze. My breath wisped out my nostrils as I stood stock still, feet planted in deep holes in the snow. I waited. I was a good distance back from the edge of a ridge that overlooked a small cedar swamp and marshy creek. Movement again, this time I could discern where it was: straight in front of me, right next to the rim. It was deer-sized, moving hurriedly. I raised my rifle, thumbing the safety and peering into the scope.

Bright sunlight filled the glass, brilliant and crystal clear in the cold. I slowly pushed the rifle along, tracing the ridge with it as I watched.

There. I stopped the rifle's gradual swing. Now the age-old question: buck or doe.

Standing in the open with my rifle raised and steadied was a chore, but I was patient. Good predators always are. I slowed my breathing and held the scope on the center of the deer. It took a running couple of steps and stops, nervous, off its game.

Doe. Not large. Nothing to be proud of. A hundred-yard shot at most, easy.

Half my tags were doe tags. I slid the crosshairs over her heart, a short movement, almost imperceptible. The trigger felt solid and smooth as I pulled it home.

She moved.

The gun fired.

She went down.

Echoes of my shot ringed the ridges around me, joining the riot of gunfire, lost in its unremarkable nature during deer season.

I held right where I was. I breathed in, then deliberately let out a breath. My eye never left the glass.

She didn't get back up.

I lowered the rifle and breathed again. The sunlight on the snow crystals was intense. I waited for a few minutes.

Crunch.

I started walking again, picking my way carefully to the doe. Nothing around me had changed. The world was as stark and loud as it was moments before.

Crunch.

When I reached her, I found she was a small doe, maybe a year old. Not more than two. She was barely alive, and she jumped the moment I loosed my round and I missed the heart. I raised the rifle again.

Another crack of gunfire mixed with the forest.

I nodded to myself, self-assured. Meat for the freezer and a predator's job done.

WHUMP.

That wasn't the sound I was expecting. I was hoping more for a cracking of wood or maybe a crunch and slam kind of sound, but no. My partner pulled back his boot from the door, leaving only a scar of black boot lugs next to the doorknob. It hadn't moved a millimeter. We both stared, surprised.

"Hit it again." I said. He looked at me, then back at the door, winding up for it.

WHUMP.

Same thing, absolutely nothing. The door didn't budge. My partner and I, clad in black body armor and silver badges, were at the front door of a rambler an hour out of the city. It was spring, so it was cool out but not frigid. A foot of snow still covered the ground. What my partner and I were doing is modernly called "warrants," but most people know it as bounty hunting. People would skip on their court hearings after being released, and eventually their file would end up on my desk with their name on my nightly worksheet.

Today, like most days, we were looking for a mether. Meth ravages people, and they chronically make criminally stupid decisions, like stealing people's stuff to feed their drug habit. This particular mether was a guy in his late 40s, but his picture on my clipboard made him look like he was over 60. Pretty much the standard look of all our clientele. We usually didn't kick in doors, either. We had a lot more tricks in our bag to get into a house ... but this place wasn't cooperating with any of them. Kicking the door was a long shot, because it's a lot harder than you think. This is why the police have big steel battering rams to bust open doors. We were not that sophisticated; a boot was all we had.

I shrugged. "I'm going to go around back again," I told my partner. I had cased the home already, and I knew the only other exit was a sliding glass door opposite this front door on the back side. As I walked around the house, I stared at the windows along the way, seeing if one of them was unlocked. I didn't see any. But what I did see was a number of cheap security video cameras evenly spaced around the house, covering almost every angle of approach. Whoever was inside, and someone had to be since the truck owned by our man was in the driveway, had been watching us from the moment we pulled up to the place. This wasn't entirely unusual.

As I rounded the backside, I spotted motion and my head turned with a snap. Our man was 100 feet away, slipping out that back sliding glass door. He saw me and changed from a quiet 'let's-sneak-away' to a full-out run.

I love it when they run.

As my feet ripped away at the snow-packed ground, I was already crunching the numbers in my head: 50 yards of snow to the tree line, which was what he was going for, but that won't help him. I know how to move fast in dense forest, and I can track him. He's got a 100-feet lead on me, but I have the angle, and I'm aiming for an intercept right about … there.

Down he went.

He was now face down in the snow as I pulled his hands together behind him. He had given up at this point, not at all resisting, so the cuffs went on easy. I quickly got him back up and walking around to the front of the house. My partner looked vaguely surprised, though I couldn't tell if it was because I got our guy, or because I was still grinning madly from the chase.

The local police arrived: one squad car, one male officer, one female. We dumped the mether temporarily in the back of the squad car while we, and the police, had a pleasant conversation about whose problem he was now. When the police showed up, I preferred to have them transport the criminals to jail. They had those great cages in their cars, and I didn't have one in my truck. They could handle the pile of paperwork, while I preferred that they just sign my custody transfer form so I could go home. Plus, they were getting paid to sit at the intake for the jail … and I didn't get paid by the hour, only by the job. But, in the middle of this discussion, the cops brought up the wife. Apparently, she was a mether too, and though she was not on my worksheet, the cops wanted her as much as the guy. They insisted she was in the house.

Okay, fine. We'd get her too.

So I went back to trying to get into the house. In his rush to escape, the guy had left the sliding glass door cracked open. Bingo: non-destructive entry. I called over the cops and my partner. This is where it got a bit surreal. This job affords you a look into the gaping maw of a terrible part of society. The house was a disaster: trash everywhere, destroyed furniture, dirty clothing, rotting food, you name it. We quickly figured out why the front door didn't budge: the mether had taken four-inch deck screws and screwed the door to the frame. But the worst part was the baby toys. As we proceeded through the house, I went down into the basement in search of the wife. I came upon their last-stand holdout room. It was a windowless space in the basement with a queen bed (don't touch it), folding chairs, and a long dresser covered in trash and drug paraphernalia. Meth pipes, bongs, lighters, baggies half-filled with off-white powders. Among all of this was a baby bassinet, child's toys, children's clothing (none of it clean), and old, dirty baby bottles. Nothing was fresh or new. Across from the bed was a folding table with a row of four small TVs, all showing the grainy black-and-white feeds from the security cameras around the house.

I had studied the guy's rap sheet well before we started work that day. It read like everyone else's: pages long, felonies on down to misdemeanors throughout the last 20 years, and multiple times in jail. The record included this line, which stood out in my memory suddenly:

124. 12/19/2002 609.378 NEGLECT OR ENDANGERMENT OF CHILD

As I stood there, I scrolled back through the list of convictions in his record and filled in the spot in time where Child Protective Services probably took the couple's two young kids.

We eventually found the wife hiding under the blown-in insulation in the far back of the attic. The female cop and I went up there, dug her out, and crab-walked her across the long center beam to the hatch. After handing the mether's wife down, I coughed from the insulation while the male cop cuffed her and told my partner and me to take them both to the county lockup. So much for a short day.

Again, balance is always maintained. In service of that balance, invariably, are competing drives. Those drives push into every possible niche, some of which we consider bad.

Bad is a very human concept.

Bad people will always exist, bad things will always be done. If there is a way to gain an advantage, it will be taken. When the balances shift, new advantages will be found.

The balances against deer overpopulation are the predators: take them away and a more brutal balance will come about.

The value of a life is a relatively recent human concept. Only we can appreciate the concept of value. Most of humanity's history has paralleled nature, and human life has been cheap and brutal. We're trying to do better. So we don't end the lives of these methers. We stop them, take them out of their surroundings and put them in jail; and, most importantly, we give them another chance. That substitutes for the predator's kill in human society: a forcible removal from the environment with the expectation that the prey will change. A hard stop and rehabilitation. It's kinder than hanging.

I preyed upon the worst of the worst.

We picked up a guy on a double-murder charge committed during a home invasion. He killed two of his friends after breaking into their home. He was so dangerous that the sheriff's department wouldn't take him in without a judge signing off on it. His sentence was federal prison for life. But he's the exception, and not even the worst of the worst. The absolute worst are the ones who have chosen to spend a lifetime teetering on the edge of going away for good. They're perpetual criminals, and the damage they do to their families, their communities, and the world around them is enormous. Consider which of these will keep you up at night? That a friend of yours will show up to shoot you while at home, or the tweaked-out mether neighbor that'll break into your garage and steal your lawnmower ... again.

Which returns us to balance. In the wild, predators kill the sick and infirm not because the predator is taking care of the herd, but because the kills are easy as they're weak. It just happens that the easy ones are the ones that really need to go. That couple who barricaded their house needed to go, and it was quite easy to take them. Every one of the people I brought to jail needed to go, from the double homicide to the hundredth charge for driving after a revoked license. Every single one needed a hard stop to how they lived their lives in order to stop the damage they were doing. They didn't make one mistake, but a lifetime of mistakes. They needed to be hunted down so they could have a chance at the reset button in life. Maybe, given enough chances, they'd figure it out. But helping them figure it out is not the predator's job. I'm just there for the arrest, the kill. That's how balance in nature works.

Back at the house, I pulled up gently on the chain between the mether's cuffs, guiding him out of the back of the squad car. His thin, navy blue nylon windbreaker ruffled in the slight breeze as we wordlessly walked the distance across the wet, ice-covered gravel driveway to my truck.

I felt great. The cuffs were warm after he sat on them for so long. It was a nice detail to notice against the breezy chill of the spring. I smiled.

He stepped up the running board and dropped into the rear seat behind the driver. I left the door wide open, an invitation to run if he tried. He didn't. I pulled out an aluminum clipboard and started filling in boxes on the work order. That's when I noticed his incarceration record. The county had built a new jail recently to replace a decrepit one, and the record showed he'd served time in both.

I laughed slightly and looked up at him. He met my gaze sullenly.

"So, do you like the old jail or the new jail better?"

I must have hit a nerve, because I got a written complaint for that remark. Another predator's job well done.

CHAPTER SIX
WORLD TRAVELER

Every commercial aircraft has an ambiance that is unique to the model and build. The CRJ has a comfortable, touch-too-intimate cabin. I've never seen amenities on one, but the flight to Palm Springs onboard a CRJ is relaxing enough without any extras. The 737, the real workhorse of the world, is a city bus. There's never seatback entertainment, a small bag of pretzels accompanies your mostly-ice cup of soda hurriedly thrust at you, and a child is screaming, maybe not next to you, but somewhere. What stands out is the three-by-three seat arrangement that everyone envisions when they think of commercial flights. That's three seats, an aisle, and three more seats per row. The A320 has the same arrangement, but it's the 737 that everyone remembers.

That's because of its awful feature: the middle seat. That no-man's-land between the Koreas or the old Germanys has you watching both sides in desperate hope no one becomes a leaner; or worse, that person is big enough to crowd what little space you have. No one wants the middle seat.

My first experience on a wide-body was on a DC-10, and I was not prepared for its immensity. Sure, there's two aisles, but I could never shake the feeling that I was sitting in a poorly designed sports stadium. Most of the seats are in the middle section: windowless, industrial, and uncomfortably close in exactly the way a CRJ isn't. This might as well be a 15-hour time-share presentation in a Holiday Inn meeting room with no natural light.

I stared grimly at the pixelated seatback screen in front of me. Grains of crust in my eyes made me squint at the little plane symbol in the center of an all-blue map display. I zoomed the screen out to the maximum to find still only the featureless blue representation of an ocean. Seat 46B onboard a Cathay Pacific 747 had exactly that feeling of both the 737 middle seat and the cramped sports stadium of a DC-10. They call the

747 the Queen of the Skies, but they are airplane aficionados, not a young consultant eight hours into a 16-hour flight to Hong Kong that has slept exactly zero hours. To my left was an uncommunicative Asian woman, young and, thankfully, slight in build. To my right was a very different story.

The mound of old knitted blankets contained an ancient Vietnamese woman who had installed herself at the last possible moment before take off, dashing my premature hopes that I'd have an empty seat beside me. She had ambled down the aisle slowly, then equally slowly sat herself down next to me and began an ancient burial rite with the blankets. The scent was intense. Egyptians buried their kings with scented oils. Ancient Vietnamese women apparently buried themselves with an industrial variant of Bengay. The delicate aroma of wool aircraft seats and stale food was erased by the chemical burning of my sinuses by a not-at-all-delicate bouquet of volatile organic compounds.

I remained awake and uncomfortable for all 16 hours. I learned two valuable lessons in my first trans-Pacific flight: never will I sit in the middle seat again, and avoid looking at the map. It moves almost as little as you do.

Switching flights in Hong Kong, I found myself suddenly more awake in yet another middle seat on a what might now be seen as a short ten-hour flight to Kuala Lumpur. Not surprisingly, I walked out of the boarding area at the Kuala Lumpur airport bleary-eyed and barely conscious. Luckily, my client had sent a car: a woman was holding a sign with my name written in thick black marker. Perfect.

I sat in the back of the car, a Malay brand that tried to impersonate a Toyota Corolla, but with the features smoothed over to look even more generic. As the car waded through throngs of mopeds, my mind wandered. I had this huge question hanging over me: I hadn't worked in Asia before, so how had I ended up on the other side of the world?

Weeks before the flight, I had been in my office when someone with a thick Chinese accent called me. He explained that he had heard great things from one of my previous clients and he'd like me to come out to Kuala Lumpur to take a look at their operation. That was it. No statement of work, not even a "Hey, this is what we need you for." Just this general "Come on out and see us!" All I had were tickets for a 32-hour flight and the knowledge that this company built auto parts.

My driver eventually pulled into a side street among large warehouse buildings. There was activity all around: people moving things, loading trucks, shipping containers stacked along the side of the road next to the cavernous entrances to the rusty steel buildings. It was warm, sticky with humidity and bright with the noonday sun at the equator. I was ushered up a set of stairs by the driver as someone else grabbed my luggage and disappeared. Beyond a set of doors into a conference room chilled with air conditioning, I was dropped off, alone. Muted industrial sounds were drowned out by the strain of air conditioners barely keeping up with the heat. The humidity felt like a cold, wet dishrag pressed to my skin. The room was filled with an arrangement of folding banquet tables made into a low-rent approximation of a spacious conference table surrounded by cheap office chairs. The outside rim of the room was lined with cardboard banker's boxes that overflowed with disused papers. One of the long walls consisted of mostly dirty windows facing the busy foot traffic of the city street outside. In a lot of ways, it resembled any other manufacturing company's conference room. In more subtle ways, particularly its grimy cheapness, it was a lot worse.

All at once, from a door on the opposite side of the room, flowed a sea of people: men and women of unidentifiable races, some in suits, some in workwear jumpsuits covered in grease, all with smiles and waves directed at me as they spread out around the conference table. A cake appeared before me: "Welcome Lion!" written on it in frosting. Well, this was nice.

Then the rear door opened again, disgorging a disheveled, morbidly obese American as the room fell silent to the unrelenting air conditioners. He trundled toward me, smiling.

"Hello, Lion! I'm Gerry! I own the plant!" He reached me in the middle of the room and grasped my hand meatily. "Welcome to Malaysia, welcome to Kuala Lumpur, welcome to my factory!"

I shook his hand vigorously, summoning my last dregs of energy to put forth the right impression. "Hello, Gerry. Thank you."

"Let me introduce you to my employees. You've already talked to my CFO, Kelvin Wang." A middle-aged Chinese man in an ordinary blue polyester suit stepped forward, nodded at Gerry, and offered his hand to me.

"Hello, Lion, it is a pleasure to see you in person."

I shook again, keeping up the sparkle while simultaneously fighting off being awake for over a day and a half. "Yes, nice to see you." Kelvin was the one who had put this together weeks ago, and then worked through all the details in bringing me out while carefully avoiding the obvious question "why."

Gerry pointed while Kelvin stepped back into the group. "This is my sales manager, Danny Nguyen." I actually didn't catch Danny's last name initially, or for about three years into the project. Had I heard Gerry's quick slur of Danny's last name, I might have figured the short, slight Asian man was Vietnamese. I'd learn his nationality far before I learned to pronounce Nguyen properly. Danny stepped forward from the group surrounding Gerry, lowered his head slightly at Gerry, then turned and did the same to me.

I nodded from afar. "Hello, Danny."

"Hello, Lion." He took a step back, returning to his place.

"And this is Maggie Lu, my office manager." An older Chinese woman stepped out of the group, and people made space for her as she strode deliberately toward me.

She stopped closer to me than I expected, head tilted back, sizing me up. "Hello, Lion."

I looked down at her, meeting her gaze. "Hello, Maggie. It's a pleasure."

"So Lion, what is your birth year?" She remained staring at me.

I knew where she was going. "Oh, of course, Maggie, '74, I'm a tiger."

She stepped back, surprise tinged with concern on her face. "How do you know that?"

I smiled charmingly. "It's written on the placemats at my favorite Chinese restaurant."

A look of confusion washed over her face. "Oh, I see. Well, nice to meet you then." She spun and began her march back to the group.

"You as well." Of all the Chinese zodiac signs, the tiger is the third to cross the fabled river and the absolute last on anyone's list of what sign you want your child to be. Something about being independent and not getting along with others.

The list went on while my propped-up sleep-deprived enthusiasm waned. Yet I noticed how Gerry's employees reacted to him. They were silent when he was talking, their faces a well-practiced sheen of intent listening. Their deference permeated the room. It was intense. Eventually we sat down to cake, leaving me to eat in silence.

The man who was clearly in charge creeped me out. Physically, he was in terrible shape, his obesity causing diabetes by the look of it. Still, he was eating a giant slice of cake and laughing loudly like the stereotypical gregarious fat man. People drifted off, out through the doors and back to work.

Gerry pushed his oversize leather office chair away from the end of the folding-tables-turned-conference table. "Okay, Lion, time for a wedding!"

He wasn't joking. I was rushed into a minivan and we hustled off, Kelvin and Danny in tow, to a traditional Malay wedding. I wondered, where did my luggage go?

The wedding was beautiful, huge, lavish, and conducted in a language I didn't come close to understanding. The bride wore a gorgeous dress, natch, and the groom looked sharp in an expensive tailored suit. I had no idea who they were, but everyone knew Gerry, and I was with Gerry, so I was treated as someone important. I vaguely remember snapshots of having a great time in the hours-long celebration.

After that came a tour of the plant. It was late and time for a shift change.

Then dinner. Everyone seemed amazed that I could use chopsticks effortlessly.

Then karaoke and drinks. I remember being surprised at how well the Asians could sing American pop songs. Accents disappeared in an act of incredible mimicry, only to return to straining to understand everyday dialogue.

I do not remember going to bed.

This was the routine for working with Malaysia Gerry: long, unrelenting days of work followed by late nights of food, liquor, and entertainment with the office crew. Japanese karaoke, Pakistani restaurants, Chinese spas, Afghan inns, Malay hookah bars, everything imaginable. Every night I'd be deposited at my hotel in downtown KL respectably drunk, pass out, and join the circus anew the next morning. It was a lifestyle that came with a price: Gerry did have diabetes. He'd make comments about how important it was to eat healthily at every meal, how the wait staff must respect his illness, and then he would gorge himself on anything within reach.

His business wasn't any different. I reviewed failing financial statements, tissue-thin product portfolios, barren client lists, anything that I could get my hands on to show how much trouble this place was in. I took reams of notes, put together detailed outlines, and devised some long-term plans. Inventory management, line worker restructuring, daily tasking of the line, new product development, time and materials tracking, and lots more. My work was that wide-ranging. Not because Gerry needed a generalist, which is what I was, but because Gerry refused to take real responsibility for his own factory.

His problem wasn't the manufacturing process. It wasn't the client list. It wasn't the accounting.

It was the person.

It was Gerry.

Several hundred people bet their livelihoods on Gerry doing the right thing.

On some level, they knew he wasn't.

Three weeks in, Gerry held another party and presented me with a wood and pewter clock. Upon it was an inscription:

ROARS LIKE A LION!

HE WILL GUIDE US THROUGH THE STORMS OF THE NIGHT TO SAVE OUR COMPANY!

After a month on site in Kuala Lumpur, I was ready to present my comprehensive findings to Gerry. We sat down in the office one evening, and I covered everything I had in my outlines and project proposals. Gerry seemed impressed. I began with the small stuff, giving him a chance to show that he was committed to making the changes necessary to keep his factory, and several hundred people, in the black. He wouldn't move on any of it.

Four weeks later, after questions, a detailed assessment, after all that work, Gerry finally told me why I was here. His products were being sold at auto parts stores throughout the United States, and Gerry sold them by the shipping container load to very large distributors. Not individual shops, not regional warehouses, but a handful of nationwide billion-dollar distributors. Which meant that every three years he'd have to go renegotiate the terms of those contracts. Each contract was worth about 20 million dollars, which meant there was a fairly big production every time one had to be done. He wanted me to lead the negotiations.

Leadership and vision didn't enter into Gerry's mind when food and liquor were close at hand, which they always were. Standing up for himself would require respecting himself, and that was not happening anytime soon. When contract negotiations came up, he got taken to the cleaners because he didn't have someone that could stand up to pressure. The distributors knew this and took advantage of him. They placed him in artificially high-stress situations and he'd crack. He'd still land the contract, but not at a fair price. Not that Gerry went alone to them, since he had an entourage just like he had back in KL, complete with the restaurants and bars. Stateside, his most trusted rabbi was flown in from New York, a couple of technical consultants that knew the product lines, and sometimes some seemingly random add-on person that never said much. This was a Japanese man at one point that only sort of knew Gerry. Other times, it was his head of sales, Danny. He, too, said very little. And then, of course, me.

These were difficult talks at first. But something went sideways after we got past the initial discussions and I started digging into the numbers: cost accounting. Everywhere I've worked that used cost accounting didn't have any idea what their products actually cost to build. To me, cost accounting is one part Excel wizardry and two parts numeric theater. It was difficult to have an honest discussion about what we needed to charge when we didn't know what we needed to make on each unit. They made some half-assed attempts to understand the costs, including a takt time study that only showed they didn't understand what takt time was. I was in the dark. Now add to this wild copper prices. Back then, the Chinese were buying up copper like crazy and inflating the price. If you built electrical motors like Gerry, copper was a big deal. It was hard to plan for three years with that going on. The distributors knew that and played that up to Gerry as well.

My first negotiation in Virginia showed these problems quickly. Gerry's numbers wouldn't line up and the talks dragged out over weeks. Gerry went back to KL. A few months later, all three of us were to meet again in Las Vegas at an industry conference. But Gerry was having none of it.

"Hide me," he said in the middle of the show floor.

I looked at him, confused. "What?"

"The distributor's guy is over in the next row. We need to get to the other side without him seeing me."

"Look, we can just talk to him. We'll set up a time to meet."

"No, you need to hide me."

I ended up pushing Gerry through the curtains behind a row of booths and into the back area of the show. I guided him through piles of empty road cases and boxes, maneuvering around a perfectly reasonable person from the distributor's side, and then pushed him out onto the floor again right where we needed to be. We shouldn't have to hide from our customers. But, as I was learning, this was Gerry.

After a few days of pointless cat-and-mouse, we finally sat down to ink the deal. I could only suspect that we got taken once again.

This continued over the next few years. I'd go out to KL, inventory the projects that needed to be done to improve the company's footing, Gerry would listen to my increasingly passionate pleas to fix things, and then he would ship us all back to the States and I'd do another broken negotiation. In Atlanta, Gerry fell asleep in the chair next to me as I was working a 20-million-dollar deal. For another contract, Gerry demanded that it be limited to a single page. The distributor thought the microscopic font and a wall of text were hard to read. They were right. That one was signed too, but not without me playing the part of a fool.

So Gerry was a problem. But Gerry's people weren't much better.

When I arrived in KL the next time, I was ready. I did my usual cursory poking at the business, but what I was really after was to figure out the people. Specifically, the management team that Gerry relied upon to run his business. I had them go through an all-day exercise to gauge their ability to think, plan, and work together. I didn't see anything obvious that was bad. But, also, nothing that was good either. That was unusual.

I sat down with each department head. We talked about their role, the processes they used, and their interactions with the other leaders. Again, I got bland answers. Several people did break the facade and started complaining about Gerry, but that was the exception. What I started to see was gross incompetence. The people Gerry relied upon were almost as bad at their jobs as Gerry. The CFO, Kelvin, was a nice guy, but when we started to dig into the finances, he barely held his own. Gerry spent cash like it came out of a firehose, but Kelvin wouldn't show the figures to me.

Danny, the head of sales, didn't know his own products. A good 80% of Gerry's manufacturing capacity was tied up in a single product line: an automotive starter called the 10MT. I wanted to know what the install base was for the 10MT; how many vehicles were they in, when were they built, what countries use them. Danny didn't know. Turns out that the 10MT was primarily used in the '70s and '80s in U.S. domestic trucks. And I'm standing at a plant that makes them in Kuala Lumpur in 2005. As I dug in further, I found the top of the bell curve of 10MT usage had passed a long time ago and there was nothing to look forward to. I mean, absolutely nothing. It was all downhill from here for sales. Danny didn't know this, and even when I told him, he didn't care. No one did, including Gerry. They didn't want to face up to the fact their primary product was going away in only a few years.

I tried several initiatives to develop new products. I got passive resistance there too. The head of manufacturing half-assed every experiment, the line boss couldn't get it through her head that she needed to weigh in on retooling, and sales wouldn't research markets for new products. So, if Gerry was semi-incompetent and all his people were semi-incompetent, who was keeping things afloat?

A new consultant showed up from Australia. I'd worked alongside many other consultants before and they all had one thing in common: their three-ring binder. This was their secret sauce, their playbook. Not everyone had an actual three-ring binder, but when you brought in a consultant what you got was their trade secrets, and they'd never tell anyone what they were. This consultant was pretty bland all in all. He agreed with all my conclusions, but he never tried to fix any of the problems. He was content to take Gerry's money while enduring the crazy atmosphere.

I started to realize something. If all the people Gerry chose to surround himself with were as bad as Gerry, what did that say about me?

Eventually, I had enough of Gerry's late night activities and convinced a young Malay secretary to be my driver during my stays. Her name was Nur Atiqua Affedni, or just iQa (eek-ah). She was very nice to me and it was great to have a friend in KL besides Gerry and his useless lieutenants. We toured the city. She tried to teach me the Malay language. As I got to know iQa, I learned more about the company and about Gerry. He grew up in New York, and as a young man in the merchant marine, he got off his ship one day in Kuala Lumpur and never went back on board. The stories she told about Gerry were edged with some very dark emotions. Some 20 years ago, Gerry had knocked up his first secretary, Maggie Lu, now the head of the office, and she had given birth to a son. Gerry sometimes talked of his illegitimate son in quiet tones to me. He kept Maggie on, and over time the office filled up with an entire age range of secretaries. I had assumed the big workforce was a local custom, a throwback to '50s'-style offices in a less-modern part of the world. Yet, iQa was the latest addition to the pool, and her father, a devout Muslim, had put her to work for Gerry to pay off some old debt. The realization of what was going on chilled me. iQa wasn't doing just secretarial work. Gerry lived in a few back rooms at the factory, refusing to leave at night, even though he had a beautiful home in the suburbs. She waited on him there, behind closed doors and out of sight. I never asked her the obvious question. I didn't want to know the answer.

Over the weeks, I came to a conclusion: I had to get her out. Knowing what had happened to the rest of the office staff, I couldn't let young iQa fall into that.

I started counseling her to quit Gerry's company and go to college. She wanted a more direct route: marriage. To me. I was single at the time and iQa's desires were flattering. She would have made a very obedient wife, as was the tradition there. But that's not what I wanted. However, I could use her desire to an end, and so I played a terrible game. As I left KL again, I told her that I'd come back for her soon, but she needed to get out of Gerry's company, go to college, and find a new job. She was disappointed I wouldn't take her home then, but she took up the challenge with the expectation that I'd be her knight in shining armor someday soon.

I had time to think on that long flight back to the States. Everything else could be solved, but Gerry and the people he surrounded himself with stood out. I realized that Gerry held on to bad people because he could control them. I played back a memory of a frank conversation with the Australian consultant when he explained exactly why Kelvin, the CFO, was not up to the task. Kelvin couldn't get a job anywhere else even as an accountant, much less a CFO. Gerry used the position and the money to control Kelvin. That matched the control he exerted over his office staff and everyone else around him. Allimalar Sugumaran, the plant manager, was a lesbian in a country that stoned women for it. She couldn't leave Gerry either. Gerry must have something on everyone, even if only their poor self-image.

While on the road together as we negotiated contract renewals, I was left alone in the Aussie's hotel room one evening, and I noticed a familiar diagram poking out from his stack of notes. He had copied the product development lifecycle diagram wholesale from my three-ring binder. He had spied on me. Damn, he was just as bad as Gerry.

This is how nature works: every niche in the ecosystem is pursued, every opportunity to succeed is attempted. Nature has no consideration for human concepts like right or wrong. If a blight can grow, succeed, and take over, it will. Species will die, landscapes will change, new niches will appear to be exploited.

Again, we are not separate from nature. Morals are an individual concept, and they vary person to person. Right and wrong don't matter when a niche in the human environment opens up and the opportunity appears to succeed at the cost of others.

Gerry and his people were weak. His herd was riddled with blight, and the herd was already dying.

It didn't start that way. Gerry didn't show up on the docks of Kuala Lumpur and decide to be the loathsome man he is today. That took years of the blight slowly growing unchecked. In the beginning, Gerry was able to get away with small things: annoyances and inconveniences to his workers. Habits that his employees would look at and consider a reasonable price to pay for working for Gerry. However, blight grows, that's its nature. So, with every year that passed of Gerry getting away with bad behavior, without being checked and stopped, Gerry simply did more of it. Then, in the presence of Gerry being bad, his employees had no reason to behave any better. They, too, developed their own habits. The blight was spreading. Eventually, Gerry manipulated and damaged people so much that his herd was ready for slaughter by the economic forces overwhelming them.

Organisms that destroy their environment have nothing to hold them up in challenging times. They are directly in conflict with the world around them. This weakness makes the herd worse, also leaves it susceptible to harm, and when tough times come, the herd's survival becomes less certain.

Malignancy always starts simple. A bad idea is left unchecked, unbalanced. Take the guy who's constantly running down the company he works for. He'll tell you how bad things are in the break room, he'll explain how he hates management to you at your cube, he'll take any opportunity to slam the company: its products, market, whatever he can get his mind wrapped around. He doesn't like what he's doing, but he doesn't do anything to change it. He won't quit and go somewhere else because the workplace is not the problem, it's him. He is pernicious to the herd, riding the line of 'dangerous yet not bad enough' to fire. This is weakness, and this is what predators hunt.

Weak prey comes in a lot of different forms inside companies. They build silos. They hoard knowledge. They attack their own. They make themselves indispensable and then get away with murder. They slow things down, dodge responsibilities, or wield process like a cudgel to hurt people. They freak out when something goes wrong, but they don't pitch in to fix it, and sometimes they even encourage the disaster. They're lazy, they don't think, they do the absolute minimum to not get fired. None of these helps the herd. All of them make the herd weak. And all these ideas can spread.

Nature has an answer to this: the predator. Weak prey are easy to kill. Easy kill attracts predators. Balance will be maintained.

CHAPTER SEVEN
THE DOCUMENT RIOT

I KNOCKED GENTLY on the open door frame to her office. Light shone though the big windows high up in the building, bathing the room in a warm glow. The view was fantastic, the city spread out below with only a few other skyscrapers as tall. You could see all the way to a huge green expanse, filled with lawn and trees, stretching around the edge of houses and a huge hospital complex. Yeah, this was a great office. She looked up from her desk.

"Hey, Maria, got a sec?" I asked as she saw me.

She smiled lightly. "Yeah Lion, come on in."

I stepped over the break in the carpet dividing the cube farm from her office and winced slightly. "Look, I wanted to stop by to apologize for what I said during our document owner meeting. I didn't mean to insult anyone or be harsh about the responsibilities." I hung my head just enough to show.

"Lion, it's alright. There were only a few people who were upset, and I think you're right. The old system has to go. So, no apology necessary."

I nodded, looking relieved. "Hey, thanks."

"Yeah, this isn't a big deal to me." She paused, looked at her desk. She was busy. "Have a good weekend, Lion."

"You too." I smiled and headed out the door.

As I cleared Maria's office, I switched to a purposeful stride and dropped the smile for a hard line across my face. I looked down at my tablet and checked a box, ticking another person off my list. This task was supposed to be humiliating, and unnecessarily so. What the hell happened? What am I doing, going around this office as a consultant, apologizing to people? How the hell did I get here? I narrowed my eyes. Well, sometimes the best way to make people understand the gravity of their poor behavior is to let them get their way. On to the next office.

Weeks before my apology tour, I had been sitting in a conference room-turned-temporary office, chatting with the CFO. Her midsize financial services company spanned a few hundred people and several states. Apparently, the company had a problem: documents. Years and years ago they had invested in Edgar Filer, an expensive Document Management System (DMS) that, well, never worked. Think of a DMS as an advanced electronic filing cabinet. Edgar Filer was barely functioning. It was thoroughly green text screen territory. User friendliness died out in this system well before the invention of a web browser. This system didn't even know what a mouse was. Yet, even though it didn't work, they still needed it. To a financial services company, documents are its lifeblood. The government regulations for this type of company lay down specific rules about how to store, manage, and keep all those documents. The old system was deeply embedded, but it didn't actually meet the regulatory requirements that had blossomed in the last decade since its installation. Just maintaining the system after the software company had stopped supporting it was looking like a NASA-sized budget. I was supposed to handle this trouble. The CFO had sponsored the project under the approval of the CEO, who approved bankrolling my expensive consultant time.

The CFO was well aware of some of Edgar's deficiencies. But the total picture wasn't clear. I was let loose with the objective to dig into Edgar and figure out whether they simply needed to make better use of Edgar or if they should replace Edgar completely. Between the CFO and I, we agreed that I would plumb the depths of Edgar within their company. I was to determine fitness for purpose.

Fitness for purpose is a great concept people use all the time to evaluate systems they have to work with. The most common expression of fitness for purpose is the idea: "To a hammer, everything is a nail," a short way of saying that sometimes a tool doesn't work so well for what you're asking it to do. While you can, for instance, build a deck with a hammer, that's not the best tool anymore. An electric screwdriver is. And that Phillips-head screwdriver? Yeah, well, it's maybe not as great for building a deck as a star drive screwdriver. Will the hammer work? Well, yes, but it may involve your deck coming apart years later as the nails pull out.

That's what we were looking for: "Is this the tool for the job?" It doesn't matter if you're building a deck, repairing a car, or doing financial modeling. So, I started off evaluating the Edgar tool with a tool of my own: the survey. It's really that exciting. A free-form open survey is a great way to kick off an evaluation like this. I don't do "rate Edgar Filer one to five" or anything like that. I ship out emails and pieces of paper with open-ended questions that start with, "What tools do you use?" and, "What strengths do these tools have?" I want people to write, to compose thoughtful responses. Sometimes, I even get a few. I find, too, that people are initially happy to participate in whatever the "fix the Edgar problem" consultant has planned. Everyone knows Edgar sucks; they wouldn't have hired a consultant if they didn't. Which means, like doing warrants, by the time it gets on my daily worksheet, Edgar is already a serious problem.

But do I actually get useful answers out of a survey? No. What I'm really looking for is the inventory of all of the tools. Edgar doesn't exist in a vacuum. It works in conjunction with a large collection of other tools. Is Edgar a lone problem child? Or is Edgar a symptom of greater failures in the organization? The more tools they have, especially ones that do the same job, the more fragmented the culture tends to be; and the less coherent their strategy.

This place was getting around Edgar in a massively old school way. They knew they had to use Edgar for electronic documents, but if they didn't have any, Edgar wasn't required. This explained the cancerous growths of filing cabinets throughout the offices and hallways. Apparently, there was a mysterious basement room filled with documents going back 80 years. No one put this down as a problem, but I could see the absence of document management within the organization by how they filled out their surveys. Combined with a walk around the office, I knew what was actually going on.

Next came the interviews. During an assay, I will sit down with a target set of people. Sometimes, it's the people on the line or in the cubes. Sometimes, it's middle management. Often times, it's upper management and the C-suite. The line, middle, and upper groups give you distinctly different pictures of an organization. After some initial poking around, I decided on cutting a broad swath through middle management. It was apparent that the line people didn't interact with Edgar, the upper people knew how Edgar was being used but never used it themselves, and the middlers were the ones that actually engaged with it.

It would have been simpler for me to take a close look at Edgar and get a laundry list of Edgar-can-do-this-but-not-that qualities. I could apply those to the organization's stated needs and come up with a reasonable idea, fairly quickly, of whether or not Edgar was up to the job. But Edgar and the company's ecosystem of tools do not exist in a vacuum. How you use a tool is just as important as the tool itself. The processes surrounding a tool could tell me an enormous amount about the tool without ever asking people, "How well does this tool work?"

Imagine you're building a deck for your house. You've got a brand-name WUXING BEST battery-powered drill. If I ask, "Did this tool meet your needs?" you might say "Yeah, I finished the deck, no problem." If I ask you, "Tell me the process of building the deck with this screwdriver," you might respond with, "First, I let the screwdriver charge for at least eight hours. Then, I line up about ten screws, hold the screwdriver firmly while in a comfortable position, and wait for the screwdriver to put in a screw. After ten screws, I then re-charge the driver for another eight hours." The process tells you the real story.

This is why I do interviews and why I don't approach them head-on. Edgar's been around for a long time, just like the employees. I may not get good answers if I ask them about Edgar directly. So, I start with a basic enough question: "Starting anywhere, tell me about how you do your job." This gets them telling a story, specifically the story of how they interact with the tools.

The interviews show that Edgar is far more complicated than I thought. It's everywhere in the organization and never used the same way twice. Almost every department has a different idea and a unique home-grown process. There are some commonalities, but only of the most general types. "We put documents into Edgar" would sum up the entirety of the situation nicely. I noticed the distinct lack of, "We also get documents out of Edgar." Huh. So, it looked like we needed to do some serious process mapping to get a handle on how documents actually flowed around the company. I sent out for a Business Process Management (BPM) expert to dig into the details.

Meanwhile, I needed to broach a touchy subject with the executives: the company needs to admit it has a document problem.

No one likes to hear they have a problem; they tend to take it very personally. It's often seen as if having a problem is some kind of deep, personal flaw. I don't think that way. I need to know the past and its failures so I can understand today. I just want to fix problems. So, my problem was getting upper management and the executives to be on board with the idea that Edgar sucks but, with some effort, the situation can be fixed. The CFO was now much more acutely aware of Edgar's issues due to my regular updates. She needed me to push the document management issue at an upcoming executive offsite retreat. I had two hours in front of everyone to make a go of it.

So, there I was, in a posh meeting room at a four-star hotel looking at my laptop, slowly burning. Well, not exactly on fire, but the PowerPoint presentation I had meticulously built was refusing to load. It was completely corrupted. Damn. I looked around the room at everyone and simply told them the truth.

"Hi, everybody. It looks like my PowerPoint got trashed, so I'm going to do a lot of handwaving in the hope that you don't notice I'm missing my slide deck."

I had the organizers tape up large sheets of white posterboard across the front of the room. This was my whiteboard. I held my big black marker tightly and smiled to the room. "Let's figure out this document thing, shall we?"

Over the next hour and a half, I had people explain their document management process while I drew it out on the board. Every time we'd get to a tough spot, like working with Edgar, I'd laugh and encourage them to continue. I rolled in humor with my responses, drawing crazy lines and confusing diagrams on the board, exaggerating the lunacy of the situation. Every time someone responded with humor of their own, I seized on it, drew it out, and then made callbacks to the joke. The first person was nervous and shakily raised her hand, but after a while the hands kept coming up enthusiastically. We built a nice repertoire of in-jokes by the end. I turned the painful knowledge that people were not doing well into a cathartic release. I got them to joke about it, and even admit that, yes, the real documents were stored on paper in "a locked, fireproof file cabinet." In the last half hour, I told great stories about how we could come to know how things flowed in the organization, and to work better as a team because we didn't have to hold ourselves to this very bad Edgar standard. At the end, I made a sweeping, hopeful statement:

"If we can figure this out, between all of us we can start to build ..." I spread my arms wide, leaned into the audience and beamed, waiting for an answer.

A gal immediately spoke up. "Love?" she questioned, on the edge of a smile.

I nodded at her. "I was going for understanding, but love works too."

As far as upper management was concerned, the problem was well on its way to being solved after that. What I had done here was to bring together the three pillars of an organization. Tools are one: these are the things we use to do our work. Process is another: it is how we use those tools. And, finally, the people: everyone engaged in the organization. All three of them are tightly coupled. Upper management was uncomfortable because they knew they had fallen down on document management and let the Edgar situation go on far too long. By talking about their tools and their process, I could address the last part of the equation indirectly: the people themselves.

If you change any part of this triangle, the other two have to change as well. Change a tool, you adapt the process, and the people need to embrace the change. And not just simply, "Hey, we have a new tool," but, "How do I best use this tool?" Change a process and the tool needs to adapt. The people need to be engaged in the new process and, again, not in a, "Oh, new process" way, but, "How does this make things better?" And people? Well, change people and everything changes.

Examining process and tools tells me a lot about people.

The executives green-lit me going to the middlers with a new initiative for document management. Until now, they had used Edgar as an excuse for poor performance. They didn't say that directly, mind you, but their interviews spoke volumes of what the people were like. I was going to stop them from avoiding work because of a misused tool. I would make them "document owners." They would be responsible in every way for the document types under their control. Quarterly reports? All of them are yours now. Customer financial goals and plans? That's yours now. Each one of these middlers would have the authority to decide how their documents were stored, how they were created, and how they were handled. They could decide the best process for the job. They looked at me in a state of shock as I presented to them the "document owner's guide" that detailed their new responsibilities at the kickoff meeting.

In the grand scheme of things, it was an excellent plan. With everyone coming up with their own document management processes and strategies, we'd see a huge diversity of implementations. From there, the document owners would reconvene every six months to present their system and learn from each other. I was building an ecosystem of process and tools from which best practices for this company would emerge. They'd all learn together; it would end up being coherent.

They didn't get that.

I stood before them that day. "One of the important parts of your document management plan is retention. Some of you have legal requirements to keep certain documents for some amount of time. You must have that as part of your plan. You must also have why that retention period is required in your plan."

A woman spoke up, an edge of defiance in her voice. "I have tax documents, which are a seven-year retention. Everyone knows that. I don't need to justify that."

"Look, you need to know the reg for that. You can't just go on 'everyone knows.' You can't just guess. You have to know for certain and cite the reg. Otherwise, how do we know what we're doing is right?"

The room buzzed quietly. I swept it with my eyes and was met with a few glares. Out of about 40 people, less than 10 were upset enough to argue with me. They pushed all sorts of crazy excuses, including "It's too hard to know the regulations!" Wait, what?

After a while, I had said my piece and the room cleared. I didn't quite get the closing "love" that the executive meeting had. No, quite the opposite: the middlers were pissed. Well, a few of them were.

The next morning, I appeared before the CEO, and she demanded I go back to everyone that was at the meeting and apologize, in person. The CEO was emphatic, practically frothing at the mouth for how badly I had done and how much I'd pissed off the entire middle management cadre. It was complete bullshit. I had the option, as I always do, of walking out. But there was still money on the table.

Which brings us to me walking around the office apologizing. That was as educational as any of the other methods I had used to figure out the company's people, process, and tools. My forced apologies divided people from the CEO. A number of them understood what I was trying to do and agreed with me. I had made friends by calling the bad people out. And, as I learned, there were only three. Three women who had their cushy low-responsibility world challenged and had freaked out. I never apologized to them.

It may sound clichéd, but to hunt prey, you need to know prey. You need to know the environment prey works in. I carefully study the area where I'm hunting. I need to know my prey's patterns, where they go, how they move, how they behave. And, while I refer to prey in a general sense, prey are always individuals. Every prey is different, every hunt has a unique environment. And I can assure you that the prey know their environment very well. On some level, they know the interplay of people, process, and tools. Weak prey use those to their advantage.

Weak prey sees their world from a specific perspective, one of being inside the herd. They use anything they can to get their way. Prey might bend personal bonds, manipulate people, play people off each other, or simply bully people to get what they want. Prey may even see it all as a game. Knowing weak prey, it's not even a delicate and thoughtful game like chess; it's more like a game involving watermelons and sledgehammers. And, like the front row of a Gallagher show, the people closest to prey already know what's coming: they know the sledgehammer always wins.

Prey is very good at their game. Don't play prey's game, you'll lose. Make them play your game.

This is why you can't go at the problem directly.

While deer hunting, I will often change the environment, cutting down trees or building blinds, to catch my prey in their habits. In a company, I will change the environment by adjusting people, process, and tools to bring weak prey into the open.

I had an idea of who the problem people were after the interview cycle of asking about process and tools. I could tell who was weak prey in just how process and tools had been bent around them. But my knowing who's the prey isn't enough; the organization needs to know. They need to see weak prey for what it is: weak. So, I used the triangle against them: I changed the process. I then removed all requirements for a tool, eliminating using Edgar as a shield. That left them cornered and exposed. When you corner prey, prey loses it. The first person to lose it, loses.

I waited out the couple of weeks to the end of the contract with busy work. The project was going nowhere due to these people. The fight wasn't worth it. I did achieve something of worth, though: a much deeper organization-wide understanding of who caused the document management problem and who had to be fired to fix it. That's my purpose. Oh, and money. I made money.

CHAPTER EIGHT
DO YOU WANT BLOOD?

"Be-beep." My desk speakerphone hummed with the open line into the conference.

"Hi, who joined?" I asked automatically. It was a silly thing to say. This was a conference call for two people and one of them was me, so the joiner had to be Vinod.

"Hello, this is Vinod." Yup, right on time. Vinod had been with the technology division of this multinational bank for a whole two weeks at this point. I had no idea where he was right now, but he was at least somewhere in the same city as me. This wasn't true of the entire team; many of us worked remotely. Even the interview process was done largely via phone. Hence, the conference call. I was seated at my desk in my home office in the suburbs. This was where I worked most days; I had a comfortable chair, a set of giant monitors staring at me, and who'd want to be in the downtown office at 9:00 p.m. on a Thursday night? This is the way of things when you're taking servers down after-hours for maintenance.

I turned my head to address the phone on my desk. "Hey, Vinod, this is Lion. Welcome."

"Hello, Li-on."

"So, you've been working with Joe on your on-boarding and training for the last couple of weeks, right?" Joe was our team lead, a good guy that got me the contract gig with the bank during a huge project that needed extra people. A shotgun wedding between this bank and another at the government's behest tossed a wrench into the works; all of a sudden, you have to be one big company and have one set of tools and data. I've been part of this project for a year now. Vinod's part of this big push too, just a lot more recent one.

"Yes," Vinod responded.

"Great, how did that go?"

"Oh-kay, Li-on."

"Great. What we're doing tonight is pushing new updates to the servers. You'll find the ticket number BAR-4318 in your inbox. I've already let everyone know that we're working tonight by email, and that announcement should be in your inbox too. So, what I'm going to do is have you drive and I'll walk you through it. That sound good?"

"Oh-kay, Li-on."

"Okay, go ahead and share your screen."

I had every reason to believe I would have an easy time training Vinod. He had gone through the same interview process that I had; which is to say it wasn't hard, but management did remark a number of times on how few people passed it. You had to play along with a scenario, pretending you were working on a problem with the servers, while the interviewer asked what to do next and then told you the results of your actions. It was kind of like playing an IT version of *Dungeons & Dragons*. If you win this game, you go on to the money-making level: a 12-month contract and maybe an extension to 18 months. With that comes a cube in a downtown high-rise and two weeks of sitting with the team lead, Joe, learning the basics of the millions of dollars of technology you're suddenly responsible for. I had a cube down there too. I was never in it after my first two weeks.

Vinod's screen share request took a good minute to pop up on my laptop.

I nodded at the mirror copy of his computer's screen displayed in front of me, just a normal desktop with the bank's logo front and center. "Great, thanks. All right, we're working on the servers BAR Pre-Prod one through eight. How about you log into them now?"

I heard a quiet hiss of the idle phone conference line on the speakerphone. I didn't see anything happening on Vinod's screen. He was not even moving the mouse.

"Uh, Vinod?"

"Yes, Li-on?"

"Can you log into the servers?"

Again, a hiss of the conference line and nothing else. I saw his mouse cursor in front of me, right of center on the screen. It continued to remain still. I stopped paying attention to everything else and focus intently on that white arrow. Why was it not moving?

Vinod spoke up. "I do not remember how." He paused just long enough to let the sentence hang there. "Can you do it?"

"Okay, give me control of your screen."

A few moments later he did. Vinod not being on the ball wasn't all that unusual, two weeks in. If you're a fresh contractor and maybe not used to working for one of the biggest banks in the world, the environment can intimidate you. I remember my trainer at this point getting frustrated with me for checking every little command twice before proceeding. Tonight, Vinod and I were going to work on brand-new stuff to him. His introduction with Joe would only have taught him the basics; I had to finish his training on the real deal. I could understand the hesitation on his part.

"All right, Vinod. I'm going to log in." Eight green-on-black windows appeared on his screen. "So, all I did was execute the macro you have here." I circled the icon on his desktop with the mouse cursor. "It opens up terminal sessions to all eight servers and logs us in."

The speakerphone quietly hissed at me.

"Okay, so at this point you can look at the ticket and know what directory the files are in and what version we need to upgrade to. Why don't you get us into the directory we need to be in?" I was okay with gently walking Vinod through this, again—he's a first timer. I took my hands away from the keyboard and mouse and watched the blinking underline of a cursor on the screen.

All I heard was the quiet hiss of silence.

"Li-on, I do not know where to go."

"Okay, Vinod, that's fine, I'll take it." I guessed that could be legitimate. The stuff that he needed was buried in the ticket, and maybe he didn't know it yet.

I continued. "So, I'll just change the directory to here." I typed a long sequence of keys. "This is the normal place we start our work and, while it's in the ticket, you should probably take note of it." I pulled my hands back from the keys so Vinod could copy the information on his computer.

Silence.

Or maybe he was writing it down.

Silence.

All right, I thought, that's been enough time for him to jot it down in a notebook. "So, now I'm going to find out where the server is running and kill the process. The process starts with 'jre-bar' and there should be ten of them running on each server. So, I need to grab the process table, I can do that with 'ps,' right?" I was feeling a little weird about the lack of interaction, so I was checking in with his level of knowledge. Vinod should know the basics of this—we were not entry-level support desk guys, this was production engineering. They didn't hire people with no experience.

Still, nothing but line hiss as several long seconds dragged out.

Okay, moving on. "So yeah, I'll just do 'ps' and grab the process ID." I click away on the keyboard. "There it is, good. To shut down the service, I'll send it SIGHUP with the kill command." Basic sysadmin 101, again, I'm trying to get recognition from Vinod on something, anything.

Silence.

"All right, signal sent, now we take a look at the log files while it shuts down. Then we know when it's done." I typed in more commands. My window suddenly filled with text as the logs scrolled away, the service doing its thing. I punched the volume button on my phone, pushing it up to the max. I wanted to hear pen and paper sounds, maybe typing on another computer, something to tell me Vinod was still there.

"All right, I'll use 'ps' again to make sure it's not running." I ran the command. Nothing came back on the screen, which was good. Still nothing came back over the phone, which was bad.

"Okay, it's down now. Now I can clean up the directory." I typed more commands followed by silence.

"Now, remove the links to the old data." Yet more commands, more silence.

"Check that the server is clear of old data."

My gut was telling me something was wrong. That feeling was based upon a lot of learned behavior in life where similar situations went badly. I would give someone a set of instructions, they listened to you, and then went off and completely botched the job because they never really got it and never asked.

But I tend to go a lot further than just a feeling. I've gone to great lengths to understand the people around me, which in turn allows me to make predictions about them. In some way, we all do this during the process of getting to know someone and developing expectations about them. The longer you know them, the more your expectations line up with reality. I happen to be a lot more formal about it in my head. I call the process predictive modeling. What I do is imagine a kind of "paper doll" of everyone I meet in my head. The paper doll, or model, starts off very generic. My objective is to take that blank, person-shaped piece of paper and fill in as much detail as possible, up to the point that I can now start making decisions about that person and predicting what they're going to do next.

But people are unpredictable! Well, yes and no. Try this for an example. The freeway is a great place to study prediction in people. If you've ridden a motorcycle, you've found yourself in a dangerous world of multiton vehicles that don't always see your few-hundred-pound bike. So, how do you stay safe? How do you keep at least a step ahead of the other drivers? By predicting what they're going to do. One of the phrases I've heard is, "Don't watch the driver, watch their front tires." What the tires are doing is leading the rest of the vehicle. Watching the driver doesn't help—who knows where their head is at—but if the tires start changing position, look out. The tires tend to move unconsciously before the driver has fully realized their decision. This happens all the time on the freeway. A game I play is to bet when the car ahead of me is going to exit. The rules of the game are to predict if the driver will exit at the upcoming exit or not. If they are, the car unconsciously drifts to the right near the white line, telegraphing an upcoming exit. If you're paying attention to speed, the car might slow down gradually, which you can perceive as a slight narrowing of the following distance. This is a good 30 seconds or more from the exit. If the car isn't exiting, it won't drift to the right, and often it'll hang center or just slightly left in the lane and maintain speed. It's subtle, but once you see it happen, you won't be able to unsee it. Things like this make up my base model of all drivers.

Again, everyone does this. While selecting a line at the grocery store checkout, I see an old woman is going to pay with a check. I won't wait in that line. The family with three kids at McDonald's isn't going to order quickly: I won't wait in that line either. I make a point of trying not to engage the teenager behind the counter at the gas station in a quick discussion of world macroeconomic issues either. Because, in each of these cases, my model predicts poor outcomes. But notice how quickly I get to decision-level prediction just based on stereotypes. My paper doll never starts off completely blank. I consider stereotypes like filling in the paper doll with crayons. It's not going to be detailed, but it provides some color and shape to your model. If I need to interact with someone, I need to refine that model a lot more.

On the job, I start my model off with two stereotypes: reasonable person and base competency. I assume that, just by being here, I'm working with a reasonable person. This means I expect them to do reasonable things, like understand and use basic logic. In my mind, it's important to assume reasonableness in everyone. To assume unreasonableness leaves me on the defensive all the time, expecting people to do bad at any moment. That's not a fun place to live and it gets tiring. The same thing goes for base competency: if I'm working with you, you've made it up the ladder to the point that you're at least competent. No one should get this far up in an organization without some ability to get the job done. Now it's time to refine the model so I can make specific predictions.

I started Vinod's paper doll with reasonableness and competency. I worked with the team that interviewed him, and I knew he had to play IT *Dungeons & Dragons* and win. Yet, here Vinod had gone silent on the other end of the conference call. Up to this point, he had not demonstrated competency. So, to verify that part of the model, I had to test him.

"Okay, Vinod, I'll let you take the next part. It's easy."

Silence.

"I've got the new service files right over in this directory. They need to be in the service's directory. Okay, go ahead and copy the new files into place."

I paused. Nothing happened for several seconds. Finally, I saw movement of the mouse cursor on his screen, but nothing that looked like what I had asked him to do. He didn't need to use the mouse for this.

I continued, "Vinod, just copy the files from the distribution folder into the server folder."

"Oh-kay, Li-on."

A few tentative keys got pushed, letters popping up on the screen, but the wrong ones. I didn't even know what command he was trying for.

"Vinod, are you okay?"

"I am oh-kay."

"Can you copy the files?"

Pause. A few more wrong keys were pressed.

"That's not the copy command." Things are going south, fast.

Pause.

"Vinod?"

"I am not knowing what I am doing."

What I had asked him to do was very simple; I had set the whole thing up, and even a junior worker would have been able to take the next step. Vinod couldn't get it done. He just trashed the competency part of my model. The reasonable person assumption was also shot. If he didn't know what was going on, why didn't he say so?

Speaking of asking for help, Vinod spent two weeks with Joe. I opened an Instant Messenger window:

IM OPEN TO JOE

LION

Hey Joe, I'm working with Vinod tonight and something's really not right.

JOE

What's going on?

LION

Did he do okay in his initial training? Did you see anything?

JOE

He did fine, I think. I was pretty busy.

LION

But nothing struck you as a problem?

JOE

No, not really.

At this point, I suddenly paid real attention. I imagined Vinod working with the team on our day-to-day tasks. He couldn't get the work done, so more of it fell on me. But, more so, he would have to be closely supervised and gently handled so he wouldn't break things along the way. Our department was already stretched incredibly thin, the project was millions over budget, and we all were working 12-plus hour days and weekends. Vinod made the situation worse. The constant hand-holding and lack of trust made more work for everyone rather than lessen the load.

This is the power of predictive modeling: you take your model and place it in a situation in your head to see how they will respond. Vinod's model showed he was a massive net drain on our overworked department. I had not come to this company to hunt prey, but one had stumbled right in front of my nose.

Mind you, I was only a contractor for this one big project. I was not an employee, not a manager, I had absolutely no authority in anything. However, as the team lead, Joe was well respected and, most important, a full employee. He had a lot of say. And he already told me that he barely remembered Vinod. So, I didn't have a personal relationship to fight on this chase. Realizing what I was about to do, I got a little shot of adrenaline. Time to be a predator.

JOE
What's going on?

LION
He can't do even the most basic stuff. I think he's really lost.

LION
He kind of begged off from driving tonight, which is fine, but I kind of prodded him with easy stuff.

LION
He didn't get any of it.

JOE
How?

LION
He's been totally silent on me and when I'd ask questions I get nothing from him.

JOE
Like what?

LION
He can't copy the new BAR files onto the server. Like, he has no idea how to copy files at all.

JOE
Really?

There's the setup. I'd known Joe for a long time. I consider him a good friend to this day. He'd believe me when I said these things. Therefore, he was the quickest path to the kill. Time to start the chase in earnest. I jumped in with an easy one, a personal concern.

LION
I don't think I can work with him. He's got no idea how to do anything.

JOE
Let me talk to Brad.

Brad was the manager, with hiring and firing authority. He was a nice guy, a bit weak on things, but that worked to my favor tonight. Joe had a pretty strong personality. Joe couldn't push Brad around, but Brad would know Joe tends to be right about the things he believes in.

I'd been letting Vinod hang there on the call while my keyboard was banging away. "Okay, Vinod, I'll do it, and you just watch along."

"Oh-kay, Li-on."

As I worked, Vinod was still watching. Joe was likely to be on the phone with Brad for the next 20 minutes or so. I was a bit jacked up, trying for a kill after all, but I was surprised too. Here I was, hunting when I said I wouldn't. It just landed in my lap!

My instincts had already pushed my rational mind to the expected conclusion, but maybe Joe or Brad might need more. Time to roll out the bullshit and see if any of it stuck. "Vinod, I need to link this file over here. I can use 'gcc' for that, yeah?"

No, no, I can't. This doesn't even make sense.

"Oh-kay, Li-on."

I fired off the proper command. A moment later I stopped, randomly. "How about this indicator here? What does this mean?" What indicator?

There's nothing on the screen but the last few commands and my half-finished one.

"I don't know, Li-on."

"Okay, well, tell me about the command I used here." I use the mouse cursor to point to a command I issued a few lines ago.

"I have not seen that before, Li-on."

Right. So, I continued the work, but every step of the way I ask Vinod what I should do next. He couldn't answer. I asked him what commands I should use. He had no idea. I asked him what my command did, even in a general sense. No clue. I made random stuff up. He still said nothing.

LION
> This guy has no idea what he's doing. I've pushed him to show any knowledge at all. He had nothing. I don't think he's seen or done any of this before.

LION
> His training was really okay?

JOE
> Yeah. He seemed quiet.

LION
> No shit, quiet. He's keeping his mouth shut because he doesn't know anything.

I pushed Vinod more and more, getting increasingly basic with the tools and task at hand. He still didn't understand any of it. I had enough to finish the kill now. I was confident this was the right prey. If my predictive model was right, he was going to be hell for all of us until eventually his contract ran out in 11 months and two weeks from now.

LION
> This guy needs to go. He doesn't have the chops.

JOE
> Are you sure?

My heart was racing, eyes wide staring at the Instant Messenger window. I was fully in the moment.

LION
Yeah. Fire him. He's not going to work out.

JOE
Okay, I'm letting Brad know.

My fingers banged away on the keyboard. My work continued silently for the next 10 minutes of eternity.

JOE
Fired.

That was it. I finished my night's work with Vinod wordlessly riding along on the speakerphone. I said my goodbyes to him, mentioning nothing of what had just happened. I told him I'd see him online tomorrow and hung up.

After a couple hours, the adrenaline ran out. I went to bed that night smiling.

The next morning, Vinod showed up at his cube and was promptly escorted out by security. He didn't have time to unpack his bag or set up his laptop. My coworkers, including Joe and Brad, ended up cleaning out the little that was left in his cube. They found a notebook left behind in his hasty departure. It contained a completely constructed history of work experience and a lot of answers to potential technical questions. A page in the notebook had the following scrawled in all capital letters:

KUMAR WILL DO YOUR INTERVIEW ON WEDNESDAY.

Vinod had someone else sit for his interview. Damn. The entire department was shocked they'd been so taken. The contracting agency offered a refund for the two weeks of time they'd billed. I don't know if they ever recovered the damage to the business relationship that followed. No new contractors were offered up. No one replaced Vinod. No one quite understood how it all happened. Did the agency play this game of getting people hired and then hoping they'd turn out? Did Vinod have Kumar play the game for him and keep the agency in the dark? Nobody knows, or at least nobody said. Somehow this guy got through everything and ended up in front of the exact right guy for one short evening: me.

This was the easiest and shortest kill I've ever made. It lasted no more than two hours. Brad had HR turning over the paperwork that night while I was still on the phone with Vinod. Again, in no way was evaluating other employees an official part of why I was at the bank. I wasn't even expecting to make a kill there; it was a huge company with lots of well-entrenched people. A consultant like myself had little, if any, leverage. Yet, my predictive model of Vinod showed only bad outcomes. Now, I admit there were a few lucky factors that made this an easy kill, like knowing the team lead well, but the largest factor was Vinod's incompetence. Incompetence is a great start to a hunt.

THE PREY

This event opened with emotions: shock and horror. As I tried to work with Vinod, his incompetency became clear. What we were doing didn't have room for sophomoric training, much less gross incompetence. The pace of work was so fast that, if anyone couldn't keep up, they were going to take everyone else down.

I canceled vacations, nights out with friends, pretty much everything in those two years as part of delivering on that juggernaut pace. I wasn't alone: we were all barely keeping up. I recall many long weekends awake for 30-plus hours and then tagging one of my teammates in about the time I was going to pass out. Then this guy shows up.

I felt I had to do my predatorial job, not only because of who I am, but for simple self-preservation. Vinod was going to work on the same things as me, which meant I was the front line in dealing with his massive inadequacy.

He had to go.

THE HUNT

The core mechanism of every kill is to emotionally rift the prey from the rest of the herd. Emotional distance must be forcibly created, tearing the prey away from the herd's natural bonds. Friendship becomes acquaintance, acquaintance turns to distance, distance results in mistrust, mistrust instills a sense of threat. The prey becomes debonded. Rarely is the predator empowered to make the firing decision themselves, but someone that belongs to the herd is. Remember back to the retail lightning rod story, Martha. What got her fired was the herd turning on her. I didn't even know why it happened or what she did, but I watched the whole store make her out to be a bad person and then, one day, she's gone. The herd will figure out the exact issue to get the pink slip written. All the predator needs to do is separate the prey from the herd and let nature take its course.

Vinod's hunt was easy: I had a massive gut reaction to his incompetence. If I felt it, then I could take that exact same emotion and transfer it to those who write the pink slip. There are two factors I had to consider: Vinod's bonding to the organization and Vinod's importance in getting the work done. The bonding part was easy; Vinod was new. He hadn't had time to fully bond. On the other hand, the expectation that Vinod would take up some of the workload was acute. Even if he was not fully part of the herd yet, he might give the team a weekend off.

So, the basis of the rift has to be a sense of the effect he'll have on the team. The feeling I got right away is: this guy will hurt us. Now, I had to be careful; emotions are tricky things. I couldn't swing for the fences and freak out, hoping that the message would connect.

This hunt was made much easier by having worked with Joe for many years. He knew what I was capable of. That meant he trusted me in evaluating Vinod's performance. So, I needed to assess Vinod's performance professionally, and let Joe come to his own emotional conclusion as to the effect on the team.

That's the key: I can never tell people how to feel. The effect is far more powerful if you bring them to that feeling on their own. Their self-internalized feelings are way more compelling than just trusting yours.

THE KILL

HUNTING PREY IN nature is without convention and rules. No one makes agreements of what is acceptable in a fight for survival, from either violence or starvation. But these conflicts do have boundaries, physics being the principal one. Speed, maneuverability, stealth; they all play into what range of tactics can be used and what shapes the consequences. There are some laws that you can't break and still walk away.

In the office world, it is no different. There are no rules, only consequences. In this hunt, I take advantage of my coworker and friend, Joe. He is a part of the terrain I use to gain an edge over my prey. But, instead of physics intersecting with raw earth, I must chase across the psychological expanse of relationships. There are things I can do, and things that have consequences.

Take Joe. With him, I run a delicate path between concern and complaint.

I check in with Joe right away. I want to be sure I'm not about to burn his friendship by going after someone he might have hit it off with in those first two weeks. After that, I remain guarded. I could tear into Joe, pushing hard without caution, aggressively reaching my conclusion. But I know I can't turn around his opinions that fast, due to emotional inertia. That's where consequences would come in. I am being mindful of the terrain. It's not worth losing a friend's respect over prey this small.

I express only my concerns with Joe, never making them complaints. To him, my worry is rooted in my direct observations, not unfounded opinions. I have evidence. My view is also personal. I don't project that worry onto anyone else. I am just a contractor. I have no long-term buy-in from the team, because I am not fully bonded with the full-time employee herd. I am aware of my place and its limitations. I use the terrain to my advantage while being mindful of the physics of relationships.

I am counting on Joe knowing and trusting me, more so than anyone else on the team. That's what gives me the edge. So, while I keep everything on a personal level, he knows that, if I'm concerned, he also has a reason to be concerned. I am able to bridge the gap and communicate that visceral emotion of what the future holds without complaining, projecting, or telling him how to feel.

My approach gets all wrapped up in the killing blow: "I don't think I can work with him. He's got no idea how to do anything."

"I don't think I can work with him" is heavy. Implicit in that statement is Joe's knowledge of my abilities. The unstated conclusion is that, if I can't work with Vinod, no one else on the team can. After that, "He's got no idea how to do anything" sums up Vinod's incompetence. This starts the process with Joe that leads directly to Brad, then HR, and finally no more Vinod.

JOE
    Fired.

CHAPTER NINE
ARE YOU NOT ENTERTAINED?

SIX MONTHS REMAINED UNTIL PROJECT DELIVERY.

It was one of the most beautiful conference rooms Garrick had ever seen: plush chairs made of real leather, a thousand-stone dark wood conference table, and the government's seal built of polished and shaped bits of wood, glass, and metal occupying the far wall. It gleamed in the sunlight. In front of the logo was Stefan, Garrick's new boss, and the seated group of people were the board for The Big Project.

"Obviously, the election is critical. With the rollout of Windows 10 on new laptops just after the election, everyone— the old and the new MPs—need to be trained." Stefan was warming up the room for another overview of The Big Project. As with every big project, there were a lot of people involved. Garrick was the new hire that would mostly work on other parts of the business, but help out on The Big Project. Overall, he was here to draw up the way technology works in parliament. Not public policy-wise, but how individual members of parliament use their laptops, send email, and store files. The stuff any organization does. But this wasn't a workforce chained to their desks: MPs went everywhere, and Garrick and the rest of the team needed to deliver on that work-anywhere promise.

"Again, our lead architect, Hubert." Stefan stepped aside as a heavy-set mid-40s man in a generic blue button-up shirt stood up in front of the nine people in the room.

"Hello. We have full approval to move forward with SharePoint Online in the cloud from leadership. This is where MPs will store everything, including all their files. I'll have a report on the plan in a few weeks. Thank you."

Early on, Hubert's idea was almost a classic story in industry: let's take the parliament to the cloud. Then, we don't have to worry about anything. Then, we don't have to maintain anything. Well, that's how it was pitched anyway.

Deb, along the far side of the table, spoke up. "Hubert, how about the conversion process for our returning MPs? Will it be hard for them to get their files into SharePoint?"

"That is a task suited for support," Hubert responded. Maybe there was something here Garrick didn't know. Support wasn't this department, it was BAU: Business As Usual. Projects for the parliament worked in a straightforward way: leadership identified a need; architecture (Garrick's team) came up with the design of the solution and got it approved by leadership; engineering built it, and it was up for grabs who in the department put it into the hands of the users. That was all the customer solutions department. After that, it fell onto support to keep it running and everyone happy—that is, BAU. What confused Garrick is that solutions and support were two different departments with two very different budgets. The BAU budget wasn't part of The Big Project; that's the regular ongoing stuff that happens every day, like support. Garrick didn't consider The Big Project "every day," nor did the project directors who controlled his department's budget. Hence, his confusion. But hey, he's new.

Deb nodded, accepting what she'd been told, then looked back at her laptop. "Anything else?" Hubert asked. No one responded. He continued, "Overall, we'll create users in SharePoint Online in advance of the rollout of the Microsoft Surface tablets to the MPs and their staffers. So, when everyone gets their new Surface, they'll already have access to SharePoint Online. We can phase in the users in groups and validate that everyone works step by step. Microsoft has already..."

Garrick lost track of Hubert's lecture. In his three months with Parliament Customer Solutions, Garrick had seen Hubert's talk on this five times. This meeting should be important, but it wasn't going to be. Leadership in the room wanted to hear Hubert's plan again, and so everyone in the department had to listen to it again. Garrick had a whole laundry list of his own questions, none of which Hubert had gotten anywhere near answering in these meetings. The election was now six months out; the project had been under way for 18 months already. Garrick's take was that a new system this big needed a lot more of a plan than "step-by-step validation" and "support will handle it" with a generous sprinkling of "that's Microsoft's problem" thrown in.

The bright symbol of the parliament was behind Hubert; Garrick feigned attention but looked right through the man into the detailed artwork.

FIVE MONTHS.

THE GRAY SKY outside the conference room did little to brighten up the government's crest. Garrick had no need to stare at it this time, as he was much better prepared for the project board meeting with Hubert. Garrick had his laptop. By now, most people in the room, save for Stefan, had their laptops too, and Garrick was well aware that none of them were taking notes or working on The Big Project.

Stefan, the head of the department, introduced Hubert again. Hubert started off on his standard speech.

The election was a well-known event, a date that everyone had planned for. Five months from now, everything, including The Big Project, would have to be ready. Go-time. Garrick's experience told him that something really wasn't right. While Hubert went on about his usual generic stuff, nothing actionable was happening. Garrick expected that, five months out, there would be demos, testing, or even trials with select users. All of this was missing. After the election, 100-or-so MPs and their staff all would need new laptops, their files, their tools, and all of it working right out of the box. The part of solutions responsible for the rollout of the laptops was already doing some of the big prep work: they were issuing the new hardware. Every once in a while, Garrick would see an MP staffer with their brand-new Surface about the grounds. He didn't see any progress like this from The Big Project.

Garrick had obligations elsewhere anyway. As an architect, he was responsible for that important step of "design a solution and sell it to leadership." The normal way this was done in solutions was through a paper: a document that explained the problem, the solution, the technology, and the methods used to solve the problem. To Garrick, these were weighty business documents. To leadership, these represented binding contracts:

the things solutions would do and how much they would cost. After all, they dictated what engineering would do, what support would manage, and how the MPs would get their work done day-to-day. To build a good proposal document, Garrick would dive into the engineering resources of places like Microsoft and Oracle for best practices, work out how to apply them at parliament, develop test cases to check to see that the ideas worked, consult outside sources to have someone else give his plan the thumbs up, price not only the work of engineering but the ongoing costs to BAU, and wrap it all up in references to all his research in case someone wanted to go down the same road Garrick did. The detailed work required Garrick to spend hours, sometimes days, on the finished result for the project board.

That was what he was working on now while Hubert droned away. He looked up between reading paragraphs of a Microsoft technical bulletin to take in the room. Sure enough, the project board was seated around the table, and only a few of them were looking at Hubert. Everyone else was banging away at emails, Instant Messenger, or last night's football scores. Crucially, though, the two people that were paying attention were Stefan, head of solutions, and John, head of infrastructure. Stefan looked vaguely satisfied, but John had an ever-so-slight frown that betrayed his opinion of Hubert's plan.

Garrick put his head back down. His work had to get done.

FOUR MONTHS.

JOHN ADDRESSED HUBERT from the middle of the room. "Infrastructure needs to know a few things so we're ready for your SharePoint Online rollout."

Garrick snapped his head up from his laptop. He'd been in the middle of crafting a highly technical email when, all of a sudden, the monthly Big Project meeting had changed in tone. Hubert was standing in front of the seal, as usual, but John had pushed his chair back from the table. For the first time in months, the rest of the room was paying attention. Something new was happening.

"So, we're planning on having the MPs store all their files on SharePoint Online, right?"

Hubert nodded. "Yes. That's reflected in my paper."

"Yes, I've seen the version you produced this month. What I'm wondering is, to start, how much data are we expecting to move to SharePoint Online?"

"All of it."

"Including what's on their desktops?"

"Yes."

"Including their application folders?"

"Yes."

"How much data is that?"

Hubert paused. "I don't know."

"You don't know?"

"No, I haven't been able to run that study yet."

"When can you do that by?"

Hubert looked up at the ceiling. "Maybe by next month's report and meeting."

John frowned. "Okay, but you're sure it can all be moved? Everything will transfer just fine?"

"Certainly!"

John's department, infrastructure, was at the heart of the question. His team controlled the disk space that all the MPs used to store their files, and he was the one Hubert had to coordinate with to get any of it moved. John likely knew exactly how much data was there.

Hubert continued, "All we need to do is upload the data from each MP's storage into SharePoint Online. Once it's there, it'll work within SharePoint for them."

"Okay, but how will it get up there?"

"We'll transfer it."

"How?"

Hubert paused again. "I don't have the details. I'm still researching that."

"Okay, when will we know?"

"A few weeks for me to write the paper."

John frowned again. "You're not leaving me a lot of time."

"Sorry, John, the demands on my time are significant. This is a big project."

"You've been working on it for a year and a half?"

"Yes. It is very demanding."

"All right."

Garrick looked around. Everyone in the room was paying rapt attention to the exchange. No emails, no web, just Hubert looking indignant in the front of the room and John looking perplexed. Stefan looked out of place, still relaxed. Well, finally someone was starting to voice the concerns Garrick had about The Big Project since he started.

Garrick raised his hand and waved at Hubert. "Hey, can I get a copy of the current version of the paper?"

"Sure, Garrick. I'll send you an email."

Back in his cube, Garrick settled down to read up on Hubert's plan for The Big Project.

It was beautiful. Pages upon pages of professional-looking work. There were charts, tables, graphs, even the font selections were made to be print-ready rather than just an internal technology document. The opening told the story from the beginning: it was all Stefan's idea. Hubert had written an introduction that went through the decision process for SharePoint Online. Stefan had made the choice, and forced the project board to agree with him, well before Hubert had been hired. Hubert had made a passable attempt at justifying Stefan's choice in the face of no other information beyond, "Let's go to the cloud!" The biggest technical decision of the project, which system to use, was made by the non-technical leadership well before anyone technical had looked at it. This was not the way it was supposed to be done in solutions.

But, whatever hand-waving Hubert had done with Stefan's decision, evaporated quickly as Garrick got deeper into the document. The pretty charts and graphs hid an important truth: no actual technical design had taken place, even though Hubert was the technical design lead. The whole project was 100% vapor: lots of computer terms that essentially said "someone else will figure it out." Hubert's plans involved Microsoft taking responsibility, support taking responsibility, and in many cases, no one taking responsibility. Garrick expected hard technical details, flow charts, project plans, budgets, and schedules. He found none of that. He expected reasoned arguments backed up by sources. He found lots of references to Microsoft technical documents, but when he read them closely, they didn't make sense when used that way. A major premise, the management of files on a user's laptop by the cloud, was written based upon another version of SharePoint that was six years old and run internally by a company, not run by Microsoft and not in the cloud.

The entire paper, a year-and-a-half's worth of work, was summed up on page 43 with an infographic: a cartoon cloud representing SharePoint Online, a bright blue double-headed arrow, and a picture of a Surface laptop. Garrick estimated it took 30 seconds to make in Visio.

The next day, Garrick found Hubert sitting in a small conference room with his laptop. Garrick observed the man through the door, studying him. Hubert stared out of the big windows of the room into the courtyard beyond. He appeared lost in thought. His laptop was open, screen bright, filled with Microsoft Word with an empty file. A blank page.

"Ahem." Garrick signaled his presence.

Hubert's head spun around to see Garrick standing there. "Oh hello, Garrick."

"Hey, Hubert. So, I was looking over your SharePoint Online design document. Thank you for sending me it."

"Oh, no problem."

"So, are there any other documents? Like a migration plan or a costing worksheet?"

"Oh, not yet, Garrick, I'm still working on those."

"There's no other technical documents?"

"Nope, it's a big project, lots to design and write!"

"But you've tested this as a demo?"

"Uh, no."

"You've logged into SharePoint Online, right?"

"No, Microsoft has assured me it'll work just fine, so I don't need to test that."

"But you're the one implementing it?"

"Yeah. Is there a reason for all these questions, Garrick? I'm really very busy. My reports, you know."

Garrick stared at Hubert for a brief second, eyed his laptop briefly, then smiled. "Okay, thanks, Hubert. Cheers."

"Cheers."

THREE MONTHS.

"WE'RE THREE MONTHS out to the election. It's time to start building!"

Stefan was excited for today's project board meeting. Garrick didn't even notice the government's seal behind him now. It had long faded into the background of the endless number of meetings in this room. Stefan had sent out a steady stream of emails about today's meeting, indicating that he was going to assign areas of responsibility.

"Hubert, you're on for implementation. So, you've got the primary tasks, getting SharePoint Online working, sized and prepped."

"Okay, Stefan."

Deb spoke up. "Hubert, you'll be making sure that the new laptops are all set up and managing all the new user transitions, right?"

Hubert looked at her, wrinkling his forehead. "No, ah, I'm, ah, way too busy for that."

"Isn't that part of implementation?"

"No, no, it's not. That's support's job. Not mine."

Mike, part of the BAU team, jumped in. "Support hasn't budgeted for that."

"Well, how about the transfer of their data?" Deb again.

"Support will have to manually copy it from their old drive to Share-Point."

Mike jumped in again. "No way, Hubert. We don't have the manpower for that big a task."

Arthur from engineering spoke up. "Sounds like you'll have to do it, Hubert."

Hubert spun to face him. "Can't you guys do it? You're issuing the laptops, right Arthur?"

"No, we're responsible for issuing just the Surface and the base software."

Garrick watched the room start to run against Hubert. No heads were in laptops today, everyone was on the edge of speaking.

"But Hubert!" Deb, the project manager, looked very worried.

Stefan raised his hand. "Everyone, please." He paused. "Hubert has it under control. Now Garrick."

Garrick looked intently at Stefan, waiting.

Stefan smiled back. "You're on the handover to BAU as well as backups and document recovery. Do the standard build-out, papers for each of the processes, requirements, and budget."

Garrick nodded. "I'll get to work on it right away."

"Great."

Garrick dropped into his chair back at his cube. He was intensely aware that Hubert had no idea what was going on. What should have been the kickoff of the real work turned into the project team ganging up on him to do some actual work. And that's when Garrick's realization happened.

"This guy has to go, or The Big Project will be an absolute disaster."

Hubert was prey, easy prey. He was already on the edge of the herd. The rest of the team was backing away, clearing space around him. Adrenaline rushed through Garrick's body as he leaned forward in his chair. In his mind, he imagined a field, an expanse of grass, and Hubert just outside of the group, enough to take him. All that had to be done was to sever those remaining ties and Garrick would get his kill.

It was time to plan the chase.

First, the meager amount of work Hubert had done couldn't stand up to scrutiny. It was whitewashed, purposefully vague, and, in many cases, factually incorrect. Garrick had to assume that no one else could understand the details enough to understand just how lacking Hubert's plan was. If they had, he'd been fired long ago. But no one on the team besides Garrick was technically adept enough to see through it. He would begin the chase with performance: if he could throw Hubert's work into sharp relief against real work, it could begin to turn the organization against him. The relationships were key. The rest of the project team was under Stefan's thumb, but this meeting showed that they were becoming aware of Hubert's shirking of responsibility, so Garrick had an advantage.

SharePoint Online was a terrible choice for this project as Garrick saw it. It had looked bad from the beginning, but he was only bolstered in that belief when he found an internal paper that had laid out the huge problems of trying to make the parliament use the software. Stefan had panned the paper and told the project board to ignore it. The paper was mostly right, however. The Big Project should have been done differently. Garrick could attempt to create a rift between solutions and Hubert by going after that one big design choice; it was sure to have long-standing technical problems—but this approach would fail. SharePoint Online was Stefan's decision, not Hubert's. Stefan supported Hubert because he thought Hubert could deliver on his SharePoint dream.

Which meant that Hubert's implementation would have to be the lever. Garrick would need to stick to the SharePoint solution, believe in it and work to make it happen regardless of its limitations, but in the process sever the relationship between Hubert and the team based on how well Hubert delivered SharePoint. If Garrick could show the team, and especially Stefan, that Hubert's plan put Stefan's dream at risk, it would cut those ties and the herd would turn on Hubert.

Second, solutions only knew one architect: Hubert. This is why he'd lasted so long on the team; they had no benchmark to compare him against. Garrick had to show them that there was a better standard of performance. Once they saw Hubert's and Garrick's work side-by-side, they would get the picture that they should expect better. By raising the bar beyond what Hubert could deliver, it would eliminate the possibility that Hubert could be redeemed. That left only one option: the kill.

Garrick sat back in his chair. The chase had to show how Hubert's plan didn't work now, and then raise the bar so he couldn't get a second chance.

Garrick started by approaching the file-recovery issue. People would delete files, computers would corrupt data, stuff would get broken—that's life with computers. So, recovery steps in when that happens and gets your files back. Hubert had cribbed the infrastructure design, where and how files were stored, from a source that didn't apply to SharePoint Online. So, Garrick had to ignore that entire part of Hubert's design. It didn't even make sense. What Garrick wrote would actually work, and the resulting paper had every technical footnote carefully attached to demonstrate that it was right. The paper was detailed, down to every last nut and bolt. The process the user would take, the process support would take, the way files would go in and out of backups every day, everything was in there. He included long-term planning, budgeting, and maintenance requirements. Everything the project board needed to make a decision and everything engineering would need to make it happen. However, the plan wouldn't work with Hubert's design. At all. Because Hubert's design was bollocks.

That afternoon, Garrick gathered Stefan, Deb (the project manager), and Clyde (the head of project management) in a small conference room for an impromptu review meeting. They sat around the table, laptops open.

"Garrick, I made this request this morning. And you have it done already?" Stefan looked confused.

"Yeah. I went back to my cube and worked it out."

Deb cocked her head. "In four hours?"

"Yup. I do have some questions, though. Can you open both my paper and Hubert's side by side?"

They did so.

"So, this is where I'm confused. I wrote a recovery-process paper based on the SharePoint Online system, all using Microsoft's best practices, laid out here"—he pointed at his screen—"and here"—again pointing—"but none of this will work with Hubert's design. We're using the cloud solution. We don't do in-house sizing of storage, it's all up to Microsoft, and we don't see it. So, none of Hubert's design will work with what Microsoft says about SharePoint Online."

Garrick let that sink in for a few seconds. "See, I don't understand how this is incongruent. We should have designs that work together. They're both supposed to be based on Microsoft's recommendations."

Brows furrowed, the three managers stared at the screen.

Stefan was the first to respond. "You're right, Garrick, this doesn't look like they're in alignment. I guess I'll have to ask Hubert about it." Stefan was back smiling again, but the others continued to stare at their screens, looking confused.

"Great, Stefan, thanks. Let me know what you find out."

"Nice work, Garrick."

A week later, Garrick looked up from his screen and took off his headphones. Something had moved behind him and he turned to look over his shoulder. Deb, the project manager, was standing at the entrance to his cube.

"Hey, Garrick, I have a question for you."

"Sure, Deb." He set down his headphones and turned around his chair.

"Garrick you did a tremendous job on that file-recovery paper. Do you have time, well, can you help me out and produce a paper on how we can get SharePoint into the pipeline of issuing the Surface laptops? I'm, uh, having trouble with Hubert's schedule. Maybe you can look at it?"

Garrick smiled. "Of course. That shouldn't be hard to fit in."

"Can you have it done in the next two weeks?" Deb asked, looking sheepish as if it was a big imposition.

Garrick grinned. "How about tomorrow?"

Her demeanor changed drastically. "Really? Yes!"

"No problem, Deb."

"Thanks, Garrick!"

"Cheers."

It wasn't hard to re-prioritize his work list. Garrick dove into the paper immediately. The next morning, he delivered the paper to Deb and the project board, with a complete design for deploying the software to all the new laptops. Again, it was technically sound, detail-rich, fully referenced, and had a study of a test bench version Garrick did in his cube. He had even walked over to the offices of engineering and support to get their sign-off on their part of the plan. Everyone the paper touched was consulted and they were all on board. Deb was ecstatic. John and Mike gave their thumbs-up in person. Stefan looked impressed.

TWO MONTHS.

"OKAY, TEAM, WHAT'S next?" Stefan stood at the front of the conference room again, waving a hand and smiling, trying his best to play the part of an orchestra conductor.

Deb took the cue. "We need the design finalized and the demo site built." All eyes went to Hubert.

He slid a stack of pages across the table. "This is the final design."

Stefan dropped his arms. John scowled. Deb look worried. Mike raised an eyebrow. Garrick leaned back in his chair and watched intently.

Arthur was first to speak. "This isn't complete. We can't do anything with this. There's absolutely no discussion on how the files are moved to SharePoint from our systems. There is no way we're going to be able to do hundreds of these things by hand." Garrick knew exactly what Arthur was mad about.

A couple weeks ago, Garrick had showed Arthur a simple study he'd done: it took six man-hours to move the files of one MP by hand, deal with the exceptions, and get the laptop set up. He had timed himself doing it across two days and two sample laptops, his phone counting the lapse of hours. If that was multiplied across every MP, the total worked out to 180 eight-hour work days to do the transfers. Arthur was not happy. From his perspective, Garrick was trying to solve the problem of the files. To Garrick, this was the tip of the spear, the most graphic demonstration of Hubert's incompetence he could make.

Nothing had changed on the topic since Garrick joined solutions. The files were the obvious problem on day one, and Hubert had never produced a good answer, even though it had been asked of him many times. No one had any idea how big the problem was, especially Hubert, the chap who should actually know. Everyone assumed the problem was "big." But, now, Garrick had done the research to show how big: a problem large enough to drive a lorry through and run over the lives of several employees.

Hubert was indignant, having had this claim levied against him a number of times in the last four weeks. "Look, that's just what needs to be done. Support is going to have to sit down with each MP and copy their files over." Garrick grinned, imagining the phrase "six months" in the back of people's heads.

"Hubert, support cannot budget that kind of time!" Mike was not putting up with it, either. Arthur and Mike worked closely on a number of projects, partly because they were office mates. They shared meetings and lunches, always making sure they had adjacent projects; they worked well together. Garrick counted on his prediction that Arthur had talked to Mike and showed him the time estimates. Again, "six months" had to be echoing in his head.

Clyde steered the discussion back on course. "We've been waiting for a full design document for months. We need the details to move forward!" He now had a small stack of Garrick's papers on other projects on his desk—nothing out of the ordinary, just Garrick pleasantly and competently doing his job. By now, he knew what a solutions paper was supposed to look like. He also knew what wasn't a solutions paper.

"This is it!" Hubert pushed the stack of pages again, insistent on his work.

Clyde shook his head. "This is not it, Hubert. What have you been doing?"

"I've been very busy! The workload I have goes beyond what you assign in this meeting! I have responsibilities!" Hubert's indignation was rising, punctuating "responsibilities" like a curse word.

Deb took back the reins calmly. "Okay, okay, that's fine, but we still need the demo system built."

Hubert glared at her. "It will take two months—"

Garrick quietly spoke up, interrupting. "I'll do it."

Every head turned toward Garrick.

"What? Are you sure?"

"Yeah, no problem. Give me a couple days?"

Everyone's eyes remained on Garrick, and tension began slipping from their faces. In the last month, they had seen his work, the proof that what he was saying now could be relied upon. He could deliver.

"Sure, Garrick, take a week if you need it."

Two days later, Garrick delivered a complete design document, demo site, PowerPoint presentations for leadership, feature lists, capability examples, and a menu of choices for the project board to weigh in on. It all fit together. It had all the technical detail every department would need. All the supporting documents. Complete budgets. It all worked. And it was done in two days. He stood in front of the board, without Hubert present, and gave them a genuine working system. It did not use any of Hubert's design.

The final page had a link on it. Garrick grinned as they typed it into their laptops. "Here, go play with it." They did.

After a few minutes, Stefan looked up from the demo, realizing his dream had been saved. "Garrick, are you okay to take on these responsibilities? All that you've laid out here? We're only weeks away from the election!"

Garrick was reeling in the adrenaline of what that question meant. His pulse raced while forcing his face to remain neutral. "Yeah, Stefan, I can do it." Hubert was done. Garrick had made the kill.

Hubert was given the option to resign that afternoon, two months before The Big Project went live. If ever there was a time when solutions needed someone, this was it. But they didn't need Hubert. He handed in his resignation. Everyone on the team was pleasant with him when they went out for drinks on his last Friday, but there was no exchange of emails, no heartfelt hugs, no "Let's meet at the pub again sometime, mate!"

Two months later, the election went fine, and The Big Project was a success. Garrick wrote a small piece of software in an afternoon to transfer everyone's files without anyone having to do it by hand. He started it on a Friday night, went home, and waited for it to finish. It got done Sunday afternoon.

The team would spend nearly a year cleaning up Hubert's other messes on almost every project he had been on. They stayed true to their unspoken promise: no one rang Hubert up and met him at the pub.

A year and a half later, Garrick left to chase a bigger paycheck. He's still friends with several of his old coworkers, though none of them know what actually happened.

THE PREY

THIS STORY IS told through the eyes of the predator, Garrick, because that's who told the story to me. It's obvious that Hubert was a problem right from the beginning, simply because the predator had the intuition to sense that important pieces of Hubert's plan were missing. Chalk it up to experience in his field. He had the skillset and the awareness to question, if only to himself at first, what exactly Hubert was up to. But that's Garrick's perspective. Not everyone shares that. Consider the herd's perspective.

Hubert is common in herds: placed in a position of specific, usually technical, knowledge that the organization depends on. It's an enticing spot for prey and they may be found here often, diligently covering up for something: lack of knowledge, bad attitude, or simply the age-old quest for power. The herd has an understandably hard time with these arrangements. In this case, the prey doesn't know what they don't know, and so they go along with Hubert, trusting that everything will turn out right.

He is hired to do the very technical feat that everyone is relying on, that has an enormous impact and an unmovable deadline. And he can't deliver. But the herd doesn't know that yet.

He gets as far as he does because upper management, Stefan, had a specific agenda, SharePoint, and Hubert went with it. Management, having been incentivized by Hubert's "of course it will work" attitude, kept propping him up in front of the rest of the team, which had the effect of making Hubert unquestionable.

His plan wouldn't have worked, of course. Again, you're seeing the situation unfold through the predator's eyes, so seeing the impending face plant is easy. But, if you were one of Hubert's coworkers that was told time and time again that Hubert had it all in hand, you'd not have seen the trouble until it was far too late. Probably just days before the election and launch. That would have ended badly for a lot of people, not just Hubert.

You could say that Garrick was doing the herd a favor by hunting Hubert, but that's a troublesome assumption. Predators aren't part of the organization, they're not herd. That distinction is crucial. If you ascribe planned and specific duties to the predator in service of the herd, the relationship breaks down and opens it up to abuse. Predators are outsiders, through and through, and what they do when confronted with prey is hunt. The herd cannot co-opt that. In this case, Hubert's work wasn't Garrick's. It wasn't his deal. Garrick had no business stepping into Hubert's space. But there was prey, right there in front of him. He did what he was supposed to. Garrick is an organizational predator.

THE HUNT

I CONSIDER GARRICK's hunt of Hubert a classic "performance kill." The basics surround the performance of one's job, or in the prey's case, lack of performance. I consider this the easiest of kills. The essential part of the hunt is the demonstration that the prey cannot do their job. Once that happens, then the obvious question must be asked by the herd: "Why are they still employed?"

Performance kills are straight-on chases that can be very slow to very quick. The demonstration of inadequacy depends on the situation, specifically how often the predator can cause the prey's work to be illuminated in a seemingly organic fashion. By "seemingly organic," I mean that, while the light upon the prey's work is planned and executed by the predator, it should be seen as a natural consequence of work, not something artificial or "outside your lane." This is where subtlety on the part of the predator is critical. At no point should the herd think the predator is out to get the prey. If that happens, the hunt is over; the prey will hide in the herd against the predator, exploiting the natural defenses of the herd to keep themselves safe from an "angry coworker out to get so-and-so fired."

This often means waiting. The prey will do bad things, as they always do. For the one thing that the predator sees the prey doing wrong, there's likely to be a hundred more that are not seen. So, the predator waits for those moments in which the prey's mistakes intersect with their work in a way the predator knows is wrong. Not so that the prey can be called out, that's on the road to being labeled out to get them. Instead, those moments should generate innocuous questions or poor conclusions based on the prey's work. There is no call-out. There are honest, specific, and damaging questions to be asked that cast indirect light on what the prey has done.

For example:

"Bill's figures show a profit year over year, but my cost analysis shows us losing money. What did I do wrong?"

"Bill, I used your process, but I think I might have caused a compliance issue. Can you tell me how I was supposed to do it the right way?"

"I'm not certain I understand your directives here, Bill. Can you help me with the details I don't get?"

The prey's work speaks for itself. They will likely dodge the question or hand-wave the answer, even in the face of a predator earnestly looking for the exact details that are wrong. The goal is to get the people around the prey to quietly question the work. It is not likely that just one of these questions will do the job. Instead, the judicious application of them over time erodes everyone's faith in the prey to produce. This is why some of these hunts can be very long. You have to wait.

Sometimes, you get a break in the form of a big project or looming deadline. As the stakes get higher, the more damaging these questions become. In Hubert's case, he was the critical path on The Big Project. Failure in this situation would be very bad for everyone, so more eyes seeking the important details means far more damage to the prey's relationship when those details inevitably come up short.

Another common strategy with performance kills is simple demonstration of superior performance. This requires that the predator display competence in the same or similar areas as the prey. This works great for same-team peer kills. The predator shouldn't attempt to do the prey's work for them, but instead show work done well in contrast to the prey's work, and let the herd figure out the rest.

A word of caution for the superior performance strategy. A hunt is a chase, fast or slow, and it requires more than the usual energy the predator can command on a daily basis. If the predator shows too much performance or does too much, the herd will expect that output at all times. It is to be used sparingly, when it really counts.

THE KILL

Rifting the prey from the herd requires building enough emotional distance that it overcomes the prey's existing bond. I think of it as energy; enough negative energy is created between the herd and prey that it eclipses the strength of even the stickiest bond of familiarity. While there are a number of ways to approach the problem, I find it important to use the herd's landscape to my advantage. If Hubert existed in a stereotypically sedate government back-office world, the herd's emotions won't have many highs or lows to leverage. But The Big Project wasn't a typical government mire. It had a hard date, uncompromising deliverables, and an entire nation's worth of visibility. This is a high-energy state that Garrick would turn to his advantage.

Imagine this situation as a cliff that Garrick is chasing his prey ever closer to. The cliff can't be moved, it can't be changed, made smaller, or negotiated somehow. Either Hubert goes off it in full display of the rest of the herd, or he stands up to the fight. The greater the consequences of failure, the higher the cliff.

These conditions don't happen in every hunt. I find it's a judgment call; I have to understand the nature of the herd and how much tension can be stirred up. It might not be enough on an average day, so I keep my eyes open for that spike in elevated risk. Hubert was set up for this conflict before Garrick even arrived. Everyone understood the significance of The Big Project, even if they didn't understand how Hubert couldn't deliver. Garrick got lucky: the landscape was well to his advantage.

In these heightened states, the point of the kill is exactly when the herd understands just how much trouble they're in due to the prey, particularly if the herd feels emotions like fear or betrayal in response. That moment has to be cultivated by the predator, quietly arranged over time so those emotions land all at once with maximum impact. I have witnessed the moment of the break as the herd shifts away from the prey, bonds evaporating into nothing, leaving the prey confused and standing alone. It is unmistakable.

If that moment lands correctly, it is the killing blow. Enough energy will be present to break those bonds, to rift the prey from the herd permanently. It's over. All that is left is for the prey to bleed out while waiting for their exit interview.

CHAPTER TEN
BREAKING STUFF

It was an auspicious day for me in The Org, a random Tuesday in the fall. I sat in the middle of the room, unremarkable in the sea of uniforms, as my commander told us he was moving on and that Shannon would be his replacement. Shannon and I were on excellent terms. We'd worked together on a number of missions: relocating aircraft around the state, flying search, and a long day at high altitude relaying communications traffic. We worked well together. So, his choice of Shannon was great news. What made today auspicious was that when the commander changed, so did all the staff positions.

Shannon stood up and walked to the front of the room. None of what was going on was unplanned. My bet was that all this had been figured out well in advance, and now was the time to fill in everyone else. She looked at her sheet of notes, then spoke: "Thank you, everyone. Adam has left us in a very good spot with a lot of great people, so it was hard putting together the staff list. Some of you will stay where you are now, and some of you will take different positions. So, safety is still Joy. Finance, Mark. Logistics, Brent. Transportation, Randy."

I knew these people already. Joy was crazy, but in a good way. She liked telling morbid stories of people dying to get her point across about being safe. A walking version of "Last Clear Chance." I thought she was hilarious and her black sense of humor mirrored my own. Brent was good people, with a grandfatherly, kind manner even though he's nowhere near being a grandfather. He did a great job taking care of the new guys. Randy looked after the trucks, and that was as far as I knew. We all drove them, but Randy did the oil changes and maintenance. I think. Mark, well, I didn't know him much. Finance was not my deal.

Shannon continued, "Chris is still communications and IT officer." Chris was a mountain of a man, and as ornery as you'd expect. He had a habit of glowering at people when he wasn't hiding in the radio room. I'd never actually seen the radio room myself. It was locked tight all the time, even when Chris was in it. All I knew was the giant antennas on the roof of the hanger.

Shannon wasn't done. "Sarah, you're personnel development." Sarah grinned. She was new, newer than I was. What I have seen of her was happy and energetic. Shannon looked at me. "Lion, you're services." Services, yes! Where the action is! Wait, I mean, yes, that makes sense, I've been working in that space for a while now. Wise choice, Shannon.

Services is an interesting gig; it's their responsibility to keep everyone trained for missions, and when missions come around, they organize everyone to deploy. Once in the field, services is expected to lead teams while still managing everyone from the unit. It was a great gig for me and I was excited.

Over the next few months, I got up to speed on my new role. No one expected much right away. I was new and there was a lot to learn. We practiced all the time, trying to improve our skills in preparation for the days we were called out on emergencies, which was often. Even the actual missions were training opportunities. I would bring new people along, even if they were underqualified, so they could see the real thing in action. I always found room for improvement.

But there were limits. Missions needed gear, and gear meant radios. Radios were not within my purview. That was controlled by Chris, hidden in the comm room. Which is why, one day, I was standing before the locked door of communications clutching a handful of paper, having just knocked on that door.

The door was split in halves, with a built-in shelf in the middle. The top half cracked open just enough to see a face. It was Chris. "What do you want?"

I was not exactly thrilled to be doing this. As far as I could tell, no one hit it off with Chris. "Hey, I'd like to requisition five of the long-range radios." These were big, handheld devices, and you could talk for miles on them. Normally, we used little plastic radios that looked a lot like a kid's radio. Ours were only a small step up from them and were a demure gray instead of blaze yellow. They also ate AA batteries like crazy and only worked if you were nearly in the same room with the other party. But they were cheap to replace. The big radios were $1,500 a pop, encrypted, and had a million channels for talking to both teams on the ground and our aircraft above.

Chris didn't look pleased. To be more accurate, he looked more displeased than usual. "Why do you need them?"

I waved my handful of paperwork at him. "I have the proper form 48's to check them out. I'm going to use them in training."

He didn't open the door farther to accept my papers. "Those are for commanders when multiple teams are out in the field. You only have one team."

"I need to train with the equipment. We need to know how to operate the radios."

"You can't until you can show a need. They are expensive and we can't risk you taking them out." The door shut and I heard the click of the lock.

I stood there, taken back. I hadn't interacted with Chris much. I guess I shouldn't have been surprised at his demeanor, given how often he scowled at us. What I didn't know at the time was that Chris was a leftover from a long-ago era. His brother was a high-and-mighty muckety-muck several layers of command up from our little unit. They had joined years ago as part of an older guard that was already on its way out as commanders and staff changed. Chris had served under those guys in the beginning but, for the last few years, he didn't connect with the current staff. So, as new people worked their way through the system, Chris remained entrenched in that back room. I don't think he knew any of the new people, and he clearly didn't trust them.

So, months carried on and I got by with my little plastic radios—they were better than nothing. Every time I saw Chris, he had that same angry demeanor. I did find out that he ran a radio talk group of communications officers from around the area, which explained the radio noises late on Tuesday nights. I guess those were a requirement, so he was doing something. But, like everything that was Chris's world, it was not my problem.

Until it became my problem. As part of services, we had to sign off people on their training so they qualified to do the job. Only then could they go into the field for a serious emergency. We started having problems with the number of people properly qualified to operate the radios. It's easy to hold a radio and talk into it, but we're an organization backed by regulations. They stated that you needed to complete the proper training. Suddenly, we had a severe shortage of qualified people.

I had completed my radio training with a visiting communications officer rather than Chris. His name was Jay, and he was a nice guy. He just wasn't around much. I had asked Chris for the training, and the answer was always "later." Technically, the training was supposed to be delivered as part of a serious training class. Jay had conducted an impromptu one-on-one class with me because he had the time. But the rest of the people needed training too. We needed the full class.

Chris would not entertain doing that. Promises were half-heartedly made only to shoo people away from his door. Nothing was ever done; no plans, no dates, and, of course, no training.

I had no idea why he was so steadfastly refusing to do his job. But it was hurting my mission effectiveness, so I began doing it myself. The task worksheets for the training were available to everyone, so it was easy to see what training requirement was needed. But the supporting materials, like a PowerPoint deck and training exercises, were locked up with Chris in his room. So, I built my own. I had some limitations—two to be specific. I still wasn't allowed access to the real radios. I needed them to do the training. The second limitation was more serious: I didn't have the qualifications to do the training. Not that that ever stopped me from working the system.

After a few hours of my class, people were talking into the plastic radios like real professionals. That's what we had. Sure, the training was a little odd with a PowerPoint that had only pictures of the real radios, but people learned what was needed. Jay came to one class and he signed his name on the papers. Everyone was qualified and we kept up with the work.

After that, everything was good. Chris stayed in his room, and I ran around out in the field with the little radios.

I was totally unprepared for the summons to my commander's office.

"Lion," Shannon addressed me from across the desk, "our unit has been assigned a training. You're in charge of it."

I looked at her in shock. "Oh."

A training was much bigger than the exercises I did with our unit. Crews from a few hundred miles away would arrive at our airfield and participate in a huge weekend event designed to simulate our biggest missions. Those muckety-mucks from way up the chain of command? Here. Aircraft, trucks, and equipment from all over the place? Here. A few hundred people? Here. It would involve every department of our unit, and I would be at the center of the effort.

A big part of getting ready for the training was the staffing. People needed to be in place to do their jobs. Joy, in charge of safety, would have to make sure everyone was safe. Gear had to be provided, food had to be at the ready, and space for crews to sleep on the floor in the hangar had to be set aside.

And, with every big operation, we had to have communications.

"No." Chris started to close the upper half of the door.

"Wait, look, we need someone to run the radios. You're the guy!" Come on, Chris, do something.

"I'm not available. I won't be there. No. Have someone else do it." The door closed.

By now, I was no longer surprised. Chris was a known quantity, at least in terms of his willingness to participate with the rest of us. Everyone else was on board, even excited to host a training. There was a lot of energy, a lot of excitement going into the big event. Luckily, I would have help with communications from my pal, Jay. He'd be able to come in and work the back room in place of Chris. Excellent.

I went to see Shannon. "So, I think we should go in and figure out what we have, make sure it works, and that we're prepared for the training. Chris hasn't let anyone into comms since I've been here, so I have no idea what Jay is getting into."

Her office door was closed. I went over the plan to have Jay do the communications work, but I needed her buy-in to open the back room.

"Yeah, that's reasonable. Let's go look." Shannon had a key buried in a lockbox. Armed with that, we walked to the back room. It was late, and Chris had long left. So, Shannon and I broke the seal on Chris's vault.

"What the hell am I looking at?" I stood there, in the doorway, mouth agape.

"Uhm, comms and IT." Shannon stood slightly behind me.

"Seriously?" I hadn't moved.

She paused. "Yeah."

It had been six months since I had been appointed services officer of my unit. That is a fancy title for "Guy in Charge of Running Around Out in the Woods Looking for Things." But what was I supposed to do with the dumpster in front of me? The services officer should, in fact, be planning a huge event for out in the woods right now.

The room contained a decaying ruin of beige plastic. The smallish office had a single window overlooking another row of hangars with the runway off in the distance. I say 'small' only because I couldn't tell its dimensions given all the open cabinets and the mounds of unidentifiable sun-yellowed computer equipment. Joy would not be happy; this was a giant safety hazard. I'm certain she'd say in a black-humor way how this would kill us all. Looking closer, I could see some of it was turned on, betrayed by their small green lights. Some of the piles hummed, while others emitted the white noise of fans blowing. Not a single piece of equipment looked like it had been useful in the last decade.

My commander stepped closer, forcing me into the room without actually touching me. "So, yeah, get in there."

I looked around, bewildered. "Where does Chris sit?"

Along one side of the room was a wall-length workbench. I could see gray Formica in tiny swatches underneath papers, keyboards, cables, and empty cans of Mountain Dew. Nestled up against the workbench edge was a chair, a 1970s swivel job in blue, frayed and tattered. In among the sea of junk were hints of the radios. Big desk ones bolted under shelving. The serious radios I had wanted for months were scattered about, almost buried in the drifts of stuff. I noticed some blinking lights on boxes stapled to the wall: the internet router and network cables. Where those cables went, I had no idea. That explained why the internet was so crappy in this building.

I realized what we were dealing with: a nerd project.

That has been around in technology from the beginning. When an IT person gets free rein and no supervision, they tend to fail in one of two ways: avoid doing any real work or turn the company's IT into their own personal play lab. Neither of these outcomes is good, but the nerd project tends to be worse. So, the IT guy will play with company technology, constantly upgrading, constantly changing, always chasing some glimmer of what's brand-new and shiny. None of it is well planned. The changes are done in a "Oh, I should do this today!" way, and what tends to happen is that the system gains so much complexity that only one person can figure it out: the guy who built the nerd project.

They are fine at home when only you, and maybe your family, has to put up with the internet failing all the time. IT people need to learn new technologies, which is why having a lab to experiment with new stuff is a great idea. That lab work should not include the same stuff everyone relies on. That's just asking for trouble.

We were looking at what seemed like an excavation of a long-dead society. The nerd project itself had not been worked on in years. At some point, Chris had probably gotten bored with the possibilities of the equipment he had on hand. That equipment was years old, nothing modern or fresh. I could tell from the styling of the computers and equipment, but even the sun-yellowed office beige was evidence enough.

The center of it all was that chair, like the center of a black hole that eventually would swallow the contents of the room. While the room seemed big enough for several people, realistically you could fit two. One in the chair and one standing over their shoulder. Not good.

This was my decision point. All of this—the nerd project, the scattered detritus of someone who stopped caring long ago, and Chris himself—had to go. The reason for months of getting in the way, of not doing his job, of being a pain in the ass, became clear as I imagined him sitting in this chair, doing absolutely nothing.

I wasn't angry, I was thrilled. He'd placed himself in exactly the right spot to be hunted. The tools he was in charge of, namely the radios and the internet, were broken beyond usability. I had limped along with what I had on hand, the little plastic radios, but now I knew why he couldn't hand out the real radios. Who knew if they even worked? And if they didn't work in the field, questions would be asked. All this broken stuff, these tools, implied who Chris was as a person: also broken, at least in regards to The Org. By sealing himself back here and letting no one else check in on him, he bore the full responsibility for what he had done.

The nerd project would be his end.

I turned around. "Shannon, I don't know that we can do anything with this."

"Yeah, I think you're right."

"Let's just let Jay figure it out."

"Okay."

"I am going to call all the higher-ups in for a test run a few days in advance. Is that okay?"

"Yeah, that works."

We relocked the door behind us.

The rest of the training preparation went well. Everyone I needed was ready. The arrangements were made for food and supplies. I found a raft of cots that would work for crews sleeping on site. Jay agreed to work the radios, even after I described what awaited him behind that door.

The schedule was easy. The training would start on Friday with a lot of the staff and crews coming in. Saturday was the big day: simulated missions, planes in the air, trucks crisscrossing the ground under them. Sunday was a relaxed version of Saturday, low-key work for those who wanted a little more time behind the yoke or wheel. But, for my plan, I needed to get started early.

I had connected with the higher-ups who would work out of our facility. I was working all in the name of good coordination: "Do you need anything?" "Does this sound okay to you?" "How can I help?" were the common questions I had. Buried in several conversations was a suggested change to the schedule. I asked them if they would please come out to the site on Thursday night to get set up. I pleaded first-timer inexperience in that I wanted everything to be ready for the kickoff on Friday. By showing up a day early, I could make sure they got everything they wanted.

So, I greeted them that Thursday evening and helped drag boxes of gear into the building. I showed them around the place. Most important, I gave them the wifi password.

I left as the laptops were getting cracked open.

Around 8:00 p.m. I got the first call.

"Lion, this is Paul. The wifi is down. How do we fix it?"

Of course, the wifi was working when I left, but the moment you stress a nerd project with an actual workload, it crumbles.

"Uhm, Paul, I really don't know."

"Can we just reset the router?"

"It's back in the comm room. That's all locked up. I don't have the key. Sorry."

"Okay, we'll see if we can fix it. Thanks."

"Sure, Paul, let me know if it doesn't come back."

In another hour, Paul was on the phone again. "Yeah, it's not working at all. We can connect, but I don't think there's internet." At this point, a group of officers well above my paygrade were struggling to make the internet work. I could only imagine their frustration in driving all that way. We did all of our mission management on the web. Every crew got their orders from a set of web forms. The system worked fine. When, of course, the internet worked.

"Listen, Paul, I can't get into that room. And even if I could, I have no idea how to fix it." This was absolutely the truth. Chris's nerd project was beyond the ken of mere mortals. "I think you'll need to call Chris." I gave him Chris's cell number.

"Okay, thanks, Lion."

A half hour later, my phone rang again. This time it was Chris.

"You have to go in and reset the transparent proxy." Chris sounded pissed.

"What?"

"The computer on the floor near the battery charger."

"Chris, I have no idea what you're talking about." This was not exactly the truth. I knew in general what he was talking about. I also knew how ridiculous it was that Chris was doing it this way, but I did not know how to work on his pile of computer crap. But now I saw the way Chris's nerd project would fatally go south.

"It's an hour and a half for me to drive in. You go fix it."

"I have no idea what you've got going on in there. I can't help you, but I can tell you that the entire training management team is there right now and they can't get online. So, go fix it."

A grumbled "goodbye" was the only indication that he was about to hang up.

I heard he got home at 3:00 a.m.

Friday was the beginning of the actual training. Management showed up and went back to work on their laptops. Crews started arriving. Food was served and plans were made. I remained absent. While everyone was getting ready to hit the practice missions bright and early, I had to set those missions up tonight. That meant driving to remote places, hiking deep into the woods, and leaving things for others to find. It was a lot of fun.

I was knee-deep in a swamp when my phone rang.

"Lion, it's Paul."

I fumbled with my phone, trying to keep from dropping it into the mire. "Yeah, Paul, what's up?"

"The internet's broken again."

"Oh, seriously?" Oh yeah, seriously. I was counting on it.

"We're trying to get the missions entered, and we can't get on at all."

"Have you tried calling Chris?"

He paused. "Can you call him?"

"Yeah, Paul, I can do that."

The sun was going down, and I was an inch from the top of my waders in a swamp as I called Chris. He picked up right away. "Chris, it's Lion. The network is down again."

He sighed. That was it. Time to drive it home. "Everyone's trying to get ready for Saturday, nothing's working, and they're bitching me out. Whatever you've got going on there, you need to undo it so it works. This can't happen again."

"Fine." He didn't even mumble a goodbye this time before hanging up.

I hiked out of the swamp and drove home. It was a good day.

Saturday went incredibly sideways, and none of it had anything to do with the internet or Chris's nerd project. The training was already off the rails when I arrived at 5:00 a.m. The higher-ups were busy trying to tackle a real mission that occurred just before we started our simulated missions. By that afternoon, everyone had left for the north to be closer to the real job of finding people in trouble out in the woods. Chris and his nerd project were almost forgotten. Almost.

A couple of weeks later, after we'd recovered from the real mission, Shannon called her full staff to her office. Including Chris. The chair left for him was in the corner. He sat down, looking none too happy, but without any fight in him. He must have known why he was summoned.

Shannon started, "Chris, what you have in the back room is a problem. No one knows where anything is or how anything works. This can't continue. The work of the training team was interrupted multiple times, and there was no way to fix the problems without you driving in." She looked at me. "Lion?"

I leaned forward and stared at Chris, unblinking. "Chris, your pile of stuff back there can't be serviced by anyone but you, you took hours to come in and fix it, and it didn't stay fixed. We had a real mission show up, and your stuff could have shut that down too. You need to pull all that stuff out of there now. All the radio equipment needs to be restored to working order. The only thing sitting between people's laptops and the internet will be the router. Nothing else."

He wouldn't meet my eyes; he kept his gaze down as I delivered my ultimatum.

Shannon stepped in. "And Chris, I want all the passwords to all those computers on my desk."

Maybe he nodded slightly, maybe he mumbled something as he left. I don't remember.

A week later, Chris delivered a three-ring binder to Commander Shannon. He leafed through it while telling us that it had every software code, license, and password in it. Shannon thanked him and set the binder aside.

Then he quit. It made sense in a way; that room was his home. I think he assumed he owned it, and no one would dare step past that locked door. That was all he had left; the people he worked alongside, the ones he actually served, had long since moved on, scattered into The Org in positions of higher authority. Somehow, he never kept up. Now he didn't know anyone, much less get along with anyone, so all he had was his pile of crap and the swivel chair. Take that away and there was nothing left.

We never did open the three-ring binder he provided. We needed three trash dumpsters to empty the junk out of the room. Nobody bothered trying to find anything of value in the pile. His nerd project was replaced by a simple wifi router on a shelf that was labeled "Linksys." Half of the radios were broken. Those were shipped back for repair or disposal. Some of the equipment was missing from inventory and required a long paperwork-intensive process to officially declare them off the books. That was likely more negligence than malfeasance. For the next six years, the room was never locked and the door remained open. Chris never returned.

His replacement did a great job, and our little part of The Org turned out fine.

THE PREY

I DIDN'T TAKE notice of Chris right away. I'm a predator, sure, but that doesn't mean that every person that might be bad is worth the time and effort. There are lots of bad people and it's not my job to go after all of them. The decision to undertake every hunt is personal.

Chris was a bad actor from the beginning. At first, I didn't care. Even when he made it difficult to do my job, I danced around him by working with an outside guy, effectively making him pointless, to get what I needed. This was what I chose to do at the time. The predator's job is best served by following the gut.

For me, the prey needs to rise to the point of drawing my attention. The nerd project did it to me this time. That's a bad pattern, one that I know well, and I understand its implications: Chris no longer respected The Org. Finally, my gut kicked in. No one could argue this giant pile of junk in his locked room was helping The Org out. Chris no longer was connected to The Org, and so one side of the hunt was done. Now to rift The Org from him.

THE HUNT

THE GREAT THING about the close relationship between people, process, and tools is that, by directly stressing one, you indirectly stress another. Prey tends to bend process and tools around them or away from them, which means they're in some way responsible and you can use that your advantage. Chris bent the process of handling the radios and internet around him, making himself the sole person responsible for them. This is a very common pattern for prey: they justify their bad attitude by thinking they provide an indispensable service. They're wrong.

What I'm looking for is the weak spot of the triangle. Of the three (people, process, tools), which one breaks most easily under stress? Which one can I subject to what might look like a run-of-the-mill use case that's actually designed to break it? The idea here is to conduct business as usual: a normal activity that should be no problem whatsoever, but is really amped up in exactly the right way to break that part of the triangle. Often, since I am hunting a person, I will use their process or tools against them. When the silo they've created finally blows up, the person will be to blame. I never have to go after the person directly in these cases, and I keep an appropriately low profile.

Chris's nerd project that controlled the internet for the hangar was the obvious choice. A room filled with junk that no one else could make head nor tail of meant the only one who could was Chris. So, my job was easy. Stress the tool — the nerd project — which will in turn stress the person

— Chris — to the point that the problem comes to a head, and Chris has to face the results of his disrespect for The Org.

THE KILL

CHRIS IS A classic case. People like him use their deep internal knowledge of an important function — in Chris's case, communications — to hold the herd hostage to their poor attitudes and performance. You already know Chris by some other, if not by many other, names.

Prey like this is worth noticing; bonds are a two-way street, and Chris lives in a very one-way world. The herd knows this too, and everyone feels that disconnect every time they deal with him. The bond that must be broken is only a weak task bond: Chris does a job that no one else can. The dilemma organizations face with prey like Chris is that they are worried that the task will go undone without him. He is specialized, he's hard to replace. They don't put in the effort to do so because that's the only part of the relationship that isn't completely broken. So, nothing happens.

Until a predator arrives. Weak bonds mean weak prey. Weak prey is an easy kill. Chris makes the kill even easier by doing his job, the sole reason to retain him, badly. So, I stress the exact thing Chris is responsible for, and that takes down Chris. Easy.

His final failure can't be small. There must be enough emotional energy for the organization to overcome their fear of not being able to replace Chris. He has to fail so vividly that the herd will unconsciously think that no one doing Chris's job is better than Chris doing Chris's job.

Again, I take advantage of the terrain. I, on my own, can't bring enough energy to bear, so I will direct a force much bigger than myself to intersect with Chris: the training. I need to be sure I can make the kill, so I go for the top of the herd. I put the senior command staff in play.

Leadership dictates the tone in any organization. If they're happy, everyone tends to think all is going well. If they're unhappy, then everyone else is unhappy too. My goal isn't to have Chris fall down in front of my commander. I want the overwhelming force of the higher-ups bearing down on him. They are the true center of the herd, the peak of organizational authority. My ask for them to come in a day early made sense to them. I'm new, I want the training to go right for the bigwigs. My real purpose was to have them get angry as soon as possible so they'd carry that anger through the entire weekend.

And they did. I never touched Chris's equipment. I can't put my thumb on the scale there. Chris's failings are his own, and prey's failings must be theirs and only theirs. I created the environment in which those failings would be amplified enough to snap the remaining bonds. All prey make the fatal mistake themselves.

CHAPTER ELEVEN
BREAKING PEOPLE

Late at night, I walked into a generic three-star hotel near the airport. The darkened breakfast area with the cold waffle makers and shut-off juice dispensers was depressing. In another five hours, I could consume scrambled eggs from an unseen boil-in bag laid out on a tiny steam table.

It didn't come with meeting rooms, which was why I found myself sitting in that breakfast room lit with only the glow of a hot cocoa machine's plastic logo. Seated across the table from me was a rabbi, dressed in what I could only guess is the traditional wear of a rabbi-cum-business-advisor: the kippah and tallit katan. That'd be the traditional head wear and the tassels about the waist from an undershirt.

Rabbi Levi opened with an easy one. "How was your flight, Lion?"

"It was long. We had an overnight layover in Singapore, which was not bad at all."

Rabbi Levi nodded. "I don't go over to Kuala Lumpur anymore because of that flight. My body doesn't do well traveling that far anymore."

I chuckled. I could see that. Rabbi Levi's scraggly beard, unkempt hair, and heavy-set frame suggested he was much older than me. He looked tired, but so did I at 2:00 a.m. after a long flight. I was worn out after 30 hours in transit. Luckily, I got sleep on the trans–Pacific leg. I had been working on fixing a cost estimation calculation with Gerry's CFO at his factory in Kuala Lumpur when the alarm went off: time to get to Virginia for a contract negotiation. One of Gerry's three-year distribution contracts, it was worth far north of the usual 20 million dollars.

Gerry was a terrible negotiator, which was why he hired me to do the job. You might say that he wore his heart on his sleeve, which didn't lend itself to a good poker face. But his issue was much worse than that. Gerry had very poor control over all his emotions: good, bad, whatever. He didn't keep a good leash on himself at all. He whip-sawed his emotional fragility all over his several-hundred-person factory and everything associated with it. You'd never know when he'd cave on something or stand firm on some ridiculous idea, all while nearly on the border of openly crying. Working for Gerry was difficult at best.

"So, how has it been with Gerry?" Rabbi Levi looked knowingly at me.

"It goes okay." I'd spent enough time working alongside Rabbi Levi to get a sense that the rabbi accepted what was going on with Malaysia Gerry. The rabbi himself wasn't terribly successful in life, but he was one of Gerry's oldest advisers. He was legitimately smart, certainly smart enough to recognize that working with Gerry was a double-edged sword.

He leaned back in the cheap metal and plastic stackable chair. "Let me fill you in on the history of this distributor."

Because of Gerry's poor self-control, his distributors took advantage of him in a big way, and these guys were no exception. They were huge. Nationwide, coast to coast, with a million stock-keeping units (SKUs) in inventory. Gerry was a tiny blip on their radar. But they were Gerry's largest contract, the one that most of his business was built on. To the point that it was nearly a monoculture: one distributor paid most of the bills and called most of the shots.

This kind of relationship raises red flags immediately in my mind. Unless you're really careful, these relationships turn abusive pretty fast. In the beginning, they might lean too much on you and stress your growth. At the end, they might suddenly pull out and you're the bag holder. In Gerry's case, they had used the cash flow as a cudgel all the way through. These guys were like the Walmart of auto parts: you played their game or you perished, and they had no qualms about making sure you knew that.

Rabbi Levi explained this in a straightforward manner while I watched him sitting in the dark breakfast room. I had guessed most of this already, but it was good to hear Levi's take on them.

I had prepared for the negotiation in excruciating detail. Using the previous contracts, I tore them apart clause by clause, breaking down every sentence onto a single page, then rewriting each part three ways: a best outcome, a middle ground, and a "we're getting taken" version. That prepared me for the context of the contract. I knew what they wanted overall, and I knew where my sticking points would be. If we were dragged down into a line-by-line grudge match, I was ready. More than ready. Bring it on.

Rabbi Levi wanted to talk numbers, so we did. We should have used an Excel spreadsheet on our laptops, but Gerry's company and associates barely knew what computers were, even though the internet had been around for a decade. So, we scrawled numbers in a note pad, and I used my crappy Casio calculator to come up with our go/no go figures.

It was a very difficult time in Gerry's industry because the Chinese were buying up loads of copper and driving the prices through the roof. The parts needed to build Gerry's 10MTs were getting expensive, and since copper was the key component in his starters and alternators, Gerry had to scrounge even the old broken units for salvage. China was buying up shipping containers full of cast-off stuff called cores. It was as bad as having entire shipments get lost in transit and "Oh well, file an insurance claim" given as the response from the shipper.

Going through all the numbers with the rabbi felt vaguely useless, and I had the distinct feeling that this was more to benefit the rabbi's nerves rather than the job at hand. I'd been banging my head on the China issue for months already, and a late night in a darkened hotel breakfast area wasn't going to uncover hidden answers. Around 3:00 a.m., we packed it up and went to our rooms.

Four of us showed up at the distributor's offices at 9:00 a.m.: Gerry, his sales guy Danny, Rabbi Levi, and myself. Our hosts consisted of four guys: a vice president, a contract team lead, an account rep, and an accountant. They cordially greeted us, showed us around the distribution center on a long, rambling walk through giant rack shelving and forklifts. I didn't have much to say besides appropriately-timed compliments on the facility. It was a warehouse. A big one, but just a warehouse.

Finally, we were herded in the direction of the meeting. There had been a flurry of emails about having lunch during the meeting, the rabbi's very particular dietary restrictions, and how we were going to make that work. As a result, the first thing I saw as I stepped into the room was a folding table covered by a white cloth. On it were disposable plates and utensils, a large plate of deli sandwiches, and a beat-up crockpot that I think contained a dish specifically for the rabbi. Odd.

The room itself looked like a common business training or meeting room. It was large, generically corporate with its drop ceiling, recessed fluorescent lights, and cabinets over counters that I guessed contained office supplies. At one end was a sizable whiteboard with the usual scattering of half-dead whiteboard markers on the rail. The room likely had chairs set up, rows of them on most days. But not today. Instead, two long runs of banquet tables were set up along the long sides, eight feet apart, with chairs behind them. I instantly realized how they set up the room. It was deliberately confrontational.

"Oh, you fuckers," passed through my head.

"Please, sit here." The VP smiled as he pointed us to one row of tables.

I have done negotiations in boardrooms, meeting rooms around conference tables, offices, breakrooms, and even once outside next to a couple of dumpsters while smoking cigars. None of them had been set up to start a fight like this. Clearly, there was to be no sharing of data, no huddled "let's solve this," no cooperative reviewing of each other's information. Even a normal conversation was impossible given the huge gulf between the lines of tables.

So, intimidation was the game. All right, let's play.

I sat down last, between Gerry and the rabbi, in the center of the long span of tables. Across the room sat the distributor's team: the guys we had met already and a newcomer who sat down straight across from Gerry. That left us at four from Gerry's company and five from the distributor. I began to unpack my bag, pulling papers, pens, notebooks, and even a clipboard onto the table's surface. I had no idea what I was going to need, but I did pass on dragging out my three ring-binder with the deconstructed contract. Rabbi Levi did the same with his papers. A few distributor guys followed suit.

We did a round of introductions, with everyone stating their names in a very routine manner. The VP said a few words about having worked with Gerry for many years and the hope that today went well to continue that relationship. Also very routine.

Eventually, the introductions were done and the guy who introduced himself as John stood up. "I'll be handling your new contract today." He glared slightly, the lines in his face betraying menace. That look told me that he was the one that set up the room. This was their heavy hitter.

I stood up and waved a hand at him from across the gulf of open space. "Hi, John! I'm Lion. I'm really looking forward to working out Gerry's contract today."

Up to this point, I'd been quiet. I didn't introduce myself as the negotiator until now, having only observed throughout the tour. These guys had been used to Gerry bringing an entourage, so I doubt they ever looked at me twice until this moment. I sat back down, leaned back in my chair, and continued. "Hey, thanks for showing us around the DC. I thought the tour was great. And thanks for setting up lunch today." I waved at the card table in the corner.

John looked at me. "Sure." He sat down, then looked at Gerry. "So, we are looking at renewing your contract for distribution of the PAC 10MT starters. This is a three-year contract that we need signed today to keep the product on our shelves and flowing. If we can't sign an agreement today, we'll have to look at another vendor."

John was staring at Gerry, leaning forward in his seat, eyes unblinking, with hard lines around his eyes betraying aggression. Gerry visibly shuddered, then looked at me. He was already afraid.

"John, yeah, hi, no problem," I said. "I'm certain we can come to an agreement. I think that's what we're all expecting, so we just need to get into the details. Does that sound good?" I nodded my head slightly, breaking his glare at Gerry. I pushed back my chair slightly so I could see both John and Gerry in the same field of view, but I kept my focus on John.

John turned his head to face me. "All right," he said slowly. He looks down at his papers, then returned to me. "So, three years, with 250,000 units per year."

I nod. "Okay, that's 750,000 units, that's great. That's the same as the last one."

"We stipulate that we'll buy a minimum 200,000 units."

I raised an eyebrow. "In previous contracts, the minimum buy was at least 80% of the total contract." I checked my Casio calculator and punched buttons. "You want 27%?"

"That's what we require."

Gerry looked at me again, fearful. I nodded at him, silently trying to say, "I got this."

Remember that bit of how a monoculture breaks you at the end? The part where you're left holding the bag? Oh, John. "John, uhm, I don't understand this change. Can you walk me through it?"

"That's the number we find appropriate, and we don't need to justify it further."

"Right, John, sure, but I'm not understanding why you're insisting on increasing the risk to us. I'm certain there's a good reason for it. Help me understand. Please."

"We can't commit to the previous minimums, that's all." He stared at me now like he did at Gerry a few minutes ago.

I nodded. "Okay, so let's work on this then. If your minimum quantity is only 27% of the contract, then we need to remove the exclusivity clause. If you guys underrun, we still need to place product coming off the factory floor."

The exclusivity clause had been sitting on my hit list since the beginning. So, this seems like a reasonable exchange to me. Exclusivity is a big deal in manufacturing and distribution. The idea is that, if you make a good product, the distributor doesn't have to compete with other sellers in moving that product. Imagine if Target said that Crest toothpaste could only be sold through Target. Then they wouldn't have to compete with Walmart on price. The downside is significant to the manufacturer. While a distributor can stipulate to a minimum purchase, it means they're tying up a production line for only one client. That risk shows up when the distributor can't sell the product any more for any reason, even if the reason has nothing to do with the manufacturer, such as pricing the product out of the competitive market. They stop ordering the product from the manufacturer, and now the manufacturer has to find a new product and re-tool. That's a huge problem. And that's why contracts have a minimum order quantity. That quantity has to be worth it. This wasn't.

John looked at Gerry, ignoring me again. "This will only be an exclusive contract, and it's 200,000 units minimum, and that's it." He said this forcefully, far more than necessary for this discussion. This wasn't a parent laying down an edict on his kids. This is a roomful of professionals with millions of dollars in factories, workers, and logistics at stake. John was playing his attack card.

On the drive over, I had told Gerry to let me do the talking. He wasn't to say anything during the negotiation proper. So, he was now caught under John's stare and showing signs of freaking out. Gerry was not a healthy man, far from it. He was morbidly obese, and now I could see the sweat beading up on his face. No wonder they were able to steamroller him in the past.

"Hey, John, look, this is a concern for us in the risk department. I really need some help understanding the thinking on this one. I'm sure you have a good reason, and it'll all make sense if we work through it."

He looked back at me, now with a slight frown. "And the new unit price will be $36.50, flat across all units."

Whoa, okay, well this was where he was going with this. These guys were paying $38.90 a unit. So, amid the copper crisis, in which they had to be feeling the pressure from other manufacturers too, John wanted to lower the per unit price. He leaned back, having delivered his ultimatum.

"John, let me run some numbers here." He watched as I punched away at my Casio and scribbled figures. "So, that's a loss of 1.8 million dollars off the top end."

"If that's what you say." He looked pretty self-satisfied over there.

"We might have trouble making those numbers in today's environment."

"That's our offer."

I nodded. John had done quite well to give me the rope I needed to hang him. He'd approached this meeting with a series of demands, not unlike a hostage situation. The thing about demands is that they're not collaborative. The world isn't that way anymore. It's no longer push-and-be-shoved, it's the age of peers and partnerships. We're all on the same team, we're supposed to work together.

So, to win I was going to collaborate and be very reasonable. Brutally reasonable.

"Okay, so let's work on that, then. I've got my parts inventory list here, we have time. Let's go through the parts lists and my costs and see what we can cut to make your price. I'm certain we can reduce on something to meet that goal."

John smiled at me with a touch of a sneer. "We can build them in-house for $36.50. We're giving you a deal at that price."

That was exactly what I needed. Gerry grabbed my clipboard and a pen and started hurriedly scrawling. Seconds later he pointed at the page:

"I'm going to lose everything!"

He looked apoplectic. I silently mouthed, "We're fine." to him, then graciously smiled at John.

"Fantastic! Then I know for certain that we can meet your numbers. We're just going to need some help."

John stared. "No, you don't, that's the price."

"Your guys can do this for that number, so we must be missing something. But we're very ready to learn. We'll meet your price if you can help us get down to it." I held up the paper ream of parts and costs. "Somewhere in here is what we need. Help us find it, please."

"No."

"I'm sorry?" I faked misunderstanding, then continued to pile on the brutal reasonableness. "PAC has had a long history of bringing in engineering consultants. We'd be happy to put up a couple of your guys to help out our guys get to that goal."

John stared at Gerry, ignoring me. "Take it or leave it, Gerry. Now." His voice was getting a little ragged, betraying him being upset. I was calling him on his bluff and he knew he couldn't deliver.

John had a touch of wild eyes. I spoke up slightly to grab his attention off Gerry. "John, I'm just asking for some help. The contract is fine as long as you can show us the way."

He whipped his head to face me, now livid. "NO. I am not sending people to KL. I am not helping you out. You take this or you can leave!" He'd raised his voice, he's yelled at me. Perfect.

Time to drive the knife in a tiny touch further. "Please, just collaborate with us a little." I betrayed no tinge of sarcasm or disappointment. I was cool and calm. I'd tuned my demeanor to ignore the outburst and carry on with reasonableness as if I was dealing with another professional and this was just a normal meeting. It was throwing John into stark contrast from me. Everyone in the room was watching me be relaxed, calm, maybe a little bit confused, and John losing his shit.

My first rule of negotiation is: whoever loses their shit first, loses.

John stood up, with his hands on the table in fists. Yes! I thought. He's winding up for something! Bring it! Then my tunnel vision on John was shattered. Another voice, the distributor's VP, out of nowhere said, "Hey, everyone, why don't we break for lunch?"

I broke eye contact with John and said to the VP, "Hey, that sounds great."

The tension in the room slowly faded as people started shuffling papers and standing up. Gerry looked at me questioningly.

"What just happened?" he whispered.

I leaned closer to Gerry. "I don't know yet, we'll see."

The distributor's people met in a quiet huddle on their side for a few minutes as Gerry's side of room, sans me, headed to the card table and the waiting pile of sandwiches. I sat there and watched, patient. Rabbi Levi was first to the card table and started fussing with the selection of food. Everyone else from Gerry's party quietly lined up behind the rabbi. John and one other person broke off from the huddle, gathered their things, and ducked out the back entrance to the room. The VP and the accountant started toward the lunch table as my guys sat down with their food.

"Can I join you?" the VP asked as he dragged a chair to our side. Rabbi Levi welcomed him over. Meanwhile, the accountant came over to me and leaned in to talk.

"Lion, do you have a few minutes to come back to my office?" he said softly.

"Sure." I stuffed my documents into my bag and got up.

"I'm Brian." He extended his hand.

"Hi, Brian." Brian led as we headed out the door and down a few halls, passing cubicle farms, to an office.

"Have a seat, Lion." Brian gestured as he sat down at his desk.

After I got settled, he continued. "So, I've been given the authority to negotiate on my company's behalf. So, from here on out, you'll be working with me. Does that sound okay?"

"Yeah, Brian, that sounds fine. I just want to make sure we're all working together on this stuff."

Brian nodded. "Yeah, for certain. Uhm, do you want to do this today or can we just get this done by email?"

I chuckled. "I'm totally down for email. I don't think this is going to be hard."

"Great! Here's my card, send me an email soon, and we'll get this taken care of."

"Yeah, Brian, I'm looking forward to it. Thanks a lot for stepping in."

"It's my pleasure."

Lunch was pretty uneventful after Brian and I returned to the conference room. The VP ate with our guys, leaving the far line of tables completely abandoned. I guessed that the VP had talked to the rest of our people about the change in plans. Gerry was looking relaxed for the first time in a week, and Rabbi Levi was talking about some esoteric intersection of his religion and food. Brian and I picked up our own plates, sat down, and joined them in conversations about the flight from Malaysia, the weather, and the other usual small talk.

When lunch was over, we lined up to say our goodbyes in the hallway. The other distributor guys had come back, including John. In that moment, I let myself go the tiniest bit too far. I shook John's hand vigorously. "Thanks for your hard work today, John."

THE PREY

WALKING INTO THE conference room with that arrangement made it obvious to me that this was a setup. In a lot of ways, my client encouraged this. He's a wreck and a pain to deal with, so I can see how the distributor figured this is how they should treat him. It's that old adage that, if you don't value yourself, no one else will. Regardless, intimidation is a very poor way of doing business in my book, even if Gerry is a nervous pushover.

The room telegraphed their negotiating tactic. No one could miss it. So, that meant I knew something just from observing the room: this would be a one-sided, take-Gerry-to-the-cleaners kind of day. This struck me as ludicrously unreasonable. We were working on a three-year contract, after decades of contracts before this and the expectations of more to come. That meant that, if they pushed Gerry down in the mud, one day he'd not be able to get back up again. That's a serious threat to the supply chain for their customers; retooling another vendor takes time and money. This made no sense, except if some bad actors thought they could get away with it.

I didn't know who those bad people were at first. But John stepped up to make it clear he was the one. While he never stated that he set up the room, his demeanor demonstrated hostile intent right from the beginning. He practically stood up and said, "I'm the prey. Come get me," by making demands and refusing to listen. Sure, John, if you're going to announce yourself to a predator, well, you get what you deserve.

THE HUNT

So, the core mechanism of emotionally rifting the prey from the herd still applies. It's a slightly different situation; I'm not expecting to get the prey fired from their company. I just want them fired from their role in order to change the tune of the negotiation, the process. I won't allow John to come after my client this way, so I'm going to have to execute a kill to reset the tone of the discussion. Preferably, I want John out of play. To emotionally rift John, I need to turn the rest of John's table away from him. This was a play against the person to change the process. Yet, the triangle of people, process, and tools is at work again.

In my mind, this hunt took on two parts. The first was to set John in direct contrast from me. I can't play John's game of aggression at all, lest I get identified with him. If I even slightly give into it, that'll lead to brinkmanship of two wrong people. Imagine if I were to counter John in an aggressive manner; he'd be able to use that as justification that his approach is right and continue with it. So, I enable him to raise the stakes if I'm aggressive as well. I needed to think this one through. What's the opposite of aggressive? It's not capitulation, because that loses the day for my client. Gerry is skilled at doing that on his own. What I worked from is reasonableness. Brutal reasonableness without capitulation. Not only did my points need to be absolutely as reasonable as possible, I needed to remain calm and reasonable myself. Then, add in mild confusion when I'm clearly doing the reasonable thing, but I'm not getting a reasonable response and can't accept the bully's terms. This showed everyone in the room who's working for a common solution (me) and who's being a bully (John).

If John returns to reasonableness, then we win, and no one gets taken to the cleaners. Reasonable reactions mean reasonable solutions and the job is done. If he continues to push aggressiveness, he further demonstrates the huge difference between myself and him. I'm trying to get along and he's trying to beat down my client. This is half of the strategy.

Corporate culture has changed in the last couple of decades. These days, cooperation and teamwork are bywords. Every corporate mission statement has something to say on the subject. It doesn't matter what company this is. No one in the western world is going to say no to cooperation and teamwork. So, if I can prod John to stop working in a cooperative manner, he'll start being at odds with the unstated cooperative culture the distributor's herd undoubtedly had. We're all on the same team, after all. We're all trying to provide a good working environment for our employees, while maximizing value of our products to the consumer so that everyone wins. Those are base assumptions of every company. The further I move John away from cooperation, the more he's going to stress the cultural fabric and expectations of his peers. If I can push him far enough, he'll rift from them and they'll turn on him as well.

So, to hunt him I need to remain infinitely patient and calm while drawing him away from cooperative discussion. The setup of the room is all I need to know my strategy.

THE KILL

THE LANDSCAPE OF this kill was absolutely fantastic from the beginning. I didn't have to go looking for the start of the hunt, since the setup of the room laid bare the heightened intention without saying a word. I can take that antagonistic space and run the prey straight into it. I need those raw, impassioned conditions to chase them to making their fatal mistake. That distance between the tables, embodying the nature of the relationships that day, John assumed would give him the upper hand through brute intimidation. His head start in creating that gulf between the two sides allowed me to step in and calmly run him down until he was tearing himself apart.

With John, I used his own emotions against him. I needed to keep upping the intensity of the room, expecting at some point the energy would be too much to sustain. Something always breaks. John is easy prey in this manner; as long as I remain on pleasantly cooperative ground, he doesn't get the response he wants. So, he doubles down on his intimidation, expecting that I'm dense and didn't get his message. He has to run faster, using more energy, to get his point across and win. He's raising the intensity of the room. And then I get him to do it again.

Brinksmanship is a terrible game. It's even worse when you don't have someone to play against. John must double down on rage, or he risks the entire negotiation turning into exactly what he doesn't want: a reasonable discussion.

The beauty of the chase is that, once the prey starts running, it's almost impossible for them to stop. And the faster they run, the more likely they're going to trip and the harder they're going to fall. John gets so deep into his own game of brinksmanship that he loses track of his peers. He's not aware they're starting to be uncomfortable with the tension he's creating. He has brought the conflict beyond acceptability. He is rifting himself from his peers by his own actions. That distance grows with every heightened exchange.

And then he snaps. Welcome to John's fatal mistake.

Sadly, my tenure with Gerry never got easier. A few years later, when the next contract negotiation came up, our backs were against the wall even more than the years before. The 10MT line was dying off, the Chinese were doing a bang-up job making them and had solved their quality control issues, and it was clear that Gerry's business was sinking fast. Everything I had predicted had come true. The end was near.

The Australian consultant and I worked out numbers with the distributor at their office in the States. The negotiation was not going great, but not terrible either. It was likely to take days. I was settling in for the long haul when Gerry lost it. He broke down and started crying, screaming in front of everyone that he was going to lose his family and his life. I called a halt right then and there and said we'd be back tomorrow to continue.

I quit as soon as we got back to the hotel. I packed up my stuff, caught a cab to the airport, and went home. My last email to Gerry informed him that he was the root cause of everything wrong with his company. The email was long, detailed, and scathing. It was the best I could do; there was no one to rift him from, no ground to hunt from, just direct confrontation with the hope the message might land. A no-win, nothing-to-lose proposition for a predator.

I got an email back from Kelvin saying that Gerry had showed the message to him. Kelvin agreed with me on everything, but could do nothing. He admitted to being trapped. He also admitted that Danny, the sales manager, was stealing inventory and selling it on the side. Gerry never fired him, but kept him on with the threat of the police showing up at any moment. Danny was enslaved too.

A few years later, I got an email from Gerry asking me to come back. But that was a smokescreen for his real ask, buried at the end of the email:

"PS: How is iQa doing? Can you have her call me?"

I never responded to that.

But it was confirmation that iQa was free.

iQa did make good on escaping Gerry's office, going to college, and landing a decent job at Sony corporate in KL. Several years after that, she got married to a nice Malay boy. She has a normal life. She even has a child.

After all those years, the one good thing I did in that company was saving her.

Malaysia Gerry died in 2013 in Kuala Lumpur.

CHAPTER TWELVE
ONE LAST GIG

I'M OF THE opinion that every 24-hour short-order restaurant looks the same after midnight. The plastic booth seats stylistically work well with the Formica tabletops and the well-worn stainless steel basket of condiments. The salt shaker is about two-thirds salt and one-third dry rice, natch. Our waitress has just walked away, having left an acrylic tumbler of Diet Coke and ice in front of me, near three of its now empty peers. It's another late night.

Seated across from me was my roommate and friend, Scott. We were both recent graduates of university science degree programs, both starting out on our own, and both filled with the immature ideals of young men inexperienced in the real world. Our late-night conversations over low-quality restaurant food varied tremendously as we tried to apply the little we did know to the great big world of the unknown. Well, we didn't think it was all that big or unknown, but that's part of being that young. We both thought we could tease out the truth with thought experiments alone.

We had both arrived at a mutual conclusion: the world is filled with people and somehow that was important. Coming from our scientific backgrounds of physics and math, people seemed like a radical departure from what we knew. Our backgrounds told us the physical world operates on a concrete set of rules, while people are a whole other thing.

Scott set his Coke down with authority, silently bringing the rambling conversation to what I could only expect was a serious point. "I got it."

I looked back, expectantly.

"So you know how we play all these video games, right?"

"Sure." Games, particularly computer games, were a staple. I'd played simple stuff as a kid: board games with the family, cribbage with my father, then the video game world with the arrival of computers. Games, particularly video games, had advanced dramatically in the last decade, breaking off into a profusion of different genres and styles. I fought low-resolution versions of World War II countless times, and sat around kitchen tables rolling dice and imagining wizards and dragons locked in mortal conflict.

Scott pointed his finger at nothing in particular, accentuating his words. "I think I figured it out, how to succeed in life, and games are the key."

I furrowed my brow. "Go on."

Scott launched into it. "In all the games you're this guy, right? You play this person in a made-up world. And there's this big goal you have to get to, you know, the goal to win the game. To get there, you have to do all these certain things. Like, to get to the next level you need to unlock a door, right? To unlock the door, you need the key for the door. The one key that unlocks that door is the red skull key, because there's a big picture on the door, the red skull, and you have to go get the matching key. Which, you know, has that same red skull on it. There are probably monsters or puzzles or something that's protecting the key, so your job is to do all those little things in order to get the red skull key, and then, and only then, can you unlock the door and progress to the next level.

"This has to be how real life works too. Like you're in a crappy job, and it sucks, like it's an early level in the game and you're just starting. To move up a level, to get a better job, you have to find that red skull key to unlock the door that lets you change your job, your level, right? Maybe the door is a promotion, or moving to a different company, or whatever. The door's a thing that's blocked right now. But once you get that door opened, there it is, the next level. You're more powerful, you make more money, you get more stuff, you have a better life, or game, or whatever. So, to succeed in life you have to play it like the guy you play in a video game, you have to play your guy!"

"Interesting, I think I can see that."

I wasn't with Scott entirely, though. My mind spiraled off into thinking about games that had detailed descriptions of characters with abilities and disadvantages, like the stuff you might try to map from real life into a game. In the game, you might be a Formula One racer that's really good at driving cars, but you can't fly a plane. I thought Scott was trying to say that you play to your strengths in life, rather than fight the stuff you're bad at. This was supposed to be about the world of people, and Scott was trying to approach the problem of how to succeed with them.

Over the years, Scott's fascination with games would come up regularly. His starting point was chess, which he had played since he was a kid. Chess clubs, competitions, and then online play. He tried to engage me from time to time, but I never had it in me for chess. Sure, I knew the rules, but I didn't know the strategy. Scott's view of chess was all strategy. His view of people and the pursuit of his red skull key came up regularly too. This was his strategy with people, he wanted to unlock that door to get to the next level in the world. At the time, he was toiling away in a go-nowhere company doing menial engineering work. The stuff you do right out of college. But Scott was smart and where he worked didn't recognize him for it. So, day after day, he kept his head down, was unhappy, and went nowhere. That door wasn't opening.

Through those few years, Scott and I spent a lot of time together. Our late-night conversations were a staple, but we also went to engineering conferences together, went camping, hiking, and did all the great stuff friends with time on their hands do. We exchanged stories of our families, our upbringing, and the things we had in common from our childhoods. It was all you'd expect from a friendship. And then, of course, things changed.

The hum of an about-to-go-bad fluorescent light ballast kept up a constant presence in the 24-hour diner. I sopped a french fry in ketchup lazily, relaxing.

Scott wasn't so chill. "I'm leaving for California in a month."

I stopped playing with the fry. "What?"

"Yeah, I got accepted into a master's program in the Bay Area."

"Wow, seriously?"

"Yeah, I'm leaving my job, like right now, and heading to bigger things."

"No kidding, congrats!"

Scott wasn't the only friend of mine to head to Silicon Valley. A lot of my friends from back then did. It was the thing to do. I expected that Scott would do the same as everyone else and disappear, ending our friendship. But he didn't. Somehow, against the odds, we kept in touch. We continued our tradition of long philosophical conversations, now over the phone rather than in a greasy spoon.

Scott continued to apply his ideas about games to the world. He decided that chess wasn't enough of a parallel to real life and switched to Go. Scott pressed the idea that Go was a game of almost pure strategy, that it was simple to play but hard to win. Apparently, the greatest minds in the world played Go. The most successful people played Go. Apparently, I wasn't one of them. I played one game and lost in short order.

Meanwhile, Scott graduated and built the expected network of connections. He started off as one of the first dozen employees at what would become a Bay Area success story. After a few years, he went out on his own, angling to be one of the important advisers to the powerful software startup culture. At one point, I went out for an extended visit with him. I lived in his home for a month, and I got the firsthand tour of Scott's grand strategy in the game of life. He was opening the doors he kept talking about. We watched videos of startup company pitches, we drank wine and jokingly tore holes in the bad ideas. He opened his contact book to me, got me into meetings, held me up as someone who could play the game called Silicon Valley. I went home after that month a little bewildered, but deeply indebted to Scott for all he did.

A year later, I got a call from Scott that started off with an odd question: "Lion, what do you think about nepotism in hiring?"

"Well, I don't have a problem with it as long as the hiring is done according to skill. If you're hiring your worthless cousin just because he's your cousin, well, that's a problem. But if you know them and they do good work, then you have a leg up in knowing what you're getting."

"Yeah, okay. So how would you feel about working for me in Africa?"

I woke up from a beautiful chemical sleep onboard an Airbus A380 bound for Dubai. The flight from San Francisco took 16 hours, and the best way to deal with it was good neck support and sleeping pills. This was the long haul to the region, and after a short layover I'd switch to the inter-Africa flight system. My first stop would be Bujumbura before heading to Kigali in Rwanda. In the seat next to me was a young woman, and by the look of her eyes she'd been mostly awake for the entire flight. Only two hours was left in the air, just enough time for a meal and landing. She must have been starved for conversation for the last 16 hours, because she started chatting me up as I put away my sleeping gear.

"Hi, where are you headed?"

I blinked a few times in her direction. I was not really awake, and it'd take some time for the effect of the pills to completely wear off. I felt very relaxed, though, so I smiled and played along. "Oh, I'm going to Rwanda."

"Oh, well, I'm going to Congo to volunteer to modernize African villages."

"Oh okay, that sounds nice." I meet a lot of these types in and around what I do. I don't work with them directly, but every aircraft has loads on them onboard and I see them at morning breakfast at the hotels. They're young, bright-eyed, and all have the same story.

"It's the best I can do to help out the poor people of Africa. We have so much, and we just have to give to those who are less fortunate."

I couldn't help but grin. The pills made it easy. "Oh, sure."

"What are you doing to help the earth and stop global warming?"

I laughed slightly, recalling having to pay for every grocery bag in California. I let the drastic subject change settle in my mind a few seconds. "I replaced all my lightbulbs with LEDs. That cut my energy consumption some."

She looked mortified. "That's not enough! If you're not doing more, you're killing the earth!"

Oh, well, that went south fast. "Look, I have a lot to do. I don't know what you expect."

"More, for one! Are you even going to Africa to help? Are you getting villages clean water or better food?"

"No." Again, I paused. "My company buys up African real estate companies and unifies them with a centralized system termed a multiple listing service. What I do is build economic infrastructure so that Africa can pull itself out of poverty by giving companies, families, and people the ability to buy and sell real estate with proper records and process and cut corruption and mistakes. Infrastructure like this is what will help Africa succeed in the long term."

She was incensed. "You're just a capitalist! You're going to destroy the planet!"

That was short. I put on my headphones, turned up the tunes, and waited for breakfast. This was not my problem. My problem was waiting for me in Kigali.

Scott was nervous that his employees would think he's playing favorites by hiring me, so I suggested he make the hiring process harder.

He did. I had a number of interviews, but in the end here I was, working in the field in Africa. I was to join another field agent: Praveen. Scott wanted me to spend six months with Praveen learning the ropes, but by contract, he wasn't my boss. He was merely there first. That's fine.

My first day with Praveen, months ago, set the tone. We sat across from each other in a conference room and he led with this:

"I don't want you talking to anyone else but me."

Wait, what?

He continued. "You may not talk to the people back in San Francisco or the London office. Only me. I'm the head of the field operation."

That's a hell of a thing to open with. Where do I begin? "You aren't the boss of me!" is an accurate gut response, but he was raising a much bigger problem than a denial of the org chart. First, I was new. I had no friends in Africa. I didn't know the rest of the team. I couldn't even talk directly to the local companies we were buying out. This left me intensely isolated. It's an isolation that's been manufactured by Praveen.

Second, I didn't understand what we were doing on the larger strategic scale. Praveen gave me financial spreadsheet work to do. That's a lot of what we do, but it's disconnected to how it's getting used in the agencies. So, I was blindly working away on something I didn't have context for, and my requests to learn more were ignored.

I was not down for this. Having Praveen in the middle of all this was not helping me get my head wrapped around the work, and the disconnection from everyone else in a new environment was taking a toll. So, I evaded Praveen's demands and talked to the rest of the team anyway. Which ended up with me in the conference room again and a repeat performance of the "you can't talk to anyone" speech.

The organizational isolation was creating some serious red flags for me. I had to believe that if I stuck it out with Praveen, Scott would follow through with his promise and I'd work independently. Scott's idea of separating Africa into territories for each of us sounded promising. I had that to look forward to. Apparently, I'd get Kenya. I could do that.

One of the sites in Rwanda was having difficulty with reconciling agent payment transactions. Their process was terrible and Praveen had gone in to rebuild it, taking their error-prone, all-on-paper system and backing it with Excel. But it still didn't work and the office still had huge problems with cash flow because the whole system was inaccurate.

The Rwandans didn't understand their business and neither did I which meant that both sides were frustrated. So, Praveen handed spreadsheets off to me. Not the project, mind you, but the spreadsheets and a list of specific problems to be fixed.

What I had before me was a disaster. I've seen terrible accounting and spreadsheets before. This was among the worst of them. A dozen or so sheets with crazy cross linking and references that, the moment you touched any of it, would break hundreds of cells across most of the pages. No wonder work couldn't get done.

Praveen didn't know what he was doing.

Okay, I can fix this. I'm good at this.

"Praveen, I'm going to rebuild your transaction sheets. I can't follow what's going on, but I think there's some good simplifications I can do to make it easier to work with."

"No, you'll fix the issues I gave you in those sheets."

"This whole thing is really fragile. It won't take long to rebuild using yours as the guide template, so it's not wasted work. It only needs to be redone with a slightly different approach."

"No, you're going to do it as I told you to."

This is a pattern I've seen before. Someone will have poor work output, but will hide that under a pretense of moving up to management. That's their only goal, and work quality isn't a consideration. If they get into management, they get out of work, and no one finds out how terrible they are at the job. Invariably, they make bad bosses. They don't understand how to do the work, and then can't empathize with their reports. That turns into a lack of solid leadership that results in more of a micromanager than a boss. And that's how it's going here.

It's not like I'd been free to be alone all this time. Praveen had been fitting the pattern exactly and micromanaging my life. A Word document and a spreadsheet are empty canvases, and to maintain coherency I use good logical layouts of the stuff I put in them. It's a discipline that pays off every time. But no one could stand up to minor gigging of their work every single day.

Was Praveen doing this to improve the product or to prove himself as the head of the field staff? I was convinced it's the latter.

I was in a tough spot. Scott and Praveen had worked closely together at their previous startup. My simple questions about the guy got back comments like, "Praveen is the best of the best!" I had to respect the serious relationship between the two. I trust Scott, so he must be right.

Yet I couldn't reconcile Praveen's poor performance with Scott's faith. For the time being, I promised myself I would not hunt Praveen, because this was Scott's company.

I stalled on Praveen's spreadsheet issues until my next rotation back to San Francisco, when I could talk to Scott directly. Scott and I had replaced our long phone calls with walks along the piers. Our conversations ranged greatly, as they used to over the phone. But this time, I had a very specific and touchy topic.

"I'm really having trouble with Rwanda's transaction system. Praveen told me to fix a few things in it, but it's a serious mess. I can't follow it. I can rebuild it, but Praveen very strongly pushed back." I'm trying to measure my words.

It was, as usual, a beautiful day to walk the piers. "Okay, Lion, what's wrong with it?"

"The calculations are spread across many pages, as far as I can tell. Parts of it are done in different locations and then linked back and forth across the whole thing. If you touch one part of it, it tends to break silently in other places. You have no idea that the numbers that come out of it are invalid at that point. It's convoluted enough that I can't audit it to ensure it's producing the right stuff."

If I were hunting Praveen, I'd get into more detail, drawing the issue out, asking questions to highlight specific problems in his work, casting indirect doubt on the work. Maybe I'd even point out the evidence of bad design habits in support of a performance kill. But I was not hunting, so I pulled my punch.

"I don't think this is Praveen's fault. I know there's been a lot of back and forth about reporting and record keeping and that it's been changing a lot. So, my guess is that this is the product of a tough time pinning the agency down on their process and converting it to ours. So, this seems to be a moving target issue.

"Praveen's good, I have no problems with him. But this is the financials. If we can't nail this, the agency goes under. They're already in trouble with cash flow, and this process might have a lot to do with it. I think it should be redone."

This was feeling like the beginning of a hunt, even though I said I would not. I lied when I said I was okay with Praveen, but I didn't know what else to do.

"Lion, can you work with Praveen's model?"

"Sorry, Scott, I can't. I just can't get my head wrapped around it." This would have been my answer if hunting. Here it was presented as a simple truth.

"Okay."

I had tried to be friends with the guy. I had asked Praveen about his past, his family, his hobbies, his friends, the usual getting-to-know-you stuff. Questions that would hopefully yield some common ground, that would give us a chance to bond. His answers were short, curt, uninformative. When we got to friends, he said he had none in a flat affect that left me without a doubt that he was telling the truth. He was almost unfamiliar with the concept of friends.

I'd ignored Praveen's "don't talk to anyone" order enough that he wasn't trying to stop me anymore. Over these months, I had learned that the guys in the home office were great. They did all the heavy lifting—all the deep process management and handling of the changeover of the agencies. They made the jobs of us field guys easy. We too had the same getting-to-know-you conversations and, lo and behold, common ground. One was a pilot, another liked hiking and the outdoors. For the first time since I started, I might have friends to hang out with when back in the States. I was excited.

When I returned to Africa, it was a different story. Praveen was frosty with me. I was certain he and Scott had a conversation about our talk on the pier, and Praveen was not pleased. Six months had gone by, past the date Scott said my time under Praveen would be done. But there was no change in Praveen's dealings with me. We had added two more field guys to the team, and now Praveen was taking his "I own the field" attitude very seriously. At least he wasn't micromanaging just me. The shift wasn't formal, but we kind of split up duties. I worked a bunch with Sai; he wasn't as advanced in the financials as I was, but he was eager and had a great attitude. Sai and I worked well together. We had skillsets that complemented each other, and though I had a much deeper financial and technical background, I never considered him junior. We were peers, partners.

Kamal, out of New York, was moderately skilled on the technical side, so he tended to work more with Praveen. Kamal was also a good guy—he had some great stories about his early days in finance. Hilarious stuff. But the best part was that he could work with Praveen. This kept Praveen off my back in a minute-by-minute sense, so that was a welcome relief. But it didn't stop the browbeating entirely.

We met in a conference room, and Praveen addressed all of us. "You must close all your tasks by the end of the week. If you don't get everything done, we need to talk about why you didn't get what I assigned you to complete. I don't want tasks being pushed to the next week. You must finish your work in the time allotted."

He paused. "Lion, I need you to do the closing finances report. This has been needed for a while, so everyone's expecting it as soon as possible. If it's not done right away, it'll be trouble."

This project had been avoided by our team for months. I had an idea of what it was based on the chatter surrounding it. I'd have to work with the CFO to get exactly what he wanted. Praveen had not made the guy happy with his transaction system, but I tend to get along with CFOs. It must be the math. "Sure, Praveen, I'll have it done in a day and half."

"It needs to be done sooner. We promised it to the CFO."

Whoa. This wasn't a simple job. My estimate was that a week should have been budgeted for it. And now, I'd been given the big job and a ridiculous timeline. "I can't get it done any sooner, and that's if I work hard on it." I was serious. It was a complex ask: 12 hours of work was blazing fast.

"Fine."

This was great. When I got back to my desk, I put on my headphones, cracked open Excel, and lost myself in the work. I had in my head a well-organized way to handle the numbers, one that could be adjusted quickly and easily.

Hours later, I was absolutely jamming. This was new work, so Praveen hadn't micromanaged it enough to get in the way. I was having a great time making progress. I was on time, and I knew that I'd make the deadline with the CFO. This level of enjoyment had been very rare in this gig.

So, the tap on my shoulder was a surprise. I slid my headphones off to see Praveen standing there.

"I need you to meet with a team."

I looked at him, confused. "What?"

"I need you to do a site personnel meeting right now."

"Praveen, I'm on a hard deadline. I don't have time. You know this. We talked about this."

"No, you're going to do this now instead."

Praveen had done enough damage to the relationship with the agency CFO with his transaction system that I wasn't about to miss a deadline with him.

I stared at Praveen. "No."

Praveen gave me a hard look, then left.

I must not hunt Praveen, I told myself. I can't. I won't. I owe it to Scott.

The next morning, I sat down with the CFO to show him the new data. All I had to go on was guesses as to what should be on the report, so when the CFO made some suggestions, I was ready. A half hour later, I had exactly the report he wanted, and that was made possible by a disciplined approach to Excel. If I had just "winged it" and not planned for the CFO to ask for changes, I'd need another day or more to fix it. For the first time, the guy was happy. I had delivered the first version on time, then turned around and delivered his requests in almost no time. My relationship with the CFO was starting off on a great foot. I'm fixing the damage caused by Praveen.

A few days later, Scott requested that I stay up late for a phone call.

"Why didn't you meet with the site team this week when Praveen told you to?"

Praveen must have complained. "I had to deliver on the closing report that was going direct to the CFO. I explained that this was the priority."

"You got a different priority from Praveen."

"I had blocked out those 12 hours to build the report for the CFO, and there wasn't any way I was going to miss that after the transaction issues. I need to build a good relationship with him, since the financials haven't been going right."

Scott paused. "Lion, you need to get it. Please, tell me you get it. You need to work with Praveen. You get it, right?"

What? "Sure, Scott, I get it."

I didn't get it. I just said the words to get off the call. At that moment, I started to question my friendship with Scott. Something very wrong was lurking on the edge of my awareness. Everyone in the company had come together, and we had started down the road to bonding. Except two huge outliers: Scott and Praveen.

On the next rotation back to San Francisco, I tried to engage Scott on some of the things we used to do together. We had a few standing items on the books, like the symphony, the opera, but nothing materialized. No visits to vineyards. There were no more casual chats or philosophical debates. No more walks along the piers. Scott was pulling away from me.

I was lost at this point. On the one hand, Praveen needed to go. Badly. On the other, Scott had doubled down on the guy. Somehow, the two had a connection that I couldn't understand. But Scott had been my friend for a very long time. We'd been through a lot together, and he'd supported me in the past. I felt trapped between being a good friend and doing what needed to be done, which meant I was failing at both.

Back to the road, the next stop: Lagos, Nigeria. Far from the sleepy streets of Kigali, Lagos is huge, busy, and the site Praveen and I were working on was an order of magnitude bigger. International trade means lots of expensive commercial property to deal with, and the complexity is that much larger. But some things never change. I was seated in a little section of a cube farm in among the hustle and bustle of real estate agents. Headphones and concentration were mandatory to unraveling the ingrown processes this place used to move property. There was a problem here, and we had to find it and fix it.

Again, a tap on my shoulder. Again, it was Praveen. I took off the headphones.

"Yes?"

"You broke the transaction reporting again. This is serious trouble you've caused!"

Not this again. I'd been engaged in a slow back and forth with Praveen on his bad transaction system. At some point, he wanted it brought into the tools I made for my successful closing report. But his spreadsheets were so fragile that they broke all the time. This had nothing to do with my efforts and everything to do with Praveen.

"You're supposed to make this work, and now the client is angry they got a blank report!"

After almost a year of Praveen's badgering, I was so tired of dealing with this guy. I'd not had a moment to relax, with him breathing down my neck in all that time. I didn't make the choice to be unprofessional. It just kind of happened, and it shouldn't have. I made a mistake.

"Look, Praveen it's your shitty stuff that causes this. I've tried my hardest to work around it, but it's your stuff that's broken, not the simple report runner. Fix your shit so it stops fucking up, and this won't happen."

Praveen stormed off as I put my headphones on. I pulled up my thrash metal playlist. I must not hunt Praveen. I must not hunt Praveen. This was the promise I made. Even if I wanted to, I'd be starting to be too late. I was taking the prey personally.

An hour later, I got another email from Scott: stay up late for a call.

"Lion, I need you to fix your stuff and get along with Praveen!" Scott was pissed. I was tired.

"Sure."

"I'm serious, you have to work with Praveen." There was no point in arguing the obvious: we don't get along.

"Yeah, Scott."

"When you get back, we have to have a 360 to determine fault with the transaction system."

"Sure." 360, root cause analysis, whatever you call it, it's all the same. Formalized blame. That's going be an easy one to identify: it'll be my fault.

"There's a lot on the line, everything is on the line! You have got to understand!" Scott was getting worked up.

"Okay." I didn't care.

"Tell me you understand! You *have* to understand! Do you get me?!" There was a lot of emotion in his voice.

I was worn out and beat down. This verbal tirade wasn't helping.

"Yeah, Scott, I understand." Words.

"You better! You better be getting along with Praveen by the time you get back to San Fran!"

"Sure, Scott."

The next day, the mystery behind the whole ugly experience snapped into focus. I won't forget staring out the window of my Lagos apartment the moment it happened. That scene of broken, unfinished buildings was a perfect backdrop to my thoughts. Scott was "playing his guy." He was trying to do exactly the tasks necessary to get to the next level. His game strategy told him he needed to be CEO of a company that would command respect, that would open doors. And so, he was doing exactly that. Along the way he discovered Praveen, who operated the same way. Praveen had no friends, no backstory, nothing anyone could connect to. He too was just playing the game.

Scott wanted me to come work for him because he assumed I played the game too.

Oh, shit.

Then everything changed.

The investment guys from London showed up while we were in Lagos. They were the ones that bought up the real estate agencies. They had the cash, they made the calls. It was rare that we operations guys were able to spend time with the investment guys. I had met some of them in my previous postings, but they were always on the move while we tended to spend months on location at a time. I liked them; I had joked with one guy that we should open a pizza place together in Kigali and quasi-retire there. To celebrate the teams coming together, we kicked off a barbecue out back of the corporate apartment in Lagos.

As we all sat around the pool, stuffed with food, someone broke out a joint and passed it around. I sat down next the head of the investment team, Tony, on the poolside couch.

"So why are you here, Lion?"

"Well, you get right to the point." I chuckled. "What's 'here,' Lagos or something else?"

Tony took a drag on the joint and offered it to me. I declined. I wanted to be present, not stoned. I took a big swig of my gin and tonic.

"With this company? This isn't a flashy gig."

"Yeah, well, Tony, I got this thing about infrastructure." I settled back into the couch. "See, the world is built on some seriously big stuff that people take for granted. Power, roads, financial markets, debt, insurance, legal systems, it's all infrastructure that makes the world go around."

Tony was impressed. "Wow, I agree with you! Yeah, what we're doing is infrastructure!"

I nodded. "The best infrastructure is the stuff that no one notices, it's just there, and they can build on top of it. That's why what we're doing is so important. We're building a way to manage property ownership that people can count on, which means people can plan, invest, and grow. It may seem mundane, but it's powerful stuff."

"I couldn't agree more. That's impressive. I didn't know anyone on your team thought this way. I thought it was just me."

"Well, yeah, most of the people in the Bay Area are into flashy dating apps or social media or whatever. I want to build stuff that lasts."

Tony raised his glass, I did as well, and we toasted as he said, "Hell yeah!"

We continued talking, good stuff in a getting-to-know-each-other way. I watched the joint make several circuits around the pool furniture, stopping by an outlier all by himself: Praveen. He was not connecting with the group, not talking, not taking part. He hadn't all afternoon. He didn't know how to handle this.

After a few weeks, Praveen headed back to the home office, leaving Sai, Kamal, and I in Lagos. What started that Saturday by the pool translated into everyday dealings. I was spending a good deal of time in meetings with Tony and his team and we had developed a good rapport. We got to a place I could never reach with Praveen: we joked. One of the guys wrote on a whiteboard in permanent marker, and so every meeting he'd be up there scrubbing as we laughed at him. All in good fun, of course. We made plans, we organized, and Tony and I got to know each other more.

Which was why Tony started to ask me why my side was failing to deliver. It was not an accusatory question. I guessed that Tony couldn't develop a good working relationship with Praveen or Scott. They couldn't connect with people because they're too wrapped up in their game. I knew operations was failing to deliver. I knew what the cause was without Scott's "360."

I was trapped, in a way. I owed Scott, for all he did for me in the past, to stick with his company, to make it work. That whole month of Scott showing me his world made me indebted, and I felt it every time I dealt with Praveen.

Tony was having me do meetings with them, exclusive of anyone else on our team. If I were hunting both Praveen and Scott, this was the perfect play: I'd stepped into the relationship vacuum that Scott and Praveen left open. My opinion with them was honest and open. We treated each other as if we were on the same team. There's nothing Praveen or Scott could do about this, since investing technically footed the bill for operations. So, if Tony said he's working with Lion, he's working with Lion.

Despite the investment guys, I'd gotten to the end of my rope with the entire gig. I'd been miserable for months. I suspected my friendship with Scott was over. I'd not seen my home or my wife in a very long time. I suspected the end was near as I worked my way through security at Lagos' airport on the way out. I had planned a weekend holiday in Scotland with friends before heading back to San Fran, but my conversations with Scott's assistant to book travel had become increasingly short and unhelpful, as if the bonds were already coming undone.

The 360 meeting went as expected. I explained the issues with Praveen's work yet again, but Praveen and Scott were well past listening. They concluded, as if it was some grand due process event, that I was to blame. Well, I knew that going in. I recognize a setup when I see it. What I also saw was the threshold I'd been hesitant to cross: Scott was no longer my friend. It's over. I knew this was coming, but I was left numb by this realization.

One afternoon, Scott stormed into the office and threw his wallet and some loose pens around. He ranted about the expense report software, but I knew underlying all that was his increased tension with investing about our side's inability to keep up. Everyone quietly ducked and covered as Scott had his snit, but I just laughed inside. This is who my friend really is?

A few days later, I had a call with Tony.

"Lion, what's the deal with you guys? Rwanda is falling apart, and you've not even gotten started on Lagos."

It's a valid question. I owed a real answer to Tony. My mantra played in my head, only out of tired habit: I must not hunt Praveen.

I failed. "Tony, we can do better. I know we can do better." The subtext of who exactly can do better is obvious: Scott and Praveen.

So, I arrived in the office an hour early on a Wednesday. A field team meeting was on my calendar. But in the office was only Scott, the HR gal, and a smug-looking Praveen. Oh, thank God, it's happening, I thought. The day I've been waiting for. My debt to Scott was about to be expunged.

I tried to get Scott to say why I was being asked to "resign with a severance package." We both realized the implied threat of legal trouble if he actually said something meaningful. My work quality was top-notch, I had reduced tension with Praveen by simply not talking to him, and I was doing great work for investing. Scott said nothing meaningful beyond, "You know why." I guess I did know why.

They expected me to return to work the next day.

I took the rest of the week off.

On my last day, Scott and I went for a walk along the piers again. I knew that this was coming, this echo of our former friendship. I'm not certain what he was trying to do, but I got the feeling he felt obligated to say something. He talked about us still being friends or whatever. He had a lot to say, none of it memorable.

"Scott, I finally figured out something."

"Yeah?"

"You know 'Play Your Guy,' right? In the last year, I figured out how we looked at that idea differently for all these years. I thought it was about recognizing what you're good and bad at, being honest with yourself, and using your strengths for good. You saw people as an intricate puzzle, like chess, to be played and won."

I paused. "But the thing is that life isn't a game, is it? It's way more complex than that and there are real consequences."

"Yeah, life is not a game, I get that."

I let Scott ramble on a bit more. A few minutes later, we came in view of the Embarcadero BART station.

"Scott, this is where I get off."

THE PREY

BAD PEOPLE, PREY, can come from anywhere.

It was obvious from my first day that Praveen was a problem. His attempts to control people consisted of simple, brutal, and inelegant power games. Scott's original deal of Praveen and I being peers was never going happen in Praveen's mind. I'm certain Scott had that intent initially. At that point, he wouldn't lie to me. But, over time, any mistakes or inadequacies ginned up by Praveen likely went straight to Scott to bolster his position that he, and only he, could be in charge.

It took me much longer to realize that Praveen and Scott were the same problem, and even more so, that Scott assumed I was just like him, heads down in the game against people.

No one was fooled by them. Their inability to bond didn't go unnoticed. It was right there for everyone to see. Bonding can't be faked. People see through insincerity without even realizing it. They're turned off by it on a gut level. Being genuine can't be faked either. Again, people know. People that can't bond will always be alone, and they're harmful to organizations. Herds must bond. Without it, you have nothing.

THE HUNT

A LOT OF things went wrong here, and it's not simple to draw all the lessons out into a soundbite. Even now, years later, the whole charade still smarts.

One: I promised to not hunt Praveen and that made things worse.

The beginning of the drawn-out road to being fired started with trying to address Praveen's bad transaction spreadsheets. My intentions were, in my head, good in that our business couldn't afford such sloppiness when dealing with 'The Money.' We really had to get that right. But I ignored the people-process-tools triangle and attacked the tool, which in turn attacked the person. Every one of my "I like Praveen, but …" statements was trying to disconnect the person from the tool. Of course, it backfired. My intentions were to improve the business, but I made the working situation worse by not keeping my head down. As if I could actually do that.

Two: Scott had no guts to deal with the problem directly.

If management does not deal with interpersonal problems right away, they spiral out of control. If I was in Scott's position, I would have brought Praveen and myself into a room as soon as possible and had us all work out our differences, with the expectation that everyone would get along when we were done. This comes with an assumption people seem to lose track of: if your people are valuable, they deserve consideration when relationships start to go bad. Relationships take consistent effort and leadership had better not shy away from doing that work lest you have this kind of fight develop. If caught early, it's not yet the end of the world. If you ignore the problem, you get bad prey. People who are ingrown, defensive, and difficult. Then it's the end. If you want to keep bad prey from forming, get in front of the problem. It's not the whatever at fault, it's the people.

Three: I was a bad predator.

Because I tried to keep my promise that I wouldn't hunt Praveen, I half-assed the predator's job. That drawn-out, messy engagement never should have happened. I should have kept my mouth shut on a number of occasions, like my soft attempt to cut Praveen down, or even my "We can do better" statement to Tony, which I knew would make it back to Scott. It stressed the relationship, but it didn't hit hard enough to sever the bond. If I had committed to my job as a predator, I would have had a much larger impact. My last conversation with Tony ended with:

"It's too bad you're leaving. You seemed to be the only one who knew what was actually going on."

I exposed my nature to the prey carelessly and needlessly, without planning and control.

THE KILL

THIS IS THE most important lesson from this story:

IF THEY FIGURE OUT WHAT YOU ARE, YOU ARE GONE.

This gig was bad from day one. It got worse as I inexpertly and unintentionally hunted Praveen, then Scott. Internally, I use the terms predator, herd, prey, hunt, and kill. But the herd doesn't need to know those terms to recognize the threat. They see someone undermining and pursuing their members. If you go against the herd, you are not part of the herd. In response they act, and that action is to remove the predator by force.

When it became clear I was operating in open contradiction to Praveen, I was severed from the herd, specifically from Scott. I took care to keep the other company relationships in good standing, but Scott controlled the hire/fire decisions, not them. My half-assed predation exposed a long-term attempt to discredit Praveen. I was surprised that it took so little to do it, that there was never an attempt to correct the situation, but that's an indicator of Scott's approach to our friendship and/or the relationship with his employees, not mine.

This is a risk for every predator. If you fail enough, in either execution or subtlety, you will be removed by the same system that you exploit to kill prey. They rift from you suddenly and dramatically. Then you're the one killed out of the organization. In this case, it cost me the gig and an old friendship.

I never forget this risk. It makes me careful and methodical. In building the situations where prey demonstrate their true nature at the point of the kill, I try to minimize exposure of my actions. I cloak what I do as much as I can. I try to have a good excuse for my actions that isn't the whole truth, but is true enough. I construct scenarios in my head over and over, working out how to get the kill and not spook the prey. And finally, I execute and evaluate every step of the way. If I need to get out of a hunt, I can take it. I planned for it.

The herd will never stand for predators in their midst. Don't get caught.

CHAPTER THIRTEEN
BEING RUN OUT

CHARLIE LOOKED BLANKLY at the side of the building as he drove his car into its parking spot. The building was a tall, gray concrete warehouse, vertically striped with load-bearing beams. It wasn't pretty. It was, however, a beautiful day to be out in the suburbs, in this light industrial office park filled with equally nondescript, gray, ridged warehouses. Working out here had its advantages and disadvantages. For one, there was a lot of parking and not a lot of traffic. There were cut green lawns, trees, and not a lot of fire engine sirens. After working downtown for many years, this was a welcome change. What wasn't so great was that this suburban office park existed in a food desert. The closest place for lunch was McDonald's. Not quite the "Where do you want to eat today?" of downtown. All in all, it was almost peaceful.

Once he walked inside, he entered an atmosphere of quiet desperation and low-key chaos. Charlie dropped unceremoniously into his generic cheap office chair, dug into the grease-soaked McDonald's bag, and logged back into his computer to find a reply to his email.

From: Jules Michaelson <jules.michaelson@alfredsersonmedical.com>
Sent: 20 Dec 10:14
To: Charlie Willstat <charlie.willstat@alfredsersonmedical.com>
Subject: RE: Re[2]: ROCKWALL TESTING URGENT

CHARLIE - ROCKWALL TESTING'S FOUR OFFICES ALL HAVE THE UA-167 URINALYSIS MACHINES. THAT SHOULD BE EASY FOR YOU. SINCE YOU'RE NOT

> AVAILABLE I'LL HAVE TO GO DO THEM MYSELF BUT YOU HAVE TO GET WITH THE PROGRAM!
>
> *Reply to:*
>
> **From:** Charlie Willstat
> <Charlie.willstat@alfredsersonmedical.com>
> **Sent:** 19 Dec 9:36
> **To:** Jules Michaelson
> <jules.michaelson@alfredsersonmedical.com>
> **Subject:** Re: ROCKWALL TESTING URGENT
>
> Sorry Jules, I can't get to Rockwall's stuff this week again. I have that new blood sampler to get configured for Polytech Clinic. Maybe next week?

It was no accident Charlie was too busy for his boss. Jules had been hired a couple of months ago by an act of overt cronyism by the department head, Jim. At least, that was the theory. They must have worked together for years, because Jim had dropped Jules in management without even an interview process. They both looked like they came out of the dog-eat-dog office world of the 1960s. They were older men wearing off-the-rack suits from at least a decade ago, well-stained and worn by years of chain smoking and rail vodka lunches. Charlie had to make an effort not to stare at Jules' teeth. There could have been a dentist's yacht to fix those teeth.

Jules' trailer park executive look matched perfectly his trailer park executive skills, which is to say that he was more interested in talking about work than doing work. The complete lack of knowledge of the company's medical testing and diagnostic systems didn't help the situation either. The company occupied a specific technical niche that Jules had no business being in. But here he was, in charge of the technically adept field engineers and phone support staff.

Charlie was phone support.

Jules and Jim were only part of the problem. The larger picture included Alfred-Serson Medical's (ASM) acquisition by the much larger Medtechnik. ASM had only one office, fulfillment line, and warehouse. Specifically, this gray, concrete, windowless building. Medtechnik was an international company. It wasn't clear what Medtechnik was planning to do with ASM yet. And so it goes with power vacuums: people tend to be nervous, desperate, or power-hungry. It made the office only somewhat unpleasant.

> **From:** Jules Michaelson <jules.michaelson@alfredsersonmedical.com>
> **Sent:** 3 Oct 14:31
> **To:** ASM_SUPPORT_ALL
> **Subject:** MEDI-SOLUTIONS NEEDS A FIELD ENGINNER NOW!!
>
> ALL,
>
> THE LICENSE PACK UPGRADE FOR MEDI'S BA-415 WENT WRONG SOMEHOW! I GAVE THE CLIENT THE NEW LICENSE (ATTACHED) BUT THE ANALYZER WON'T START NOW. I'VE ATTACHED THE OLD ONE TOO. I WANT SOMEONE TO DRIVE OUT THERE AND FIXZ IT NOW!
> **ATTACHED:** Old_BA415_v1034-234.img
> **ATTACHED:** New_Hemiscope-Debug and Test_Not-For-Clients_January.img

Jules had this great ability to not understand the issues in the field but, true to his nature, he talked big and promised everything. Charlie and his cube mate, Mitch, watched Jules make mistake after mistake with clients, which would have been fine except that Jules always dumped those mistakes on his staff. Like the email above. Jules not only sent them the file from a different machine, it wasn't supposed to go to clients at all.

A few weeks back, Jules had caused so many problems in the field that every field technician was on the road putting out fires. So, when one more Jules–inspired inferno came up, he came down to the phone support cube farm to demand Mitch get in his car and drive, bright and early tomorrow morning, Saturday.

Mitch refused. Jules raised the topic to Jim. Jim later addressed the rest of the team. "I'd take Mitch outside and kick him up and down the parking lot!"

> **From:** Jules Michaelson <jules.michaelson@alfredsersonmedical.com>
> **Sent:** 17 Oct 11:09
> **To:** ASM_SUPPORT_ALL
> **Subject:** GO INTO THE FIELD
>
> EVERYONE:
>
> I DON'T CARE IF YOURE A FIELD TECHNICIAN OR PHONE SUPPORT! YOU MUST GO INTO THE FIELD WHEN TOLD BY YOUR MANAGER! NO EXCEPTIONS! GET IT TOGETHER!

Hunting Jules didn't turn out to be that difficult. It had become common back-room knowledge in the field and support departments that Jules was incompetent. But, given everyone's boss was Jules and he reported directly to his crony Jim, the department could not do much. But the field team and phone support group hardly worked in a vacuum. Sales and marketing were close by, both in collaboration with support and in the fact that they were in the same cube farm. This gave Charlie lots of chances to ask questions of various sales managers.

> **From:** Charlie Willstat <charlie.willstat@alfredsersonmedical.com>
> **Sent:** 15 Nov 16:21
> **To:** Jo Kellogg <joanna.kellogg@alfredsersonmedical.com>
> **Subject:** Re: Order of service kit for HS-198
>
> Hey Jo,
>
> Jules ordered this service kit for Upton Clinics. But there isn't one for the HS-198. Does he mean a refill kit instead?

Reply to:

From: Jules Michaelson
<jules.michaelson@alfredsersonmedical.com>
Sent: 15 Nov 16:02
To: Charlie Willstat <charlie.willstat@alfredsersonmedical.com>
Subject: Order of service kit for HS-198

CHARLIE — ORDER UPTON A NEW SERVICE KIT FOR THEIR HS-198 FOR NEXT DAY SHIPPING. HURRY

From: Charlie Willstat
<charlie.willstat@alfredsersonmedical.com>
Sent: 10 Dec 09:53
To: Jason Selge <jason.selge@alfredsersonmedical.com>
Subject: Re: NEW UA-222

Hey Jason,

This is your customer. Did Jules tell them we don't have any of those model machines in the warehouse? And that the shipping container is still about 20 days out from arrival?

Thanks,

Charlie

Reply to:

From: Jules Michaelson
<jules.michaelson@alfredsersonmedical.com>
Sent: 9 Dec 17:16
To: Charlie Willstat <charlie.willstat@alfredsersonmedical.com>
Subject: NEW UA-222

CHARLIE — FRANKLIN BIOMED HAS DONE THE

ESIGNR FOR A NEW UA-222. GET THE INSTALL SET UP FOR THIS WEEK RIGHT AWAY.

From: Charlie Willstat <charlie.willstat@alfredsersonmedical.com>
Sent: 19 Dec 14:31
To: Jo Kellogg <joanna.kellogg@alfredsersonmedical.com>
Subject: Re: REAGENT KIT - FAIRFIELD DOCTORS AND ASSOC

Hey Jo,

Sorry to bug you again, but I'm confused on this request for one of your clients ... what's Jules talking about?

Charlie

Reply to:

From: Jules Michaelson <jules.michaelson@alfredsersonmedical.com>
Sent: 19 Dec 13:43
To: Charlie Willstat <charlie.willstat@alfredsersonmedical.com>
Subject: REAGENT KIT - FAIRFIELD DOCTORS AND ASSOC

CHARLIE — NEXTFIELD HOSPITALS HAS RECEIVED THEIR ORDER OF A DS-011 AND A BA-197 REFILL KIT BUT NOW THEY DON'T KNOW HOW THEY FIT TOGETHER. THEIR PULL TICKET INDICATES THERE IS ANOTHER UNIT ON THE BILL OF SALE BUT THEY NEVER RECEIVED IT. YOU NEED TO GET ON THE PHONE AND STRAIGHTEN THIS OUT RIGHT NOW SINCE THE CLIENT IS PISSED! THEIR ORDER NUMBER IS 011837A

That wasn't a valid order number, and Nextfield had actually ordered a case of refill kits that arrived without issue. Neither Charlie nor Jo were able to figure out what Jules was going on about, but they never followed up with Jules either. It didn't seem worth it.

Over time, this strategy of looping in other departments had the effect of weakening sales' confidence in Jules as he gained a lot more company visibility of his daily work. But it wasn't enough. While the field technicians still scrambled to keep happy all the clients Jules had touched, phone support took a very different tack.

Which is why Charlie had sent Jules that email saying that he was unavailable. He and Mitch were almost always unavailable now. He had watched Jules for months, patiently building his predictive model. That detailed paper doll gave Charlie insight into Jules' work. Eventually, he got good at seeing failures coming: he knew what Jules could and could not do, knew the clients and their setups of equipment and needs, and then watched for the inevitable collision of Jules' inability and a client's ask. Charlie was one step ahead and made sure he and Mitch were already occupied on other customer issues by the time Jules' next fire came down to them.

By schedule alone, Jules was forced into the field by himself.

With no other options and a big promise to deliver to a client on the line, Jules had to set up urinalysis machines that all had to work together for a big client with four clinics. Every one of the four clinics was set up in ASM's standard way, but having them all talk to each other was unusual. This was not even in the ballpark of Jules' capability. It wasn't even on the same continent.

All four of Jules's sites were broken for a week by the time the account executive, Lisa, stepped in. Charlie had done great work for her clients in the past already, so when something went wrong, she looked for Charlie personally. This was what brought her down to the support cubes to work something out: she would drive to all four offices and be Charlie's hands while he fixed everything by remote.

It worked. They were done in six hours, and most of that time was spent driving.

The next week, Medtechnik's officers met in ASM's big conference room in a closed-door session. Closed door, but open blinds in the window to the hall. Not by accident, Charlie walked by that window a couple of times. He saw Medtechnik's people talking sternly to Jim while a number of sales managers sat on the sidelines: Lisa, of course, with others in the sales department, even the marketing director, Sara. This was big.

Jim never saw it coming that he'd have to fire his friend Jules. Charlie sat back in his cube and beamed. One down.

> **From:** James Fredo <james.fredo@alfredsersonmedical.com>
> **Sent:** 6 Jan 9:43
> **To:** ASM_SUPPORT_ALL
> **Subject:** Upcoming Changes!
>
> Everyone,
>
> While Medtechnik considers their options on who to head up ASM, I am proceeding to get a number of improvements done around here to make us more efficient, more cost-effective, and provide the best customer experience possible for our clinics and hospitals. I have plans to reorganize the support process and bring us closer together so we can make our clients happy!
>
> Look for my initiatives and be ready to turn on a dime! It's go time!
>
> Jim

In the wake of Jules' sudden departure, Charlie had expected Jim to slow down a little. But he didn't. This began a litany of emails from Jim with promises of improvements that everyone saw as an obvious attempt to be promoted. The only real thing to change was Jim getting more involved in day-to-day operations, meaning that, instead of Jules, everyone had to deal with Jim. It was hardly better. In a lot of ways, it was worse.

"I don't care! You say it works that way! Well, I don't! Just get it done! Now!" Jim was up to his usual in-your-face management style: Mary was backed up against a cubicle divider with Jim bearing down on her, yelling. Mary looked like she wanted to bolt. Which is exactly what she did. She quit the week after. ASM had been shedding people over time, first because of the acquisition by Medtechnik, then under Jules; but now that

Jim had taken more direct control, staff were leaving as if quitting was a bus they were late to catch.

> **From:** James Fredo <james.fredo@alfredsersonmedical.com>
> **Sent:** 13 Jan 8:57
> **To:** ASM_SUPPORT_ALL
> **Subject:** New support staff!
>
> Everyone,
>
> Please welcome Stan, Melody, and Ishaan to the ASM support team! I expect everyone to assist them in getting up to speed quickly!
>
> Jim

To solve the problem of people leaving in droves, Jim was hiring lots of new staff to try to keep up. It didn't stem the tide; it was still a net exodus. The experienced people were quitting and the new people had no idea what they were getting into.

> **From:** James Fredo <james.fredo@alfredsersonmedical.com>
> **Sent:** 28 Jan 14:27
> **To:** ASM_SUPPORT_ALL
> **Subject:** Get tickets closed in the phone support queue!
>
> Phone Support!
>
> The open tickets in the system are now over 200. You need to close them faster and then get on to the next ticket. This is everyone's responsibility! If the new hires are not closing fast enough, you must help them get trained up faster.
>
> Jim

Morale was low in the office by the time Medtechnik did something.

> FROM: James Fredo <james.fredo@alfredsersonmedical.com>
> SENT: 3 Feb 8:19
> TO: ASM_SUPPORT_ALL
> SUBJECT: Welcome our new general manager from Medtechnik, Alan Reyerson.
>
> Everyone,
>
> Alan is a well-respected member of the Medtechnik team and is here to be our general manager. Please welcome Alan at 2:30 today in Conference Room B.
>
> Jim

Charlie took the approach that what had worked for Jules' kill would work to hunt Jim. He began hunting Jim by casting the same light on Jim's work.

> FROM: Charlie Willstat <charlie.willstat@alfredsersonmedical.com>
> SENT: 25 Feb 15:10
> TO: James Fredo <james.fredo@alfredsersonmedical.com>;
> Alan Ryerson <alan.ryerson@alfredsersonmedical.com>
> SUBJECT: Re: Ticket Queue at 400!!!
>
> Hey Jim and Alan,
>
> I just wanted to let you know that we got the ticket queue down to 350 today! We're doing our best to keep up and train the new people at the same time.
>
> Thanks, guys!
>
> Charlie
>
> **REPLY TO:**

> **From:** James Fredo <james.fredo@alfredsersonmedical.com>
> **Sent:** 25 Feb 12:33
> **To:** ASM_SUPPORT_ALL
> **Subject:** Ticket Queue at 400!!!
>
> Everyone!
>
> The ticket queue is at 400 open! Get to work closing customer issues! Man up and get your nose to the grindstone! No one's going to hold your hand!
>
> New people had better be getting training from the experienced staff!
>
> Jim

And Jim kept on being himself.

> **From:** James Fredo <james.fredo@alfredsersonmedical.com>
> **Sent:** 4 Mar 16:21
> **To:** ASM_SUPPORT_ALL;
> Alan Ryerson <alan.ryerson@alfredsersonmedical.com>
> **Subject:** New Client - Heartfield - up and running!
>
> Everyone!
>
> I want to announce that I have completed the Heartfield Labs deal. That's 16 machines, supplies, and training for the lab techs. Go ASM!
>
> Jim

Charlie knew who actually did the work, both from sales and from the field techs that got all that equipment installed over a long weekend. Of course, it wasn't Jim. But the new GM, Alan, probably didn't know that. Jim brought up a lot of things Charlie was able to ask questions about.

From: Charlie Willstat
<charlie.willstat@alfredsersonmedical.com>
Sent: 11 Mar 11:51
To: James Fredo <james.fredo@alfredsersonmedical.com>;
Alan Ryerson <alan.ryerson@alfredsersonmedical.com>
Subject: Re: New Support Manual Initiative

Hey Jim,

I was wondering about your new online manual. Support hasn't had tiers before because we tend to get really technical questions from the clinics and lab techs. Some of us are really specialized in some of the product line, so we pass clients to them when they need help with those things. Will that be part of your new system? Just thought I'd ask.

Charlie

Reply to:

From: James Fredo <james.fredo@alfredsersonmedical.com>
Sent: 11 Mar 10:19
To: ASM_SUPPORT_ALL;

Alan Ryerson <alan.ryerson@alfredsersonmedical.com>
Subject: New Support Manual Initiative

Support,

I'm starting a new support manual system. This will provide the lower tiers of support the ability to quickly close or escalate customer issues by giving them a flow chart in which to diagnose customer issues quickly and without extra time. We'll do this new manual in software where the support technicians will need to check off each question, step, and decision in the tree before they can hand the client off to a higher level support person. This will make your jobs easier!

Jim

Charlie was one of those highly specialized people; he knew a whole family of complex diagnostic machines that no other technician had the background to work on. Charlie's role was so important that he went to department meetings just to report on how those machines were doing in the field. Other support people had similar roles, again, with deep technical knowledge down to the science of how ASM's technology worked. They were critical.

From: Charlie Willstat
<charlie.willstat@alfredsersonmedical.com>
Sent: 24 Mar 17:31
To: James Fredo <james.fredo@alfredsersonmedical.com>; Alan Ryerson <alan.ryerson@alfredsersonmedical.com>
Subject: Re: Software Ticketing System

Jim,

I'm hoping this new system can really help out. The metrics you've been using have been for a full department like we had at the beginning of the year. We have half the people now, so anything you can do with this system to help would be a huge deal. Thanks.

Charlie

Reply to:

From: James Fredo <james.fredo@alfredsersonmedical.com>
Sent: 24 Mar 9:38
To: ASM_SUPPORT_ALL;

Alan Ryerson <alan.ryerson@alfredsersonmedical.com>
Subject: Software Ticketing System

Support,

We will be switching to new support ticket management software soon. I am identifying the new solution, with the expectation that we will close tickets faster with less overhead while maintaining a

> higher quality of service to our clients. Be ready to get it in gear, support! No more excuses for the long ticket backlogs!
>
> Jim

The new system never showed up, nor would it have ever helped. Jim's concept of how support worked was limited to his own experience of talking to his cable TV provider's customer support line. It didn't have any application to ASM's skilled and knowledgeable customers. But the metrics, and the forceful demands to perform to those metrics, never stopped.

The lunch kitchenette became the de facto gathering place to escape the grueling work conditions Jim was pushing. As Charlie walked in with his empty water bottle, he saw Lisa, Jason, and Melody, all from sales and support, gathered around a table.

"I don't know how much longer I can take this." Lisa had her head in her hands as she mumbled to the others. "I have more and more clients angry at me." She looked up. "What can I tell them? That we don't know anymore? That we're way behind schedule? That we have half the people we should?"

Melody leaned in. "I had one guy bitch me out for at least a half hour."

Lisa looked straight at her. "What are we supposed to do here? Sales is not supposed to be the punching bag of the company!"

Jason laughed sullenly. "I've stopped taking calls from one client already. Jim sent two other field techs to do an annual service for all their machines last Saturday, but never paid attention to the inventory. They got there, realized none of the maintenance kits had been shipped, and then got yelled at by the lab manager for not doing the work. Now he's been trying to call me. What the hell do I do?"

Lisa dropped her head again, nearly sobbing. "Jim screamed at me this morning. Something about mixed-up orders. It wasn't my fault."

The group didn't even take notice of Charlie as he filled his bottle from the tap and left.

> **From:** Alan Ryerson <alan.ryerson@alfredsersonmedical.com>

> **Sent:** 10 April 13:26
> **To:** ASM_SUPPORT_ALL
> **Subject:** Weekend client work must be approved.
>
> Good Thursday afternoon, everyone,
>
> I want everyone in support to know that any weekend work for clients not currently on the schedule must be approved by Mark or myself before being calendared with the client. Medtechnik understands that sometimes a client's needs fall during off-hours, but we do not wish that off-hours commitments become standard procedure.
>
> Thank you all,
>
> Alan

Alan's voice of sanity into Jim's world was short-lived.

> **From:** James Fredo <james.fredo@alfredsersonmedical.com>
> **Sent:** 10 April 13:52
> **To:** ASM_SUPPORT_ALL
> **Subject:** WEEKEND POLICY
>
> Support,
>
> It is my policy that weekend work will still continue. Alan is incorrect in addressing support; this is for another department. Not us! You will not need approval from Alan or his AA. You will not be restricted in servicing the support queue. Get back to work!
>
> Jim

Charlie slid back from his desk and poked Mitch in the shoulder. "Look at this." Mitch saw the email on Charlie's screen, then looked back to his own to read.

After a few moments, Mitch turned to Charlie and grinned. "Were we going to do National's install this Saturday?"

Charlie nodded slowly. "Yeah, I believe we were."

From: Charlie Willstat
<charlie.willstat@alfredsersonmedical.com>
Sent: 10 April 14:49
To: James Fredo <james.fredo@alfredsersonmedical.com>; Alan Ryerson <alan.ryerson@alfredsersonmedical.com>
Subject: Re: WEEKEND POLICY

Jim and Alan,

Mitch and I had planned on doing National Lab's DX-440 install this Saturday, but we never put it on the calendar. Should we wait on this one? National won't mind if we do.

Charlie

The next morning, Charlie noticed the conference room was packed again: Alan, Jim, the department heads, sales team heads, and Sara from marketing again. Charlie didn't linger at the window: the email was on the conference room projector.

Back at his cube, Charlie kept a low profile for the next two hours.

From: Melody Kirkpatrick
<melody.kirkpatrick@alfredsersonmedical.com>
Sent: 11 April 10:05
To: Charlie Willstat
<charlie.willstat@alfredsersonmedical.com>;
Mitchell Wilson <mitchell.wilson@alfredsersonmedical.com>;
Sara Nelson <sara.nelson@alfredsersonmedical.com>
Subject: Jim

Security just walked Jim out.

Two down.

Charlie sat back in the conference room, watching the weekly department meeting unfold. As each department or specialist reported their news, Alan would cap their input with simply, "Great, thanks." It was no different for Charlie's.

"So, the infrared laser spectrometer series is so far doing fine after last year's release. I think we're finally getting off the initial bad software they were shipped with, since customer support calls for the KV series are down a good 15% this quarter. The bad laser collimators that were shipped last quarter should be all replaced now, and the manufacturer says a new coated-glass version is available with less dispersion." Charlie paused, then looked at Alan. "We have the choice of the current ones or these others. Which one should we use?" He looked at Alan expectantly.

"Yeah, great, thanks Charlie. Sara?"

Most of these meetings went this way. Someone would present something, and Alan would move on. If the topic wasn't technical, Alan might have something to say. But if it was, he moved on to whoever was next.

Eventually, Alan would announce his own plans. "I have been working with the vendor on the chromatograph line, and we'll be starting the new CX-200 series next month. The vendor assures me there's a lot of market interest, and we should be stocking this new series as soon as possible."

Usually when Alan gave his update, no one had any questions or comments. Maybe it was because every update was light on details or, as in this case, was something the vendors told him and he repeated. Or maybe no one was paying attention. But Charlie was listening and tended to say something.

"Excuse me, Alan, but support hasn't had a single person trained on those yet. They're nothing like the old ones, and Genitech's training is only once a year. Support isn't ready for those going into customer sites."

Alan looked cross. "Just use the manuals, Charlie. Okay, everyone, that's the meeting for today. Have a great week."

Charlie hadn't intended to hunt Alan, but week after week the plans Alan made on his own didn't intersect with the reality on the ground at ASM. Alan might be yet another bad director, or maybe he had a poor understanding of ASM. However, while the majority of the room tuned out Alan's updates, several people tended to pay very close attention to

Charlie's questions: Alan, natch, and Sara, head of marketing and the de facto head of office gossip.

> **From:** Aquasel Medical <aaquasel@gmail.com>
> **Sent:** 14 May 10:54
> **To:** Jason Sorenson <jason.sorenson@alfredsersonmedical.com>
> **Subject:** Re: BG-011 Blood Gas Test Station
>
> Thank you very much Jason!
>
> Go ahead and order one of the test stations. Our old one is on the fritz and we're really anxious to get going again! Thanks a ton!
>
> Mike
>
> *Reply to:*
>
> **From:** Jason Sorenson <jason.sorenson@alfredsersonmedical.com>
> **Sent:** 6 May 11:07
> **To:** Aquasel Medical <aaquasel@gmail.com>
> **Subject:** BG-011 Blood Gas Test Station
>
> Mike,
>
> Thanks for the call earlier. I have good news after checking with the rest of sales. We can get you the new BG-011 right away. It comes with a five-year warranty from us and the manufacturer, which includes the metal catalyst.
>
> You'll be our first clinic to have this installed. It should fix the problems you have with your old unit. We'd be happy to remove the old machine as well, even though it was bought from another vendor. If you have any questions, let me know right away!
>
> Have a great day!
>
> Jason

A sale like this was not a big deal to ASM, another expensive unit to ship and install involving support and the field team. Normally, this would be taken care of quickly and without fanfare. So, life at ASM went on as usual: understaffed and overworked, slipping sales and high turnover, even low stock and supplier problems. Another month of Charlie questioning Alan at department leadership meetings passed before the issue showed up again.

> **From:** Aquasel Medical <aaquasel@gmail.com>
> **Sent:** 18 Jun 7:49
> **To:** Jason Sorenson <jason.sorenson@alfredsersonmedical.com>
> **Subject:** Re: BG-011 Blood Gas Test Station
>
> Jason,
>
> When are we getting the station installed? I haven't heard from anyone, and it's been a month since we ordered it.
>
> We were invoiced for this already as well.
>
> Thanks,
>
> Mike

The sales agent, Jason, shipped off the email to the rest of the team. The issue bounced around the office quickly.

> **From:** Alan Ryerson <alan.ryerson@alfredsersonmedical.com>
> **Sent:** 18 Jun 8:25
> **To:** ASM_SALES_ALL;
> ASM_SUPPORT_ALL;
> **Subject:** Re: RE: Re: BG-011 Blood Gas Test Station
>
> Where are we with this? Why isn't this installed at Aquasel already?

> **From:** Jo Kellogg <joanna.kellogg@alfredsersonmedical.com>

Sent: 18 Jun 9:14
To: ASM_SALES_ALL;
ASM_SUPPORT_ALL;
Subject: Re: RE: Re: BG-011 Blood Gas Test Station

I billed Aquasel already at the time they signed, so someone in field support should have done this.

From: Denise Gorton
<denise.gorton@alfredsersonmedical.com>
Sent: 18 Jun 9;41
To: ASM_SALES_ALL;
ASM_SUPPORT_ALL;
Subject: Re: RE: Re: BG-011 Blood Gas Test Station

I'm the only one that can install these, but I haven't seen the work order yet.

From: Charlie Willstat
<charlie.willstat@alfredsersonmedical.com>
Sent: 18 Jun 9:50
To: ASM_SALES_ALL;
ASM_SUPPORT_ALL;
Alan Ryerson <alan.ryerson@alfredsersonmedical.com>
Subject: Re: RE: Re: BG-011 Blood Gas Test Station

Alan and everyone,

I told everyone three weeks ago in our staff meeting that the manufacturer was out of stock. I then repeated this after the meeting directly to you, Alan. We should not expect delivery until the end of next month.

"Charlie!" Jo had appeared at the entry to the cube only minutes after he had sent the email. "You need to call Aquasel now and sort this out with them!"

Charlie slid his chair out and stood up, staring her down. "Jo, this is Not. My. Problem. I'm not even involved in this sale. I don't install or support those machines, why are you asking me?" Charlie was visibly upset that Jo was trying to push this on him.

"You know what's going on with the supplier! You have to call Aquasel now and tell them!" Jo wasn't calm either.

"All I know came from a bulk email from them. What am I supposed to tell Aquasel? That you billed them without knowing what's in stock? That everyone was told it was not in stock?"

"Charlie! Call them now!"

Charlie crossed his arms. "No. I won't."

Jo stormed off and left Charlie fuming. He turned to Mitch, who had watched the whole thing. "I'm gonna get some air."

A half hour later, Charlie and Mitch had retreated once again to the lunch kitchen. This time, it was free of sobbing employees or thousand-yard-stares of quiet desperation. They were alone.

"So, what do you think Jo's going to do?" Mitch had a bottle of Diet Mountain Dew.

Charlie leaned back on his chair. "I have no idea, and I don't care. Every time someone does something around here, it goes wrong. No one listens."

"Of course not. That wouldn't be the ASM way. First Jules, then Jim ... But shit's still not looking up."

"Alan's not much better."

Both their heads turned to the sound of footsteps on the linoleum. "Oh, hi Sara." Mitch was quick to turn up a smile on his face, masking their discussion.

"What're you assholes up to?" She laughed. Charlie and Mitch knew well enough to change the topic. This was the office queen of gossip, and she wielded it like her own personal staff of power. People she favored were talked up; people she had deemed unworthy got talked down. Being the head of marketing meant little in terms of technical skill, but that wasn't required for her job. That hardly stopped her from straying into the deeply technical world of support. There was gossip there too, after all.

Mitch kept the smile going. "Not much, just chilling for a few minutes. You?"

"Gotta grab a coffee!" She popped another pod into the machine and started its chugging sounds to produce a cup.

Mitch smiled away, Charlie kept a neutral face, and eventually Sara left the room.

"Back to it, I suppose." Mitch stood up and pushed in his chair.

"I guess."

Two hours later, an email arrived.

From: Gail Townsend
<gail.townsend@alfredsonmedical.com>
Sent: 8 Jun 11:46
To: Charlie Willstat <charlie.willstat@alfredsonmedical.com>
Subject: Report to meeting room C immediately.

Charlie, report to meeting room C right now to speak with HR.

"You've been suspended, effective immediately." Charlie was on the phone in the meeting room talking to Gail, head of ASM HR. "You've acted inappropriately to a member of staff and are being placed on suspension pending an HR investigation into the incident. You will be supervised by security to your cube, where you will get any personal items you need, then be escorted from the building."

"What am I being—"

Gail continued, not even bothering to acknowledge Charlie. "You may not talk to anyone in ASM, from this moment on until the investigation is over. Your benefits will still be active, but your pay is suspended starting tomorrow. This conversation will be followed up with a letter to your personal email with the formal details. Do you understand the process that will be done right now?"

"What am I being charged with?"

"That will be covered at a later time. Do you understand the process that will be done right now?"

"I'm not going to be told what's going on?"

"Please follow the security guard. Good day." With that, Gail hung up.

Two weeks to the day he was walked out, Charlie sat at his desk at home in front of his personal laptop. It had been two weeks of crushing silence. ASM had not contacted him at all. He had no idea what was happening, or if he still had a job.

> **From:** Gail Townsend <gail.townsend@alfredsersonmedical.com>
> **Sent:** 26 Jun 14:48
> **To:** Charlie Willstat <cwill1971@gmail.com>
> **Subject:** Re: Written confirmation?
>
> Charlie,
>
> We are still collecting information and will respond to you shortly.
>
> ***Reply to:***
>
> **From:** Charlie Willstat <cwill1971@gmail.com>
> **Sent:** 25 Jun 17:52
> **To:** Gail Townsend <gail.Townsend@alfredsersonmedical.com>
> **Subject:** Written confirmation?
>
> Gail,
>
> I still have yet to receive written confirmation of my suspension.
>
> Charlie

Two more weeks, for a total of four, passed. Charlie wasn't doing well at first, caught in the limbo of having a job and needing to hit the bricks for a new one. But, during the interminable wait, his view started to change. After talking to friends, Charlie was convinced that his conversation with Jo in his cube was the cause. Refusing to call the customer and tell them the expensive bill they had paid wasn't going to result in a new machine anytime soon had to be the trigger. But he was in the right. He had stood his ground in a game of pass-the-buck from someone who had screwed up. The more he considered this, the more intent he became. Did more lurk behind this than a heated discussion in a cube?

> **From:** Gail Townsend <gail.townsend@alfredsersonmedical.com>
> **Sent:** 11 Jul 10:37
> **To:** Charlie Willstat <cwill1971@gmail.com>
> **Subject:** Notice of Disciplinary Investigation Hearing #CSM212-043
>
> Charlie Willstat,
>
> This message is to inform you of a disciplinary investigation in which you are named as the subject. This investigation covers the following allegation(s):
>
> That on Wednesday 18th June, Charlie Willstat spoke in a wholly inappropriate manner to another ASM team member.
>
> An investigation into this allegation is underway, which includes:
>
> Gathering of relevant evidence, including emails, memos, paper notes, etc.
>
> Interviews of complainant(s), witnesses, and other person(s) involved. Summary documents of these interviews will be kept.
>
> Reviews of HR records of yourself and prior work history within ASM.
>
> Any other information or data as we see fit.
>
> You will be expected to be interviewed as part of this investigation. HR will contact you as to the time and date of this interview.

So, it was the incident with Jo. This set Charlie's mind at ease, finally knowing the reason. Nothing else was on the table, and that benefited Charlie immensely. All he had to do was to fight this one incident. He wasn't fighting for the job anymore. By this time, it was certainly lost. Office gossip—at the hands of Sara, no doubt—would have taken its toll on any hope of decent working conditions at ASM. He was now fighting for closure and unemployment. If they fired him for cause, he'd be denied unemployment while he searched a new job. Which he needed after all this time.

It sounded like interviews were going to happen, but only written summaries would be taken. He frowned at this, knowing that there was no way they would represent him well. The only sensible response would be recordings.

> **FROM:** Gail Townsend
> <gail.townsend@alfredsersonmedical.com>
> **SENT:** 11 Jul 14:46
> **TO:** Charlie Willstat <cwill1971@gmail.com>
> **SUBJECT:** Re: Recordings of interviews
>
> Charlie,
>
> Recording interviews is not our policy. The summaries taken by me will be completely accurate.
>
> *REPLY TO:*
>
> **FROM:** Charlie Willstat <cwill1971@gmail.com>
> **SENT:** 11 Jul 11:29
> **TO:** Gail Townsend <gail.Townsend@alfredsersonmedical.com>
> **SUBJECT:** Recordings of interviews
>
> Gail,
>
> I formally request that audio recordings be taken of all interviews.
>
> Charlie

After five weeks, Charlie requested the interview summaries while hinting at retaining a lawyer. HR was required to provide all information in his file, with this investigation process included, but nothing had shown up and Gail had continued to be quiet.

After six weeks, an email arrived with a stack of PDF attachments. The required investigation interview summaries were included. Finally provided with a way to clear himself, Charlie went to work.

There were a total of five interviews, all about a half hour each. These involved Jo, who was the other side of incident, and four others in the cubes nearby. Mitch wasn't on the list, even though he was in the same cube and a witness to it all. As promised, the summaries were only notes taken by the HR person, not verbatim transcripts of the conversation. The interviews were laid out over a series of days, all time-stamped and cataloged with the participants and allegation in the header. Two people ran the show: Alan Ryerson, ASM general manager, and Gail Townsend, from ASM HR.

Charlie had to work with roughly a dozen pages of questions and answers. He had time, so he pored over them, carefully working his way through what Gail had assured him were "completely accurate" summaries.

The stack started off with the interview with Jo. She was the first person they talked to, and the questions were directed to how she saw the incident. After the basics of names and places, Gail got to the heart of the matter:

"So as far as the incident itself, we have the statement of another witness in a previous interview who said Charlie berated you. Did you feel berated or belittled by Charlie? Was Charlie aggressive?"

"He was saying it wasn't his problem, that it was someone else's. He was waving his arms around and had raised his voice. He was very aggressive. I felt embarrassed and intimidated."

"Well, I just want to say that this isn't your fault. If Charlie would have behaved himself, none of us would have to do this."

Curious, Charlie thought, that a previous interview had taken place prior to the first interview. It didn't stop there. A trend emerged among the questions Gail asked. The statements leading up to these questions were benign, such as talking about their working relationship to Charlie. Then, suddenly:

"Was Charlie acting in an aggressive manner? Did you find him intimidating?"

"Why do you think Charlie is so angry and aggressive?"

"Why was Charlie so aggressive and intimidating?"

"Would you consider Charlie angry, aggressive, and intimidating?"

"Why would you say [Charlie] was so angry that day?"

Two responses to these questions stood out:

"He was waving his arms around and had raised his voice, he was very aggressive. I felt embarrassed and intimidated." (Jo, from above)

"Charlie was being loud and aggressive, waving his hands around in an intimidating manner. He was really aggressive."

The others didn't follow the narrative:

"No, he wasn't aggressive at all. I'm shocked this process is taking place."

"That day was more frustration than anger. It's what we have all been feeling."

"He wasn't angry, he was loud, but he's always loud. That's just him."

In the middle of all this was an interview with Sara:

"I'm the one who made the complaint because I'm looking out for Jo."

Sara wasn't even on the floor at the time.

It all made sense to Charlie. Sara had seen everything go down with both of his kills, Jules and Jim. Alan had seen Charlie's work on Jim as well. And they both saw Charlie's continued pointed questions about people in ASM, particularly Alan. This investigation wasn't an isolated event, because that's not how things work in herds. Charlie was a nebulous threat to Alan and a sidelong threat to Sara's opinion factory.

On an overcast day in August, Charlie drove to a Holiday Inn. Walking past the front desk, he noted the signs to the meeting rooms and followed the arrows to the back of the hotel. In a nondescript, windowless hotel conference room he sat across from Gail and Tom. Gail had the reins of today's show, while Tom was a new face, an HR person from Medtechnik. With the usual pleasantries exchanged, Gail started in on the case.

"So, the alleged incident on Wednesday, June 18. Can you tell me about it?"

Charlie tilted his head. "So, I've not really gotten a clear message on what I've supposedly done. I read about wild hands and aggressive behavior, but that's not registering as a reason for suspension."

"You threatened Jo at your desk about an order you were supposed to contact the client over. Do you recall that conversation?"

"Certainly not one that involved me threatening anyone. Jo stopped by with an issue about a piece of test equipment bound for a lab that Jason had promised, Alan had approved, she had billed, and we had nothing of the sort in stock. She wanted me to contact the customer and tell them that it was going to be a few months before their equipment would arrive. I declined since this was not my area of responsibility, and I had no involvement in the process except for a statement near the time of sale that the manufacturer was out of stock.

"After that, she just walked away. She seemed angry at me, which I was bothered by since she made it seem like I wasn't doing my job. I went outside to the smoking area after that to get out of my cube for a minute."

"Do you recall being loud and intimidating?"

"No, not that I was aware of."

"Were you animated in your conversation?"

"I'm normally pretty animated, so I can't recall, but it's possible. That's normal for me."

"Could you have been perceived as aggressive by anyone else?"

"No, this situation wasn't unusual for what support deals with—except for Jo's response, of course. Which I had forgotten about after going outside anyway." He paused. "I'm having trouble understanding why Jo would file a complaint over this."

"She didn't."

"So, who did?"

"Sara."

"She wasn't there."

"Correct."

"So, you're telling me that the complainant wasn't even present?"

"Yes."

"I don't understand. Sara even stopped by the break room shortly after the discussion with Jo. She seemed fine and said nothing about Jo."

"So, did you feel angry about being told to call the customer?"

"I was just confused. It's not my area."

"Did you feel you did anything unacceptable?"

"No."

"Do you think your behavior is justified in making people feel threatened by being aggressive?"

"Uh, no?"

"Did you consider apologizing for your behavior?"

"For what behavior?"

"That's fine. I think I've got my questions answered. Tom?"

Tom had been silent this entire time. "Nope."

"Fine, then we'll—"

Charlie talked right over her. "I need some of my questions answered."

"Okay, okay. Go ahead, fine."

"So, I've noticed some irregularities in the statements you have provided."

"They're summaries."

"Yeah, and you said they're completely accurate, yeah?"

"Yes."

"So, how is it Jo was told that someone else had an interview before her? Did you not provide me with all the interviews, or was the summary inaccurate?" Charlie pushed a yellow highlighted page across the table. "Here."

Gail looked perplexed. "Okay . . ."

"And then there's this list of questions that lead the witness into making statements that I was intimidating and aggressive, with no room for the witness to express their own opinions." He slid another page across, this time with a collection of summary clippings on it.

"We are required to use the same questions for interviews."

"Or how about you telling me that I couldn't speak to anyone about this? Was that told to everyone else?"

"Yes. That's the policy."

"So, why are these people saying exactly the same words: hands waving and aggressive behavior several times in their statements?"

"I don't know. The statements were made independently."

"Or how about this accusation of aggressive behavior when Sara, just after I returned from outside that day, called Mitch and I assholes in the break room?"

"That's not relevant."

"And Mitch was there only a few feet away. Why wasn't he interviewed?"

"He wasn't material to the process."

"And finally, why is it that the complaint has been made by someone who wasn't even there, for a supposed victim that has been coached through the process?"

Gail glared at Charlie. It was Tom who finally responded. "He's got you there, Gail." He laughed slightly.

She regained something akin to composure. "Well, the investigation is still pending, and your questions would be answered in a hearing. We haven't made a decision yet, and not all the facts are in. We'll let you know when we need to speak to you again." She stood up. "Thank you for coming, Charlie."

Charlie pointed at the pages on the table as he stood to walk out. "I'll just leave those here for you. Have a nice day."

After another two weeks and a letter from an employment attorney for Charlie, he received a response: six months' severance pay, all accrued vacation time paid, and all back pay after being put on suspension. Charlie took the settlement and never looked back.

THE PREY

WHAT'S NOT OBVIOUS about this story is that Charlie's new to being a predator. He learned about the concept six months prior to the story, and it just clicked. I've noticed that tends to be the case when someone gets told about organizational predators and prey. They either shrug it off, fail to understand it, or they realize it's a life-changing event. For Charlie, it was the latter. He'd never be the same.

Given this new understanding, Charlie was in a place rife with prey: a company going through trouble, and staff were no small part of that trouble. A few hiring mistakes led to easy prey right in front of a newly-awakened predator. Not a great combination for keeping the peace.

Jules and Jim were obviously a worthless pair. They had no redeeming qualities: they were sleazy to the core. And not even discreet about it. That takes carefully maintaining a veneer of old cigarettes and hair gel every single day.

THE HUNT

CHARLIE WENT WITH the one technique he figured out right away: sunshine. By gently calling attention to the problems the prey caused, he was able to begin the process of rifting them from the herd. No one wants to work with a perpetual, egregious failure, a miscreant, or someone who's willfully ignorant. That goes even more for management. When the decision-makers start seeing the prey for who they really are, that rift starts forming.

This chase has to be done discreetly. Charlie knew well enough that he couldn't just point fingers and scream, "Look at this guy!" Words have meaning, of course, and Charlie's words were intentionally non-confrontational:

> *Jules ordered this service kit for Upton Clinics. But there isn't one for the HS-198. Does he mean a refill kit instead?*

Or supportive:

> *I'm hoping this new system can really help out. The metrics you've been using have been for a full department, like we had at the beginning of the year. We have half the people now, so anything you can do with this system to help would be a huge deal.*

Or even celebratory:

> *I just wanted to let you know that we got the ticket queue down to 350 today! We're doing our best to keep up and train the new people at the same time.*
>
> *Thanks, guys!*

But buried in each one was enough damage if it was seen by the right people. No one could accuse Charlie of having a problem with the prey. He was a team player through and through.

Hunting can be a slow process. Charlie needed to open that rift over months to make it work. If he pushed too hard, he would be perceived as out to get them. If he was too slow, well, it never would happen. And that's the challenge of this strategy: timing is everything. You have to pick and choose when you take action. It has to count, but it can never be seen as negative or too often.

It also needs to feel honest and coherent. The herd can sense insincerity instantly. It can also tell when the predator is acting unusual. They'll pick up on the smell of something not right without even being aware of it.

It was this innate sense of the herd that turned out to be Charlie's downfall. None of them said, "Charlie got Jules fired." No one was aware of the predator. But when Charlie took down Jim next using the same methods, that sense that something's wrong kicked in. No one expressly said, "Charlie's a threat," but they'll have felt it somehow. He'd killed too often in too short a time span, and the herd took notice. Sara, gossip queen, realized that people's opinions had been swayed because of Charlie's rifting hunt. You've been made, Charlie!

But worse was Charlie using the same tactic when dealing with Alan. It doesn't matter if Charlie intended to hunt him or not. He just kept doing what he thought was right by the company: calling Alan out on his shortcomings. In and of itself, this is not a problem. It was probably even necessary. But the herd doesn't know if you're hunting, or just doing your job to keep things on the level. They'll subconsciously assume the worst: the hunt is on.

If sunshine is your tack in the chase, you need to agree to stupid stuff when not hunting. It's hard; predators are smart and will see the stuff that's wrong. But the herd needs to see a compliant, agreeable you to sense the difference between a hunt and just trying to make the office a better place. Keep those fangs on the down low unless you mean it.

Let the place cool down after a kill. We get it, Charlie. You were excited and this was a huge thrill. Hold on to that adrenaline rush and quietly kindle that feeling. Don't jump headlong into the next hunt.

THE KILL

I WENT TO lunch with a regionally-known HR lawyer once. Another lawyer friend we had in common had introduced us. I thought it would be interesting to see what the top of the HR infrastructure thought of the idea that a single person anywhere in the company could willfully drive the firing of an individual without being given the power to do so.

I didn't open with such brazen terms as herd, predator, prey, and kill. I feared the industry lingo might be off-putting. I tried to speak their language with terms such as toxic individual and termination process. That went fine, up until I tried to explain how this can be accomplished with someone who's never been given the authority and can even be employed against those above you in the org chart.

It didn't go well. She said her most common issue was toxic employees damaging companies. Apparently, few organizations know how to get rid of them. Management of all forms came to her on an almost daily basis to get help in making these people go away. The conversation then turned to more HR terms: actions plans, personal development plans, and disciplinary notices. We all know the process of finding a deficiency, writing it up, writing a plan to deal with it, and then evaluating the person's execution of that plan. This is HR boilerplate.

Every time I tried to get her to see outside of the HR process, we struggled with the conversation. I couldn't even venture past the idea of someone who doesn't have the authority. I didn't bother trying to discuss the mechanics of a kill. Lunch didn't end well.

I have to admit I don't understand HR's perspective either. Are they watching over the company or the employees? I think they see themselves as protectors, people looking out to right a wrong or make the company a better place. But I could be mistaken. In the years of doing my predator job, I've had little contact with HR unless I've made a mistake.

By the time HR is involved with one of my kills, it's too late for the prey. HR comes along to dispose of the carrion. The prey have rifted from the herd, and HR will go along with whatever the herd comes up with as a legal reason for termination. It could be anything. It's not my job to craft that for them. The predator need not worry about the process, all the paperwork and exit interviews. Sit back, predator, job well done.

But, when the predator makes a mistake and fails, things can get ugly.

Charlie put up a fight when HR decided to roll him. Take careful note of the underhanded tricks they attempted. They took on a self-identified protector role. My experience is that corporate HR tends to overextend itself when it feels justified. Righteousness, like rage, is self-indulgent. ASM was no different. They made obvious mistakes all along the way in pursuit of the threat they saw. This is the difference between them and predators: at that moment, they have a moral cause. That can lead them not to be calculating, not to be attentive to the smallest detail and, most importantly, not to be patient. But they have the body of corporate policy on their side, which influences all levels including leadership and corporate legal. They will win. If you're sitting in HR's office staring down complaints, you're rifted from the herd. Time to find a new job.

Finally, letting the herd cool down after a kill is a must, but understand this: it will never go back to the way it was. Organizations have long memories and, even if you wait years between kills, eventually you'll be found out. Always be ready to walk to greener hunting grounds, because it will happen someday.

CHAPTER FOURTEEN
SYNERGY

Brian looked around the bar with unhappy familiarity. It wasn't the decor; the dark wood highlights and Tiffany-inspired lights made for what might be considered a classy place. The few silent TVs had CNN on, rather than wall to wall basketball or football. All in all, it was a perfectly serviceable bar. It just happened to be the place everyone went on Friday to see off someone leaving the company. Tonight, it was Caroline, from pre-sales. As was the tradition, everyone was seated around the big table in the back.

Mike raised a glass and everyone followed suit. "To Caroline, may your new cube farm be greener than today's!"

"To Caroline!" everyone shouted. Brian took a sip of his whiskey, letting it pause in his mouth as he considered the moment.

Or moments. Caroline's departure wasn't the first; that unhappy familiarity came from the fact they were coming here an awful lot these days. As more people left, the send-off parties would get smaller. Given enough time, they wouldn't need the big table anymore.

The whiskey began to burn and he swallowed it. Taking stock of the table, Brian saw his colleagues having a good time. This was a rarity. He swirled the contents of the glass around, playing with it while he considered his own place at the table.

In the last year and a half, business had been a bit out of hand. For 20 years, the company ran a nationwide network of software for vehicle repair shops. A client would come in with their broken car, describe their problem to the clerk and, as if by magic, the clerk knew exactly what was wrong and, more importantly, how much it would cost to fix. On the clerk's side it was hardly glamorous. Their best customers used old green-screen computers caked in grime. Truly old school.

Yet it worked for 18 years. Or so everyone thought. Somewhere up the food chain were number crunchers and executives who had been asleep at the switch. Young startups were rolling out new systems for shops that included, of all things, graphics and a mouse. Brian's company had been hemorrhaging money by the time he arrived.

When leadership had figured out they had to update, about a year and a half ago, they held this big meeting. Brian only heard about it in places like the bar or the break room as a tale told in confidence. "Update or die!" they said. Update required a lot of new engineers, like Brian. Die had slightly less staff requirements.

He took another sip, then smiled to himself. They hadn't figured out which one yet, had they?

His first six months were straightforward enough; the company was all-hands-in getting the new product shipped. The work was intense, but Brian enjoyed the pace, and as long as the engineers were making improvements, the company was happy. Engineering meetings tended to be productive. Even though upper management was engaged in an ever-present crush to get done as soon as possible, anyone who signed on knew it would be this way. Luckily, their department head, Kevin, worked as a go-between, keeping upper management satisfied, keeping engineering productive, and keeping the big clients happy that, soon enough, they'd be able to point-and-click like the rest of the world.

Then Kevin left. Because of course he did.

No one blamed him. They had toasted him at a Friday-after-work, here at the bar, the same as tonight. Yet the company hadn't been the same since his replacement, Steve, showed up.

Brian downed the rest of the whiskey and stood. "Good night, everyone. Good luck, Caroline."

The next Monday, Brian sat in his cube with the ancient, yet private, 65-inch walls. The company's cube farm was old school, just like their product. The walls were off-gray, covered in stained fabric, and bore the marks of years of having pins stuffed in them and pages taped to them. Still, having worked in the land of 45-inch walls—or worse, open plan—Brian's 65s felt almost like he had his own office. A stack of emails stared at him, mostly concerning recent changes to customer installations of the product. That was the stack from end of Friday. What followed was the usual Monday morning bolts of hate mail from customers.

"Hey, Brian." Paul stuck his head into the cube. "Are we doing those three interviews today?"

Brian looked over his shoulder. "Yeah, we should bring Luis in on them too."

Paul edged farther into the cube. "Okay. You know the one guy has a master's in engineering, right? He shouldn't even be interviewing here. We can't pay."

Brian shrugged. "We need the people. If he wants to work here, it's better for us."

Paul nodded. "Sure, I guess."

Brian went back to the emails. The last six months had been the worst. Upper management dictated terms to Steve, and he said yessir, unaware of the strain engineering was under. The product launch was stepped up from a year and half to 10 months. The pressure went from a positive 'let's-get-it-done' to a desperate race. The software was going into the field way ahead of schedule. Steve blandly went along with everything.

Brian fired off a handful of apology emails to clients. They had changed out their green screens for brand-new computers weeks ago, but the software still didn't work for them. They ran their shops on paper now. A few other emails were simply curt "not this week" responses, leaving the customers to wait it out with the grubby keyboards and no end in sight. The last email was dropped into a folder Brian had labeled "Customer Hate" without response. He wanted to keep the angry rants, if anything for CYA purposes.

At 11:00 a.m., Brian, Luis, Paul, and a potential new hire took seats in a large cube near the end of the row. The desk had been cannibalized, but four chairs and a round table remained.

"Hello, thanks for coming in. I'm Brian, and I'm responsible for engineering recruitment."

"Hi Brian, I'm Matt. Thanks for having me."

Brian leaned forward on his elbows. "No problem, Matt. Let's kick off with you telling us a little about yourself."

Brian's eyes stayed focused on Matt's face, but he wasn't really listening. This wasn't his job. He wasn't supposed to be in charge of the hiring process. But, since Steve wouldn't do it, the duty fell on him. Brian faced an unenviable task: the company was massively failing to deliver on its promise to its clients, and Steve had run engineering into the ground from just passive ignorance. Brian nodded when he assumed it was appropriate, given Matt's body language. As Matt continued, Brian mused. More than half the staff had left, and only a sliver of people who knew the system remained. Even with as many new people that had walked in the door, they were understaffed. So, it didn't matter to Brian what this guy said. He could breathe, he could work.

Brian sensed Matt was done with his speech and focused his attention. "That sounds really great, Matt. We're all very impressed."

Two hours later, Brian told HR to make an offer to Matt. The interview was a formality, for Brian had selected him for the experience on the resumé. At least he was trying to bring in good people. Brian didn't notice if Matt ever showed up, but probably he didn't.

The same high cube walls created a ragged barrier of sorts in the parking lot below the building. These walls were far dirtier than anything upstairs. Gray gave way to a tan tinge and a deep settling of dust, with the occasional heavy grease stain. The cube walls were arranged in a rough circle in the center of the dark parking structure across the lane from the elevator doors. This was the smoker's gulag, and in January it felt like the cement depths of a Siberian jail.

Brian took a drag on his cigarette and commented, "I finished release six."

"Seriously?" Paul looked on, surprised.

"Yeah, it got sent out Tuesday." Brian let his hand rest on the back of a smoke-covered plastic chair.

"And it worked?"

"Of course."

Paul looked confused. "Wait, what Tuesday? What month is it? Will you ever get those weekends back?" He laughed.

Of course he wouldn't. The long hours, the weekends in the old cube farm—they all added up to "the new norm." But Brian wasn't the only one working late. So was everyone else, including Steve. Steve seemed to have an advantage.

"Hey, Steve." Brian passed him on the way to the men's room as Steve was walking out.

Paper towel in hand, Steve blew his nose and smiled big. "Hey there, Brian! How's it hanging?"

Brian nodded as he passed. "Just fine, Steve."

Steve did this a lot; those persistent sniffles and trips to the bathroom seemed like his common practice. Every time Steve came back out, he was all smiles and fun times. Especially late at night.

Brian had mixed feelings about Steve's apparent coke habit. Brian himself enjoyed a joint every once in a while on a Friday night, and other people in the office loved the club scene with its drug trappings. So maybe the problem wasn't the drugs. Maybe it was that Steve was so completely useless, even with the drugs. The persistent stereotype of coke heads in business is the over-achiever; these guys don't stop. They become kings of Wall Street and drive Lamborghinis. Steve drove a Honda Accord. He didn't do anything. Nothing. Sure, he said things in meetings on a regular basis, but it was all corporate word salad. And he's the team's manager. On a project that demands good solid leadership. Steve only kept a seat warm while the whole department slowly tore itself apart.

"Brian! Why is Pirkev Motors still unable to get into the GM parts database?" This was Cathy, in the cube across the aisle from Paul. She was standing at Brian's cube, looking worried.

Brain looked confused. "Uhm, maybe ask Steve? He should have talked to them."

Cathy shook her head slightly as she turned to leave. "Sure, whatever, Brian."

This kind of irritation had become everyday. Fifteen people in two rows of cubicles constantly sniped at each other over who was responsible for what and when it was supposed to get done. Brian sat there, drumming his fingers on his desk. This couldn't go on.

The core of the problem was obvious: Steve. Brian stared hard at his monitor, looking straight through his image into his psyche. It was time to hunt.

He walked over to Cathy's cube, knocked on the corner, then stepped in close.

His tone was quiet, like he was keeping a secret. "Hey Cathy, uhm, where's Steve now?"

She pursed her lips to think. "Good question. I don't know. He should probably call Pirkev himself."

Brian shrugged. "Thought I'd ask."

Leslie peered over the top of her cube into Brian's. "Hey, Brian, who's responsible for the toolkit updates? I need to see if we can push a library version."

Brian looked up, face wrinkled. "Uhm, I don't know."

"Isn't it you? Or Paul?"

"Nah, I think it got assigned to someone else."

"So, this is a Steve question?"

"Maybe. I have no idea where he is."

"Thanks, Brian."

Brian zipped up his winter jacket and pushed open the stainless steel panic bar on the door. Outside was a dimly lit place in the freezing cold: the smokers' gulag. As he approached, he lit up. "Hey there." Rick and Gary, the two integration guys, were already seated at the grubby table.

Rick waved slightly. "Hey, Brian." He turned back to Gary. "So now there's an ETL issue that I can't solve without some kind of higher-up decision."

"How long will that take?" Gary took another pull.

"I have no idea."

Brian stepped close to the table. "Hey, shouldn't Steve be around for that?"

Rick and Gary looked up at him. Rick tilted his head slightly. "I suppose he should."

Brian walked along the lane between the cubes, heading for his own. He didn't get far: Luis and Adam were standing between their cubes, and Adam looked downright hostile.

"This was not my job! You can't just assign me a task at random! I don't have time for extra work in this sprint!"

"Who else is gonna do this, Adam? Yeah, it may not be your deal, but if you don't do it, no one will!"

Brain approached them both. "Guys, shouldn't Steve be in on this? Is he around?"

Luis thought for a second. "I haven't seen him all day."

That was the beginning of the hunt. Steve had never been there for the team, so no one expected him to manage all the little infighting details. He showed at all the usual status report meetings, but when it came to the scut work of managing the daily business, he was completely absent. Brain's first phase of the hunt was to ask the simple question, "Where's Steve?"

This went on for a few weeks. Eventually, Brian had to do very little. "Where's Steve?" became a common question.

The door to Steve's office was open as Brian approached it. He looked inside to find Steve there, surprisingly. As he raised his hand to knock on the door frame, Brian saw the headset clipped atop Steve, while showing his back. Steve was on the phone, feet up on the side table behind him.

"Yes, of course." He looked relaxed. "We're making substantial changes to the system to allow you to do exactly that. We're in it with you. You'll be able to do those lookups faster and more easily from here on out." He paused. "Absolutely. You're the top priority. My guys are on it all the way." Steve twirled a ballpoint pen in his right hand. "Yes, thank you. And we'll have this done right away. Have a great day."

When Steve reached over to hang up the phone, Brain finally knocked. "Hello, Steve?"

Steve turned his chair around. "Hey Brian. What can I do ya for?"

"I just wanted to let you know that we finished ticket ENG-1233."

"Oh, okay. Thanks Brian."

There was one thing Steve was good at: customer talk-downs. They'd call in angry at the poor progress that was being made, be it delivery, features, or something flat-out not working. Steve took point on almost all the calls that got escalated out of Cubeville to management. Steve talked them down off the ledge. With every single one, Steve gave a warm performance that left the clients feeling like they were the star of the show.

He had no follow-through, however. The moment the call ended, everything he said got dropped in a vast sea of 'don't care.' Eventually, they'd call back.

"Has anyone talked to Carzone number 217?" Kashri stood outside her cube, looking at everyone else's. "Anyone?"

Chris spoke up. "Not me."

Sheila followed. "Yeah, me neither."

Kashri frowned and sat back down. A moment later, Brian quietly walked into her cube. He kept his voice low. "Hey, Kashri."

"Hello, Brian."

"Is Carzone pissed?"

"Yeah, Brian, they are very upset they didn't get their promised update."

"Oh, well, I thought Steve talked to them yesterday."

"Oh. Okay."

"Hey, Brian!" Paul had slid his chair around the divider between his and Brian's cube.

"Yeah, Paul?"

"Any word on the Steeplechase guys? I just got off the phone with them, and they are angry again."

"Oh yeah, Steve talked to them."

"I see."

Brian found Justin sitting in one of the big, empty cubes surrounded by printouts spread across the table. "What's going on?"

Justin looked up from the mess of sheets before him. "I'm trying to make sense of this set of client trouble tickets. They're not happy about something."

Brian scanned the pages. "Didn't Steve mention something about this? Wasn't he on the phone with these guys two days ago?"

"Where's Steve?" quickly turned into, "Isn't Steve on this?" or, "Didn't Steve talk to them?" It didn't take much to make that change. Brian quietly mentioned it to a few people as he saw them struggling with customers. Steve had, after all, talked to all these clients at some point, and it was painfully clear that he had never delivered. The call-backs were the proof. The idea that Steve was over-promising, never making good, and then dumping the problem on Cubeville took off.

"Oh, did I mention Quest Automotive?" Mary had put down her burger to address the table. About half of engineering was seated in a series of tables in the middle of the restaurant. "They still can't upload. I think Steve's been talking to them."

Leslie, seated next to her, dropped her head. "Shit. That's my guys."

Adam stared at her from across his unfolded burger wrapper. "I guess that's how it goes."

Brian looked over at Mary. "Well, what'd Steve say?"

"Oh, the usual, you're top priority, it'll be done tomorrow, that kind of crap."

Paul looked vaguely pissed. "That's bullshit."

"Yeah, he should actually do something."

"What does he do?"

"It's below our pay grade to know, I guess."

It was still frigid in the smokers' gulag and no one had emptied the butt can in months. It had overflowed onto the floor. Brian, Paul, and

Rick sat at the plastic table, nearly silent. A single cigarette smoldered in the ashtray. Paul had his pack and lighter out, but hadn't lit up yet. He sat there motionless, lifeless. Rick didn't even smoke. The guy only wanted off the floor for a precious few minutes of peace.

Rick spoke quietly. "I had six new trouble tickets assigned to me this morning, all broken stuff in shops."

Paul barely moved. "Dude, what the fuck?"

"All of them came from Steve."

Brian picked up the burning smoke. "Angry customers?"

Rick eyed him, looking hopeless. "Yeah, every single one."

"Again, what the fuck? That guy is destroying this place."

"Yeah."

Brian lifted the cigarette and inhaled.

It reached the point that people openly gossiped about Steve, none of it good. When given the chance, Brian simply asked a light question to keep the gossip going, to drive it to more detail and more negativity. Without exception, the conversation would lead to people being openly angry at Steve. By now, the gossip had spread to outside the engineering department. People started asking, "Who's this idiot Steve?" all around the company.

Brian rounded the corner into Steve's office, hand up, ready to knock. He stopped short. Steve was turned completely around, back to him. He had his head down, right above the surface of the rear-side table. Brian heard the sound of strong nasal sniff from across the office. Then Steve's head came up.

Brian knocked. "Steve? Got a sec?"

Steve spun quickly in his chair, grinning ear-to-ear. "Brian! Great to see you, man! Step on in!"

"Hey Steve, I just wanted to confirm that the new productivity reports go to you, the director, the CFO, and Ray."

"Oh yeah! Sure!"

"Thanks, Steve."

"No problem, Brian!"

That list of people on the org chart rose from Steve on up to one level below the CEO. The productivity reports had been started by Alex, the director of engineering. Surprisingly, they weren't onerous. Alex had a straightforward way he wanted reports on how many tickets were closed, how much was shipped to clients, and how many hours people worked. Even though the task was simple, it was beyond the grasp of Steve, so Brian was assigned to ship them up. Someone, namely Alex, might actually be paying attention.

The endgame of the hunt was approaching. Timing was everything.

During another dreary 15 minutes in the smokers' gulag for Paul and Brian, Paul went on a tear.

"Fuck Steve." Paul sat there, fuming. "Seriously, fuck that guy. I do not need to take more people screaming at me because of him."

Brian slowly burned down a chunk of his cigarette, then exhaled. "Hey, so why don't you go talk to Alex about it?"

Paul looked startled. "I can do that?"

"Why not?"

"Steve screwed me again." Chris leaned against Brian's desk.

"How so?"

"The asshole dumped the data migration for American on me with a due date of Friday."

It was Wednesday.

Brian sighed loudly. "That's a two-week job."

"Don't I know it!"

"This sounds like something you should talk to Alex about."

Chris sat there, considering. "Yeah, I'll do that."

"Hey, Jennifer." Brian had to walk around the entire bank of cubes to get to his across-the-divider neighbor, Jennifer. He could have simply leaned around the cube walls, but these days his conversations had to be subdued.

"Hey Brian, what's up?"

"I need your updated hours for the productivity report."

She looked incensed. "You have got to be kidding me. Steve told me not to count Monday night on it. I'm supposed to lie."

"Oh, huh. It's Alex's report, maybe you should ask him."

Over the span of a week, Brian told at least eight people to take their complaints about Steve to upper management. Each discussion was quiet, one-on-one, and never twice with the same person. Brian never followed up, either. Never asked of anyone, "Did you talk to him?". And then, an interesting thing happened.

In the big cube, Kashri, Sheila, and Brian were trying to make sense of scribblings on a white board. Kashri had called the meeting, and she was the one with the most questions.

"So, how do we get 12 more computers to Fresno Tire?" She had written down a list of available ready-to-go units, their promised destinations, and then a hasty chart of past shipments. "I don't think we can do this."

Brian was curious. "How did this mess happen?"

"Steve said we needed to get 12 machines to them or they're going to cancel their contract."

"It's really that bad? Do we believe them? Or is it an empty threat?"

Sheila looked up from her laptop. "There's no way, Kashri. I can't get more out this week."

"What am I going to do?"

Sheila closed her laptop screen with a click. "Talk to Alex. This shouldn't be on your head."

The next Thursday, Steve didn't show up at work. No one said anything. Rumors spread, of course. Maybe he was out sick, maybe he was on vacation, and, most of all, maybe he was fired.

Friday morning, Alex, Ray, and the rest of upper management announced that Steve wouldn't be coming back.

Around 1:00 p.m., Brian noticed the light on in Steve's office and stepped in. Steve was putting his belongings in a cardboard shipping box with the company logo on it. He didn't look his normal, happy, coked-up self.

"Oh hey, Brian."

"Hey Steve. Sorry to see you go, man."

"Yeah."

THE PREY

A MORE OBVIOUS prey than Steve is hard to find. The bad work ethic, the smarminess, the ignorance, the coke, and the way he could talk down customers only to have them blow up worse later—all those factors added up to: Steve is terrible. It doesn't matter that Steve's blandly pleasant attitude played well with everyone, including the clients. He had no substance behind it. From the perspective of this story, the predator's perspective, this comes through clearly.

From the perspective of the herd, Steve's worthlessness was not that obvious. If it was, he would have been fired long before. Yet the vacuum hurt everyone around him: his team, the company, and the clients. When the team was fighting over who should do what, when it should be done, and if it should be done at all, Steve needed to be the one keeping the peace. Steve's that worst-of-the-worst kind of person in a company: he hurts his entire team in a completely nonchalant, inattentive, and personally destructive manner, and he does so over and over again. He's so effective at his style of damage that no one knew he was causing it in the first place. Even the customers were snowed by Steve's casual wickedness.

All of this damage hurts the organization terribly. No one's happy; even worse, they're at each other's throats. People are quitting, people aren't staying after being hired, and all that's left are the bitter and the ignorant. Even they won't last long.

Steve had to go from the herd's perspective. Steve hurt them and would continue to hurt them.

That is not the same as the predator's perspective. They are opposite sides of the same coin; different, but vitally linked.

The predator's perspective has nothing to do with the health of the herd.

The predator's perspective is never about what's good for the herd.

The predator is not better than the herd.

The predator does not get to decide what's best for the herd.

The predator hunts because they are a predator: the reward is the thrill of the hunt and the passion of the kill.

The predator's perspective was that Steve is easy prey.

Easy prey tends to be the members the herd needs to lose. In this lies the balance in the system, predator and prey. Bad predators get run out. Easy prey gets killed out.

To a predator, someone causing damage to an organization is a sign of easy prey. It is not a moral cause to save the organization, the project, or even themselves, although sometimes damage has to happen personally to the predator for them to wake up and see the easy prey in front of them.

This is not to say that a predator can't be happy that the herd is better after a kill, or even be happy that their own work experience is better as well. But "for the good of the herd" is a dangerous justification. Predators need to do their job: hunt and kill.

THE HUNT

Brian's approach was designed to keep his personal risk to as near zero as possible. That's impressive. It's extremely rare that a predator can keep themselves out of harm's way as well as Brian did. He instead turned his coworkers into unwitting predators; they had no idea they were being recruited for the kill. Why should Brian stick his neck out when many small attacks would do? This was a kill of many teeth, many claws. Nice job, Brian.

He laid the plan out in the beginning with three distinct phases.

The first phase raised the staff's subconscious awareness that Steve was not present. Since no one was used to him being around anyway, Brian had to get people to actually notice his absence. The department was fragmented, with old and new people, staff fighting among themselves, and no direction. Brian provided that direction in the form of asking, "Where is Steve?" This is a subtle move well in line with Brian's strategy: all he asks is the whereabouts of Steve, and everyone else fills in the implied, "He's not here and he should be."

A slight against the herd travels quickly, which meant that the "Where's Steve?" message spread amongst the staff in no time. From then on, people knew who Steve was: the manager who didn't show up.

After they realized that, it was time to bring Steve in close so the herd could see him for who he is. Phase two kicked off the "Steve talked to them" and "Steve was on that" messages. Brian was showing the herd that Steve was causing problems for everyone. Because Steve was never around, everyone assumed the problems were theirs. By telling people, at the right moment, "Hey, Steve is supposed to be on that," the staff became aware that the problems were not theirs, but Steve's. Steve was making their jobs worse. The herd was now incensed, as Steve is working against them. He's betraying them. The rift begins.

The gossip that followed was a natural, expected, and desired by-product. Brian gently stoked the gossip with a simple question here and there designed to keep the conversation going. Brian gave them neutral encouragement to dig further into their resentment. Questions like "Well, what did he do?" drew details from people, and often the details could make people even more upset. The more upset they are in the moment, the more resentment they will carry with them.

Throughout all three phases, Brian kept a careful watch of the conversations around him. This allowed him to judge the effectiveness of his hunt. When he started hearing others raising the discussion against Steve in the same manner as what he had put out there, he knew it was working. The message was spreading on its own. All he had to do was start the process off and the herd would do the rest.

Now that Brian had made the herd aware of Steve, and then gently incited anger at Steve, it was time for action: phase three. This was the most delicate part of Brian's plan. He needed to provoke people, random herd members, to go to upper management in an organized manner, but in a way that looked completely organic. If people trickled into Alex's office over the span of months to complain about Steve, it would not have enough impact to make the kill. If they all showed up outside Alex's door with proverbial pitchforks and torches, Alex wouldn't be able to take that seriously, or worse, he'd try to mediate the problem. What was necessary was a consistent number of people over the right period of time arriving to bitch so that Alex was brought into the anti-Steve fold naturally.

Brian planted the suggestion that people talk to Alex very carefully. Up to this point, he'd been neutral. His questions never pushed into hating on Steve. So, telling people to go talk to Alex had to be done when it was natural, made sense, and only one-on-one. No others could be privy to Brian's suggestion, lest he be labeled as an instigator. Furthermore, Brian had a short time window to work in to get the organic effect he wanted, so he had to get out into the cube farm and seek those private moments with people. And then, once the message of, "Maybe you should talk to Alex" was delivered, he was done. He couldn't follow up, seek information about how the talk went, or anything. Again, he had to keep a very low profile and trust that the herd would follow through on everything he'd worked for.

Brian knew the plan would work the moment he heard two colleagues making the suggestion to each other to talk with Alex. The idea had become rampant in the herd.

THE KILL

EARLY ON IN this book, I told you the story of Martha, the woman who left that retail store I worked for in my college years. In her case, the slow building of the herd's dissatisfaction with her eventually turned into raw anger. This kill isn't much different, except that it wasn't a spontaneous reaction of the herd. Hunting Steve was carefully orchestrated by a predator every step of the way.

You'll notice nothing that happened in those meetings with upper management, or management's decision to terminate him, was included here. Steve was summarily fired. Brian had no idea how it all went down, so he couldn't tell me. But the predator does not need to know the actual mechanism of the firing; it doesn't matter as long as the kill has been made. Every kill is messy in some way, and it is challenging and even unwarranted to get the details of how the herd justified their actions in terminating the prey. To the predator, it's immaterial. If you were to ask management "Why was Steve fired?" you will never get, "A predator hunted Steve down and killed him out." To them, that's a ridiculous statement. In fact, their answer probably has nothing to do with the predator's actions at all. The herd will determine their rationalization on their own.

Brian never bothered looking for those answers. Nor should he have. After work on the day Steve was fired, he went to his favorite bar with his close friends and celebrated. The obvious question was asked by everyone: "Why are you celebrating?"

Not everyone's a predator, and very few would understand what he had accomplished, so Brian simply answered, "It was just a really good day."

CHAPTER FIFTEEN
A KILL ISN'T A DEATH

I GREW UP in the wilderness, far from the sounds of human machinery and progress. I went to work in the city, far from the natural sounds of the wind and rain. I never left either. Take my soon-to-be temporary office, for example. I loved it. The floor-to-ceiling windows granted a stunningly close view of another office tower in a forest of similar office towers. I couldn't see the ground. I couldn't see the sky. This was another kind of beautiful wilderness, deep in a dense forest of steel and glass. But it wasn't an office in most people's sense, it was just a conference room, and I couldn't see the world below from up on the 35th floor. I did, however, have a clear view down into the edges of a massive cube farm a couple floors below me in the next building over. The people's desks, each one a home of sorts, had innumerable little touches of personality that stood out from this vantage point. These people must be the lucky ones. They worked at the edge of the farm, near the window, able to gaze down on a similar scene stories below me in my own building.

"Lion, this is the contract, just like I sent you in email. Are we good?" Jan was a middle-aged executive and dressed the part well. As chief operations officer, she was exactly the right person to be asking that question. She slid the short stack of stapled pages across to me, SIGN HERE sticky tags poking out from various places.

That was why this wasn't my office quite yet. The contract Jan proffered was a statement of work—consultant-speak for "the things the consultant will do." It was all carefully worded to make it quite clear what this company wanted of me and what I demanded in return. In it was the provision that I was to have a dedicated conference room as my office for the next six months. That was also standard practice for consultants.

The room was set up just the way I like it: no desk, no company material, only dark wood, stainless steel, and leather. The big conference table would be my desk. I had my pick of any of eight identical comfortable chairs. One wall had a giant whiteboard and, for once, the tray had fresh markers. Consider me impressed.

The contract contained a long description of what I'd be doing in this conference room-turned-office: a comprehensive look at the company's operations. The tools it used, the processes it had, and the people themselves. The executives were out. Sales was out. The people who did the work for customers—financial analysts, bankers, and market traders—were out. What was left was everything else: legal, researchers, compliance, IT, marketing, HR, and the guys who put on the roadshow at conferences. These people made up the back office.

5. EVALUATION OF OPERATIONS STAFF

Consultant will evaluate the below listed staff for capability as it relates to their assigned role, appropriate skillset and technical abilities, corporate cultural fit, and role viability and Consultant will provide recommendations for each.

This was unusual. Normally, I'd be tasked with dealing with only process and tools, even though that invariably led to the people themselves. Prime territory for a predator. But this was different, one of the rare times evaluating the people was actually in the statement of work. I wonder how this will go.

"Yeah, Jan, this looks all in order." I took to playing "find the SIGN HERE flags" and putting my scribble of a signature next to each. There wasn't any question that I was going to sign the contract. Jan was sharp, and she had the foresight to include people in the evaluation list. Smart. The last signature sealed the deal. The conference room high up in the dense canopy of office towers was mine for the next six months.

"So, starting anywhere, tell me about what you do here." After the introductions, I kick off most hour-long interviews with the "starting anywhere" question. I want people to tell me their story, an hour's worth of each employee's personal viewpoint of work life. In large assessments, like this one, I do between six and eight of these interviews back-to-back in a day. I take notes on my laptop, diligently typing up a chaotic shorthand filled with misspellings that only I can interpret. There's a good reason for the note taking: not only do I record the stuff I need, but the people I'm interviewing feel that their story is important enough for the high-priced consultant to write down. So I dutifully banged away at my keyboard while maintaining steady eye contact with the person sitting across from me at the table.

Sometimes people start off on the defensive. The lawyers at this company had come off this way; they're lawyers, after all. No one questions them. But I'm not here to dig up their mistakes and beat them with it. I just want their stories. Eventually they warm up to me, once they realize this isn't a deposition. HR is similarly tight-lipped as they take their role and some sense of confidentiality seriously. I dig into their workflow with questions to validate that they're doing their job; nothing hard, just simple stuff to get some idea of how much these individuals know. "How many terminations have you had in the last two years?" opens the door with HR into their personal knowledge of process and corporate social dynamics. On the surface, that question looks as if I'm just getting a handle on employee churn, but that's a simple view of what I'm doing. "Okay, tell me about that" as a follow-up earns me a lot better look into how they think and perceive themselves, their relationship to the organization, and the organization as a whole.

The individual stories are important to the individuals, so my sustained keyboarding while they talk never lets up. What they tell me counts, but I'm really after a much bigger picture: I want to see the connections between people. How they fit into the organization, who goes where for what, how the triangle of people, process, and tools plays out in the organization as a whole. No one has ever directly told me, "I'm the problem in my company!" But problem people never fail to tell me who they are, albeit indirectly.

This was shown soon after I started my new contract.

"So today, we're going to diagram out your network so I can get an idea of what you work on." I stood before the whiteboard in my conference room office, marker at the ready. Across the table was Cory, the guy in charge of all IT in the company. "So, starting anywhere, walk me through it." Cory looked excited. He was in his mid-30s, which is not bad for running IT for a multibillion-dollar company.

"So, I have three switches at the top of the racks. Those all power the connections to people's offices." I drew three rectangles on the board. "Then there's the primary server, in another rack." I drew a box on the board. "And then there's the fail-over server underneath it." I drew a box under the other box. "And then there's the storage, all the disks, connected to both the primary and backup." I created another, bigger box and lines connecting them.

"Then there's the database server." Another box. "And the phone server is in a room next door." I drew a box on the edge of the whiteboard. "Then the tape backup server is in the other rack, with a test server in that rack too. The video conferencing system sits below that, I think." I kept on drawing, trying to get all the systems Cory brought up sorted on the board. It turned out to be not that many, maybe 20 at most.

This was the scope of what Cory was responsible for. The diagram I had up there, a series of 20-some boxes and rectangles, was the absolute center of Cory's job.

"Okay, so that's the equipment. How's it all connected?" I pointed at the backup system. "How is this connected to file storage?"

"Oh, through a switch!"

"Sure. Which one? There's at least five here."

"One of the ..." He faltered, then paused. "I don't know."

My face didn't betray my surprise. "Okay, Cory, well, we need to know. So, let's go to the server room and find out."

I stood a few steps inside the door of a long room in the center of the office floor. There were no windows, no desks, no cube walls. Just racks of computer equipment and the sound of air conditioning constantly running. Cory, head of IT, stood next to me.

He reached out a hand. "This is it, the server room."

The nice thing about IT departments is that the interview comes with a graphic display of the employee's execution. The server room always tells a story of its own and it never lies to me. And this server room told an incredibly mundane story: an average amount of equipment, racked up, not neatly but not messily. I can see firsthand what Cory had me put on the whiteboard, roughly as he described them. An average amount of old hardware was stacked off to the side, waiting for the day it was fully depreciated off the tax schedule. Lots of store-bought cables hung in bundles from wire trays and racks, giving the racks a waterfall-made-of-cables look. It wasn't messy enough to be a nerd project. It wasn't clean enough to be an IT director's point of pride. It looked like the kind of place serious IT guys could walk into wearing a blindfold and plug straight into the network without ever feeling around. Something in my gut told me this impression was wrong, but I couldn't figure out why.

"Okay, so how the connections are made, let's dig in."

Cory walked to the back of the equipment racks. The cable mess continued here as well. Yet another cable waterfall obscured the equipment.

Cory looked nervous. "So, in here are the connections between the systems." He made no attempt to get close.

"So, I'm going to reach in and start tracing ..." I stepped up to the mess and started pushing cables around, searching for recognizable features. "This is the back of the primary server, yeah?"

"Yeah."

"Okay, so here's four cables coming out of it. I'll trace one." I began following the cable through the mess. I was not gentle: I pulled and twisted cables, trying to keep up with the snaking wire in my hand. If I let it go, it'd be lost and I have to start all over.

After six feet of threading my hand through the rat's nest, I reached the other end, less than a foot away. "It looks like it's going to the file storage machine."

"I guess. Sure."

"You guess?"

"Yeah, the vendor set it up."

"I see."

My investigation went on that way for over an hour: I traced cables, and Cory shied away from touching anything. I didn't understand why he was afraid of his own stuff. When we got back to my office, I started filling in the lines that connected all the boxes on the whiteboard.

"So, that's it, yeah?" I stood back, taking in the map I'd created. It wasn't complex. It was actually undersized for such a big company. The diagram took up most of the whiteboard, but only because I wasn't saving space. I wanted it to be easily understandable and not just scribble on the back of a napkin.

Cory looked pleased. "Yeah, that's it! We got it all."

"Okay, Cory, so this is everything you're responsible for?"

"Yeah."

Now it was time to test him. "All right Cory, turn your chair around and face away from the board." He did. "If switch four fails, what services go down? How will the operation be impacted?"

"What?"

"Switch four, it breaks. What else breaks?"

Switch four connected the server to the rest of the network. It was visible right there on the diagram, in black and white. Any good IT guy would know his own network and know the whole company goes down if that one piece of equipment fails.

Cory finally answered. "I have no idea."

In the following months, I'd complete my first round of interviews. At that point, the report of all my findings was already up to 52 pages, spanning a number of back-office departments and naming tools (poor software), process (silos and fiefdoms, poor expectations due to incoherent business methods), and people. I had only a handful of people that needed a closer look: Cory from IT, Ryan from support, administrative assistant Linda, and John from research.

Cory relied completely on vendors, the companies that make the IT equipment, to do his work for him. He had no idea how his network actually worked. He definitely couldn't fix it—he wouldn't even touch it. He considered himself a "vendor manager" rather than an IT person. He's prey.

Ryan was one of the people in desktop support. He was responsible for answering all the "I can't print!" and "I can't get my email!" complaints. He was a young guy, which means he was inexperienced and made a lot of mistakes. He was also a bit scatterbrained—not in a terrible way, just in a young and excitable way. He, however, was very into the tech culture of young IT: anime, comics, the lot. But this company, like most big financial firms, was very austere and reserved. Ryan bought a suit to work here, but his personality stood out like a sore thumb. Prey.

Linda was an archetype of many personal administrative assistants. She worked for the head of Investments, who was the only person she was pleasant with. Investments wielded significant organizational clout, which meant that, as long as Linda stayed true to her boss, she could do anything she wanted. That power-by-proxy let Linda be casually capricious with the rest of the company. Absolutely prey.

Research was the back-office workhorse of investments. As a team, research dug into potential investments to get the details, and those details had to be right. John cut corners, even making things up, to the point where the department had a saying: "Is it true, or is it John true?" Prey.

Jan sat next to me in my conference room as we stared at my laptop screen. "I would like to try to improve the capabilities of these people." I pointed at the list of four employees. "I have some improvement plans we can run to boost their performance before I write their sections of my report. This will give us specific, actionable results." I was sort of telling the truth. The improvement projects weren't meant to improve their skills. Each was carefully designed so they would fail spectacularly at a task they should be easily capable of performing. After hours of interviews, these people had shown me the exact part of their skillset that would crumble when pressed. I tried to hide my excitement.

"Yeah, Lion. That sounds reasonable. Go ahead." Jan signed off on my plan. This was amazing. I was giddy with anticipation.

The company wanted the higher-ups to have iPads, so Wi-Fi needed to work in the office. The capacity was there in name only. Cory's vendor had undersized it badly, expecting no one to use it. So, Cory's petard would be to build a new Wi-Fi system from the ground up, without vendor help. I specifically forbade him from reaching out to vendors. He had to do the work himself.

The support process was broken well before Ryan got to it, so I'd restructure the process of triaging and fixing people's IT issues for him. I didn't set out to build something complex, only a process that would be understandable and reliable to the people in the cubes. But Ryan would be the one responsible for its execution. He had to focus on his own reliability.

Moving Linda under a new boss was a great way to break up her reign of terror. She'd work under the trading desk director for a month to "cross-train on another department related to investments." The trading desk team was high-stakes and tolerated absolutely no bullshit, which was the equivalent of putting Linda in front of a speeding freight train. She'd have to put her games aside and join the team for real.

For John, I planned a new report-audit process. For the next few weeks, I'd take the entire team and management aside for an hour and we'd select reports to review together. In the guise of, "How did our predictions turn out?" the team would encounter John's work. He'd have to defend himself.

I was busy overseeing these projects, so the time I spent in my office was rare. When I was there, the door was closed and I was heads down, lost in thought, writing the giant report the statement of work demanded.

I was startled by a knock at the door.

I looked up. "Come in."

The door swung open to reveal Ryan from support. "Lion?"

"Yeah, Ryan, come on in." He looked nervous.

He gingerly stepped across the threshold and closed the door behind him. "Lion, I know you're doing evaluations of everyone." He paused, uncertain. "I mean, everyone knows that."

I looked at Ryan with a purposefully neutral expression and waited.

"Lion, I have a wife and two young kids." He looked down at the floor. "I really need this job."

I let out a slow, silent breath. "Okay, Ryan."

"Yeah, so, please don't fire me." When he looked back up, he looked afraid.

"Ryan, my report's not written yet. I don't know what's going into it."

He stared at me for a long moment. "Sure. Thanks, Lion." Ryan turned for the door.

I nodded to him as he walked out and closed the door behind him.

Oh yeah, he definitely has to go.

After countless meetings with Cory and his boss to clarify his progress on the Wi-Fi, he finally made a decision. In the final meeting, he laid out all the options the vendors gave him, including the pros and cons the vendors provided. He didn't understand any of it. Fail.

During a half-dozen meetings, we had to define the new support process, but when it was time for Ryan to lead the directive, nothing happened. I didn't even bother to ask him when we were going to launch the new system. Fail.

Linda was asked to leave the trading department after two weeks.

The audit process showed errors across the board, not just with John. But his reactions were haughty and defensive. Before long, the whole team was fed up with him and saw his work for what it was.

The report, 52 pages of operational deficiencies and suggestions, had two additional segments stapled to the back. One was a page and a half detailing the recommendation to terminate Cory.

Addendum 1
Evaluation of IT Practitioner Cory Ward
Systems Administrator Role

It is the opinion of the evaluator that Cory Ward does not possess the required technical skillset to be successful as a systems administrator at this company. Similarly, Cory's expectations for his role are significantly incongruent with the requirements of the company for his role. It is the suggestion of the evaluator that success in a technical role for Cory would be found within an organization that has large amounts of structure and absolutely clear communication surrounding his performance expectations.

I engaged in the evaluation of Cory by asking him to define the details of the network and servers he supported. He began by drawing a network diagram on a whiteboard. He started the task by glossing over details and I had to ask several questions to clarify obvious missing parts of the diagram. I felt that, after several of my detailed technical questions, he realized that he was required to provide specifics. After a short time, Cory was unable to draw the diagram from memory and we were required to go to the server room to inspect the installation. I felt the network size was small enough to remember without aids. I asked what individual cables did in the back of the server racks. Cory was unable to answer (they were network attached storage). I asked what he did when something went wrong with this equipment. He responded that he would "call the vendor."

Later in the diagramming session, I asked Cory to stand with his back to the diagram. I asked him, "If [this] network switch failed, what services would be at risk?" He was unable to answer.

Cory was asked to provide costing for a collaboration server, to which he made the request without additional details to a vendor. The vendor quoted the highest level collaboration license (which was out of budget and far oversized) without advising Cory that collaboration foundation is no cost. I had to pursue licensing quotes on my own in order to drive Cory to revisit the vendor quote. On a conference call with the vendor, I witnessed Cory finally pushing back on the vendor and the vendor's reluctant admission that collaboration was, in fact, free with a basic server license.

Cory did perform his task well of documenting the systems in place in collaboration-based reference, following the format provided. The reference pages appear to have sufficient detail for a start at documentation. I did, however, note that Cory did not freely experiment with collaboration features, collaboration services I set up, or even formatting within collaboration.

For Cory's final evaluation, I started a project to design and implement company-wide Wi-Fi for use by laptops and iPads. I gave Cory a set of requirements, including that he shall not engage outside vendors in the design and specification of equipment. After three weeks with no progress, Cory told me that he was having a meeting with a vendor to discuss the features of two similar Wi-Fi systems. I considered the project a failure. The project should have been completed in two weeks or less, and three weeks had been used without progress; an outside vendor was being brought into the decision process in violation of the requirements; Cory had no understanding of the technologies he was expected to deploy and did little to no self-directed research to gain the required understanding. This entire project, even with little previous knowledge, would be easily achievable to a person that fits this role well.

Cory repeatedly told me he wished to move in the direction of being an IT manager and considered himself a "vendor manager." Both of these functions are to be undertaken within a technically-savvy IT manager role, which Cory is not qualified for. Over the length of Cory's engagement there is little demonstrable growth in his skillset that would suggest progression to a manger role, even when allowed little supervision and almost no budgetary oversight. An individual in that position would likely have used such an opportunity to overbuild the company's network and extend their own skillset *beyond the company's direct needs. Cory did neither, and his stagnation is prevalent in the company's trapped-in-2007 network. There is none of the expected optimization that would have come with an individual engaged in technology. Equipment is left in the least-configured state with no understanding of advanced configurations. Servers and services are not well understood and unoptimized. Reasonable and expected business needs, such as laptops, were dismissed as "technically infeasible." This lowest-possible-effort output of the last seven years shows that Cory is not fit for a management role at this time and needs additional time in a technical practitioner role.*

It is my opinion that Cory's best chance in a technical role is first-line production support for a large organization capable of fielding many similar roles. Cory needs the structure and peers to provide a clear set of expectations to ensure he places actual effort in the execution of his job. The company is too unrestricted in the practice of IT for someone of Cory's approach and will only serve to limit his opportunities in the future by not providing the detailed expectations he requires.

Ryan's termination recommendation was only half a page.

Addendum 2
Evaluation of IT Practitioner Ryan Kennedy
Desktop Support Role

It is the opinion of the evaluator that Ryan is too early in his IT career to serve the company appropriately. A candidate with more maturity and professionalism, but the same enthusiasm, will serve the company's needs better.

While I had initially expected Ryan to do well in his helpdesk role, it has become clear that Ryan's lack of technical experience and mature professionalism will hinder the execution of his role. Obvious problems, such as unprofessional conduct and communications

> *(including numerous gross misspellings in email) will reduce respect for his role and distance the company's users from the IT support staff.*
>
> *Ryan's enthusiasm for his role and technology in general is commendable and desirable in someone in the helpdesk role. He has a genuine interest in the betterment of the company's users and his own understanding of technology. While this serves him very well in being an outgoing representative of IT, his unprofessional conduct indicates he needs time in a more understanding environment before he can be successful in a place such as the company.*
>
> *Ryan would do well to seek a Level 2 helpdesk position as part of a desktop support or product helpdesk team.*

I was flying high the week I delivered the report. Three days of rush. Sure, the tools and process problems I found were serious enough to cover in detail, so the company could spend the next few years fixing them, but it was those last few pages that had me dizzy, specifically the hunt of Cory. This was to be my cleanest kill ever! I had the prey's neck in my teeth! It was beautiful! I had it all here, every last detail of the hunt laid out in black and white, ready for the kill! It was as if the world was all bright colors and happy sounds. My manic grin never left my face.

Which maybe it should have, if only for a bit.

"You have to walk him out."

"What?"

I sat at my usual spot in my conference room. The statement of work was almost fulfilled, and the last detail remaining was Cory. Ryan had been let go without anyone even noticing. Linda had gone back to her old role with closer scrutiny and heavy restrictions. John was off at a four-week remedial training class. Across from me were Jan and Thomas, who was the marketing director and chief technology officer. It was Thomas that nearly shouted the one-word question.

"Yeah, this is standard in IT."

"To fire people and have them leave that day?" Thomas was aghast.

"Yes. There are security issues if you let IT work their last two weeks. They might compromise the systems. Hack them to cause damage, leak your confidential files, or leave the door open so they can come back in later. So, you have to have security walk them out." I had a friend, many years ago, that tore holes in his company's systems when he got fired and didn't get walked out. He's lucky the company didn't press charges.

In my mind, I pictured the event: Cory picking up his things from his cube, confused and upset, as Nathan the security guy took his cattle tag and walked him to the elevators.

"That's insane!"

Stop grinning, Lion. "No, that's standard practice. That's how it's done." I wasn't making this up. Anyone that's been let go from a technology position knows this process.

Jan tried to be reasonable. "What about his two weeks?"

"You pay him, yes, but he's not allowed on site anymore."

Thomas wasn't having any of it. "He's been here seven years!"

"Yeah, and he's been causing problems for all seven."

"I can't do this!"

I pointed at an email from the high-profile multinational auditor the company used. "Even the auditors strongly agreed with my findings in my report. He has to be walked out." STOP GRINNING, LION.

"Lion, we need to think on this." Jan remained calm. I think she was agreeing with me, but she didn't want to go up against Thomas' outrage.

"No problem. He still has to be walked out—that's the only option." I wasn't letting up.

"We understand." Jan and Thomas stood, Thomas still fuming.

A few days later, I came down from my high.

With the report delivered and the statement of work fulfilled, I was done. Goodbye, conference room.

They never did fire Cory.

Six months later, I was sitting in another conference room on the other side of the city. This one looked over rooftop chillers and air-handling equipment in a light industrial park. Not everyone's a winner.

"Okay, thanks Kyle. I'll let you know if we need to chat again." Kyle walked out of my conference room and headed down the hall.

I was conducting another assessment, another eight-hour day packed with interviews, broken only by lunch. All that face time left me wanting to be alone, so I wasn't down for getting lunch with people from the client site, or even trying to meet up with friends. No, I quietly occupied a corner of a hole-in-the-wall Chinese restaurant, alone.

The food was not worth mentioning, but it matched the bland generic Chinese interior perfectly. The paper chopstick sleeve, classically emblazoned with the phrase "For important Chinese cultural" sat crumpled next to my plate. I was zoned out, my head idling while it recharged for the afternoon's interviews.

Then I saw Ryan with a group of guys at a big table across the room.

Oh shit.

They didn't see me come in, apparently. I had slid behind my corner table without making a fuss. From here, I had a good look at the group. Khakis and random shirts, mostly polos. Okay, professional, but not done up. Cattle tags. Ah, corporate IT.

This could be unpleasant.

If I were to get up and leave, I'd call attention to myself and my hasty exit. They were almost done with their own plates. Time slowed down.

They looked like they were having a good time.

I looked down at my plate—best not to stare. I would finish eating and get back to business.

I had a few minutes of silence before they stood up.

"Hey Lion!" Right on cue, it's Ryan.

I looked up, wary. "Oh, hey there, Ryan." He was grinning ear-to-ear. What was this?

"Lion, I saw you here, and I wanted you to meet my new boss!" One of the guys stepped forward.

"Yeah, thanks a ton for sending us Ryan. He has turned out perfect, just what we needed!" The guy, Ryan's boss apparently, was also all smiles.

He offered his hand. I reached out and shook it. "That's great to hear."

Ryan extended his hand. "Yeah, Lion, you did the best thing ever for me. Working for these guys is fantastic. Thank you so much!"

"That's really good, Ryan."

"Gotta get back to work, see ya!"

"Yeah Ryan, see ya."

I picked my jaw off the floor eventually.

THE PREY, THE HUNT, THE KILL, THE ONCE-IN-A-LIFETIME FOLLOW-UP

IF YOU RECALL, early in this book I talked about "the worst of the worst." These are the people that do untold damage a little at a time, day in, day out. My job, as a bounty hunter, was to arrest them, bring them to jail, and give them another chance at doing it right. I was never responsible for encouraging them to go straight, never my job to see those results through. It was enough to give them another chance to make a different choice.

I was quietly astonished for weeks after my encounter with Ryan. I didn't know what to make of it. I played the memory of the encounter over and over in my head, trying to reason it through: wow, Ryan figured it out. He made a different choice and ended up somewhere far better. He looked happy. His boss looked happy. I bet his wife and kids were happy.

It was an intense moment. I had never seen the results of what I had done before then, nor have I seen them again. What was only casual savagery on my part, a half-page in a giant report, had given Ryan the opportunity to try again. And he went for it. It had demonstrated to me that what I do works. That it can all play out so the world can be a slightly better place. The herd did their job, the predator did their job, and the prey ended up with a better life.

This memory, of Ryan Kennedy and his boss vigorously shaking my hand, remains in the back of my mind whenever I set off on another hunt. The adrenaline rush is so much more fulfilling when I know that my prey will have another chance to redeem themselves. Maybe they'll turn out like Ryan. It's up to them, after all. They have wrong ideas in their heads, beliefs they somehow come to hold that cause them to be bad, assumptions they made that couldn't be further from the truth. After the kill lies the opportunity for the prey to revisit what's in their mind. Maybe, just maybe, they'll realize that changes need to be made.

I suspect that seeing the other side of the prey's drama played out is extremely rare, and I won't have this opportunity ever again. The world is a big place and paths likely won't cross again. I'll have to trust that nature works.

Because it did.

CHAPTER SIXTEEN
THE RED QUEEN'S RACE

THE OLD JOKE goes: "How do you know there's a pilot in the room? They'll tell you." When I was reading the latest pilot safety magazine, I came across the usual pilot-in-trouble story. This is why I, and many other pilots, read these magazines: for the stories (as opposed to the pictures of beautiful aircraft). This pilot, while in flight, had his engine blow up, literally. He had no idea what exactly had gone wrong, as is common when you're not able to get out and inspect things while at 10,000 feet. Yet he made a series of decisions that saved his life. The one decision that stuck in my mind is that he left the engine controls exactly where they were when the problem erupted. See, the engine was still running, barely. He operated under the assumption that any change to the engine would mean it would shut down fatally. Which it did, when he finally landed. It seized up the moment he touched the throttle.

If you're a pilot, you'll recognize that a calm demeanor in a catastrophic situation is one of the required tools to saving lives, including your own. If you lose your shit, you die.

I was flying in a pitch-black night years ago when my passenger and I heard a terrifically loud bang accompanied by the aircraft shuddering badly. In a moment, the windscreen was covered in a thick black liquid. I couldn't see anymore.

I thumbed the radio button. "Golf Tango Niner, Tower, requesting priority landing at Clearwater. There is something wrong with my engine."

"Golf Tango Niner, declaring an emergency. How many souls on board?"

"Two."

I remembered the safety magazine article, how the pilot reported that the oil from the engine had covered his windscreen, and that was his first clue the engine was in dire trouble. So my reaction followed his: leave the engine controls alone and fly the aircraft. In the next half hour, I maneuvered to the airfield and landed, only throttling back the engine at the last moment.

We lived.

Once on the ground, we could finally inspect the aircraft. Turns out we had hit three geese in flight. One took off the end of a wing. One went straight into the wing, and one went through the propeller. If the prop hadn't shredded the goose, it would have gone straight into us. And that thick black liquid on the windscreen? It wasn't black, it was red.

Another joke goes: "How do you get a pilot to shut up about flying? Separate him from the other pilot."

That's what pilots do, they tell stories. Lots and lots of stories. Good times flying, bad times flying, it doesn't matter. Not only do we love telling stories, we love listening to them. The stories remind us, on the ground, of the incredible joy of flying, which people who aren't pilots tend to not understand.

Underlying all of those stories is a learning curve. If I hadn't read the story of the pilot's blown engine, I wouldn't have had any idea how to handle my own emergency. It wasn't that his story was a procedure to be learned by rote; it was an example to draw upon when my own life was on the line. My situation wasn't exactly the same, but remembering it helped. So now, I tell my story to any pilot that will listen. Because maybe it'll save them. Also, it's a good story.

In the United States, the Federal Aviation Administration (FAA) issues pilot licenses. But as the FAA examiner says: "This is your ticket to learn and your license is only the beginning." There's no one central authority that tells you how to fly. The FAA publishes a book of flying rules, and it's a big one, but it doesn't include *how* to fly. The only one in charge of a flight is the pilot, and absolutely everything is on them. It takes a strong-willed person to take on that responsibility. That independent will is why there's no one authority on being a pilot.

With all those strong personalities, pilot culture gravitates to stories. If you have your ticket, you're a pilot. Maybe new, maybe not, maybe experienced, maybe all you've done is fly a little bit. We're all still pilots. We don't all get along, and there are definitely pilots I will never fly with, but bad pilots are still pilots. Hopefully, they'll improve.

Pilots learn to fly in two ways: listening to other pilots' stories and doing it themselves. There is no substitute for sitting in the left seat, the pilot's seat, and doing it for real. That's where the stories come from.

This book represents what I know, and only that. These are my own stories and some I've heard from other predators. The two ways predators learn to hunt is by listening to other predators' stories and then doing it themselves. There is no substitute for the personal, solitary chase; the hunt. That's where the stories come from.

The few predators I've known have come from very different fields. Finance, technology, blue collar, and education. I've known both male and female predators. They've all had some common traits: they're intelligent, they're driven, and they stand apart from the herd and see it differently. They are all strong-willed and independent-minded. That's why there's no authority on organizational predators. There's no plastic card you keep in your wallet to identify you as a predator. That's the trapping of the herd. That's not what predators are about.

Organizations—every one of them, whether corporate, government, volunteer—needs a balance of predator and prey. There must be a check on the blight that is weak prey, bad ideas, bad emotions, and toxic attitudes. They are expected; those negatives will always be present. One of the best aspects of nature is that unrelenting push to succeed, no matter what success looks like. We achieve the good, the great, and the bad all at the same time. Weak prey will always exist in some manner. Nature doesn't judge. Nature just cleans up the mistakes.

Predator and prey is an ever-evolving dynamic. No two organizations are the same, and no two hunts will ever be alike. Prey learn and adapt in the face of predation. They always have. The herd's attempt at keeping the blight at bay, human resources, is a failure and sometimes even the source of the blight.

We all need this world to work well. The creative engines of humanity are the expression of the engines of nature. Harmony, happiness, the feeling that work matters: these are all important parts of the herd's well-being, to them producing, to humanity advancing. Weak prey break herds. We live most of our lives at work, and it shouldn't be hell.

Choose to hunt, please. No one can make you do it. No one can ever demand such a personal thing. Only you can commit yourself to the task.

Being a predator is a difficult calling. You are all alone. It is not easy to learn. It's harder to execute. You'll make mistakes at first, but that's expected. Sometimes those mistakes will put you in a tough spot. That's okay. You'll be fine. Keep at it. The world needs you, and it will never acknowledge you. Your satisfaction will come from within.

Then tell your stories to other predators. We need your stories to learn from, to celebrate, to remind us of what it feels like.

Then again, maybe this doesn't fit you. That's okay too. I hope the book was fun. I have immense respect for the herd. Your accomplishments dwarf anything an individual like myself can dream of. We all stand on your shoulders, the many shoulders of the herd.

Perhaps next time you see someone terrible being let go, you'll ask, "I wonder if a predator did that?"

My paddle, a thickly-lacquered wooden plank, marred with dings and cuts, snapped with a well-disciplined swing over the water, scattering loose droplets briefly on the surface of the lake before they rejoined the deep blue. With no delay, no hesitation, the paddle spun and slipped quickly into the surface with only the tiniest of riffles. I pulled back, hauling the wooden shaft with tense muscles, pouring power into the canoe. Near the end of my reach, I turned the paddle just enough, no conscious thought about it, and applied force to the flat edge. The canoe gracefully turned on its axis, the bow swinging right. I whipped the paddle again through the same well-worn motion, my eyes straight ahead, no attention paid to my arms—they were an extension of my will. The canoe was facing exactly head-on to the portage trail at the end of the bay, just to the left of my bowman's head.

The wind is cooler. Gone is the humidity and, even better, gone are the incessant mosquitoes. These days, I could feel fall in the air, if only briefly. This would be one of the last crews out for the season. One of the last groups to tour my home.

I looked over my canoe. It was loaded precisely: two crew people, their gear, my guide pack, and me. My loadout was perfect, finely tuned during a season of harsh wilderness travel. Poor choices don't last long out here; for gear, for crew, even for guides. Nature is unrelenting and unforgiving. I have survived storms, injury, nearby fire, loss of food, and broken equipment. There was no safety net, no emergency services. I could rely only on me and whatever crew I had on hand.

I have seen nature build up in spring, and now, as fall approaches, begin tearing down. Nothing gets an out. There are no exceptions. Life, death, rebirth, they are everyday here. Nature is not a thing that cares, it simply does because it must.

My arms keep the disciplined swing of my paddle going as I stare up into the ranks of red pines. They haven't changed, they are as immobile as the rock they're perched upon. When I had last entered this bay, months ago, I sat in judgment by the entirety of the wild. The trees stood in authority over my place, my station. But now, after it all, I recognize them as ordinary trees. A role, a place, a niche in nature, however large and tall, in an astounding system that bends the will of everything within it.

I have my place too.

I am Lion.

POSTSCRIPT

THE STORIES IN this book represent more than 20 years of my career. Not every job ended up with prey. Nor did every kill story end up on these pages. The stories were selected to show specific concepts and ideas, including the tales from other predators. All the stories are true but, as you'd expect, the names have been changed. They're all very personal in nature, from the perspectives of both the predator and prey. Few people, even among my friends, even know what I do for a living. Partly because trying to explain what a "turn-around consultant turned predator" does isn't for the faint of heart, but partly because the gory truth of my work history is exactly that: gory. I'm proud of my career, but I find it's not a light-hearted topic for an evening out with friends.

I deeply appreciate being able to share the stories that are not mine and the lengthy interviews that took place to capture them. I spent long hours banging away on notes and working on corrections to get the details right, so a huge thanks to my fellow predators that showed me the inner workings of their kills. They, too, probably can't talk about them much either; their stories are just as gory.

I had considered my career as an organizational predator over upon the publishing of this book but, after some thought, I expect it not to be. People exhibit a cognitive blind spot about things they just can't understand in contradiction to their beliefs. For instance, I witnessed a Japanese tourist in Yellowstone National Park attempting to walk up to a wild buffalo, head on, and pet it. Even when they were told, "Hey, that's a wild animal, you could get hurt!" they refused to believe the big furry cow-creature could hurt them. They just couldn't understand that reality wasn't a big, friendly, fuzzy animal. I doubt that that blind spot will go away, but we'll see.

A note on the idea of the balance of nature: many consider it being able to return to a previous "good" state. I use "balance" as a shorthand for "dynamic stability," which is more about movement and forces within a system that keep the system operating; not in spite of change, but because of change. It won't return to a previous state, but will resist total destruction of the system.

ACKNOWLEDGMENTS

To my wife:
"Keep going" was a phrase I heard at least a thousand times while writing this. I expect there to be no end of "keep going" even after this is done. I find it incredible that someone could believe in me so much as to push me and support me through all of this. We've been through so much and have so much more yet to go. Every day is an adventure with you, my love, my best friend, my full teammate. I love you with all my heart, Sharon.

To my development readers, Fox and Jim:
Thank you for all the reads, the rereads, the "Here, please read this right away!" insistence of mine after I tried something new, and the encouragement you guys gave me throughout the build of this. It all came together; I knew something was working when both of you said "Oh, I get it!" at the same time.

To my developmental editor, Amber:
Thank you for kicking me in my teeth. The right kind of conflict improves, sharpens, and brings things to a precise and inescapable point. The pain was totally worth it to write the book I needed to write. That last review was astounding. This book would not have gotten there without your honest and direct opinions.

To my editors, John and Andrew:
Thank you for working so hard on my manuscript, giving it so much polish, and not getting upset over the Oxford Comma.

My test readers:
Joel, Sean, Ric, Dave, Kurt, Lee, Dave, Adam, Blaze, and Paul; thanks

for all the feedback and interviews, as well as dealing with the innumerable spelling and grammatical problems because, you know, raisins. It took a lot of work to get the concept of the book right enough so that it could be understandable. Until you guys came along, I didn't know I was capable of telling the story of predator and prey.

DAVID L:

Thank you for saving my life. I mean, thank you doesn't really cover that, does it? I can't explain to someone what it's like to fall down a black well, never to return, only to have your fellow man reach down at the very last moment and pull you out. It is a feeling of humility beyond anything, and leaves you in awe of how precious life is and how important people are. I am proud to call you my friend, and am ever thankful that we know each other. Thanks, brother.

PROFESSOR TOM:

I will never forget that day in your office that kicked off my deep dive into breaking down group bonding. Thanks for challenging me. It worked.

Made in the USA
Monee, IL
27 May 2021